Marcel Brion is a member of the Académie Française and is a well known art historian, novelist and critic. His particular interest is Italy, and he is the author of numerous books on history and art history, including *The Medici* and the immensely successful *Pompeii and Herculaneum*.

Edwin Smith was born in London and trained as an architect. He was by choice a painter and was well known as a photographer. He co-produced about 30 books in association with writers such as Angus Wilson, Olive Cook (his wife), Stewart Perowne, David Piper and Edward Hyams. Edwin Smith died in 1971.

POMPEII AND HERCULANEUM

The Glory and the Grief

Marcel Brion

Photographs by Edwin Smith
Translated by John Rosenberg

CARDINAL edition published in 1973
by Sphere Books Ltd
30/32 Gray's Inn Road, London WC1X 8JL

First published in Great Britain by
Elek Books Ltd 1960
Copyright © Elek Books Limited 1960

Set in Monotype Times New Roman

Printed in Great Britain by
C. Nicholls & Company Ltd
The Philips Park Press, Manchester

ISBN 0 351 15422 1

TABLE OF CONTENTS

INTRODUCTION

THE object of this book is to represent in as complete and precise a way as possible the form and aspect of Pompeii and Herculaneum and the life led by their inhabitants at the period when that existence was brutally cut short by the eruption of Vesuvius, wiping out these two cities in 79 A.D. How they were brought to light again after nearly two thousand years of neglect and oblivion; and how for two centuries archaeologists have gone about clearing the stratum of lava and ashes with which they were covered, and then restoring to the ruins the actual aspect that their temples and houses had before the catastrophe: that is what this work proposes to show, while also describing the most recent finds made there, such as have endlessly enriched our understanding of the ancient world and its way of life.

Pompeii and Herculaneum are today not yet entirely cleared, although evidently the time is approaching when the excavation work will have finished unearthing those districts of Pompeii which still remain buried. As for Herculaneum, the situation is more complex and the researches are more difficult, for in the Middle Ages a new town was built upon the drifts of solidified mire that had engulfed this city, and it is not easy to dispossess the living in order to exhume a dead city.

In the description of the two cities and the way in which their everyday life went on in the first century A.D., it will be understood that new discoveries are constantly enlarging the sum of our knowledge, sometimes even modifying what we know of Roman civilization. The archaeologists' work here is in active progress. However, it is scientific etiquette to cite and discuss only such finds as have been the object of exhaustive and official publication: a publication which in certain cases occurs quite some time after the discovery proper.

With this reservation, it is the Pompeii and Herculaneum of 1960 that the reader will survey in this book. Though the book will not be dealing with problems of interest only to the specialist, it will be aimed at providing an extensive and precise historical and archaeological view of the main characteristics of everyday existence in the Campanian cities under Roman domination. To enable the reader to understand why and how these 'dead cities' became what they were before their destruction, it is expedient to give some glimpse into their foundation and evolution from the proto-historic periods up to the fatal year of 79.

The recital of excavations at Pompeii constitutes a sort of digest of the history of archaeological science itself; and the unfolding of its application in the ruins of Pompeii and Herculaneum demonstrates the new concepts which were put to work and which find here their happiest and most attractive confirmation. There will not be any question, in this book, of judging the merits of the various directors of excavation who succeeded one another in the Campanian work sites; but it is only fitting to give especial credit to the distinguished archaeologist today superintending the work at the Pompeiian and Herculanean sites: Professor Amedeo Maiuri, who for so many years has applied himself zealously and with immense erudition to the clearing of the quarters as yet unknown. Author of numerous and most remarkable books, the reading of which is indispensable to anyone wanting to understand Pompeii and Herculaneum down to the minutest details of their physical and spiritual existence, Professor Maiuri adds to his eminent abilities the faculties of goodwill and helpfulness to those who trouble him for information.

For nearly half a century, the archaeologists' aim, through restoring each object to the place it occupied at the moment of the eruption in 79, has been to create the illusion that the life of the inhabitants is starting up again exactly where it left off. Likewise they have endeavoured to match up the face of today's Pompeii and that of the ancient city, to enhance the powerful impression given to us in our visit to these buildings which are no longer 'ruins' but habitable dwellings just as they were.

So that this evidence may have its maximum effect, the reader will visit all districts of these reconstructed cities, and each monument that he looks at will enable him to explore different provinces of ancient life. In the temples and private sanctuaries he will be, as it were, initiated into the various religions which flourished in these highly cosmopolitan cities. He will walk in the Forum, where lawsuits are heard, where business is transacted and where the major events of public life are enacted. In the theatre he will attend comedies and tragedies, in the Amphitheatre he will witness the savage coursing of wild beasts and the gladiatorial combats. In company with the Pompeiians, who spend a good few hours of each day there, he will visit the *thermae* with their wonderful comfort and unprecedented luxury: the *thermae* throw much useful light on habits and manners in the Roman provinces.

To grasp the details of popular life in all their warmth and colour, the reader will enter shops and taverns, he will see the flagons and goblets on the counters, he will read the notices scribbled on the walls. In the baker's house, the loaves have just emerged from the oven; at the dyer's, the vats await their multicoloured liquids; at the home of a wealthy patrician, the table is laid for a splendid banquet. From the draper's large store, to the modest inn for wagoners, to the brothel, the elements of the life of the people, thus reassembled and juxtaposed, re-create the essential image of a provincial city, elegant and prosperous, mercantile and probably overpopulated at the moment when Christ's Apostles disembarked in the Bay of Naples. Nor has the world of the dead been neglected; for vast and often splendid necropoles extend beyond the gates, no cemetery being legally (or in fact) allowed to exist within the enclosure of the walls.

As for the private dwellings, whether huge, grand aristocratic mansions or houses of ordinary middle-class folk, each of these here described illustrates a particular corner of the life of the Pompeiians and Herculaneans, and the visitor cannot but feel the impression of intimacy created for him in these rooms and gardens. The question of the grouping and order in which this tour of private houses should be made suggests various alternatives, but it has seemed most useful to go from the least known to the best known: that is, to direct visitors in an inverse sense to that of the history of the excavations. Beginning therefore with the buildings most recently discovered, the object of the present excavations, which started in about 1950, we go back to the fairly recent ones, set in train around 1910 by new principles of restoration, preservation and presentation, and we finally reach the old celebrities, whose luxury and magnificence were extolled in works of the last century, such as the House of the Faun and the House of the Vettii, among others.

A brief survey of art in Campania (painting, sculpture, stucco, art objects) at the beginning of our era is the necessary complement of this survey, to define the essential characteristics of aesthetics and techniques such as are encountered at every turn in the private houses as well as public buildings. The unusual features of Pompeiian frescoes with their evolution of styles, the cult of everything that could create superb and exquisite decoration, the refined, often flawless taste of this wealthy and cultivated people, add to these re-created cities a grace and a brilliance of colour which constitute their greatest ornament.

The illustrations of this book form therefore an indispensable part of the picture which it is hoped to create for the reader, of these extra-ordinary, fascinating cities. I am indebted to Mr. Edwin Smith for his photography, which I trust the reader will find as brilliantly evocative as I myself do, and to my publishers for generously making this presentation possible.

HISTORY OF POMPEII

As far back as it is possible to go into the past, back to that dim period of the Iron Age, of which burial furnishings have been discovered in the Campanian necropoles of Torio, San Marzano, Striano, the shores of the Gulf of Naples between the two horns formed by the Cape of Misenum and the headland of Sorrento have been inhabited, by peoples either native to the area or not. The fertility of the land, the abundance of vegetation, the beauty of the setting, the facilities for fishing and navigation offered by the little gulfs hollowed out slightly all along the rim of the vast bay, the mildness of the climate: all this must inevitably tempt outsiders, and indeed from the time of the first founding of a town on the site of Pompeii, that town and its surrounding region were laid open to predatory designs.

What were the first inhabitants of this part of southern Italy which was to be called Campania? Probably rather primitive folk living by tillage, hunting and fishing – in the seventeenth century there were still forests abounding in game on the slopes of Vesuvius – and in very simple huts, the roofs of which were pierced in the middle to let in the sunlight and let out the smoke from the hearth. Historians of architecture recognize in these hutments with their pierced roofs the prototype of the Roman dwelling in its earliest form, which was to be elaborated more and more with the advance of civilization, but which remained centred round the main room, the *atrium*, distinguished by a roof that was open in the middle: this opening being the *compluvium*, through which rain water fell into a pool set in the centre of the room.

The actual name of the city, Pompeii, stems from a word of the Oscan language, spoken by the inhabitants of this region at the time of their entering upon the city's history, around the eighth century B.C. Who were the Oscans? An Italic people settled here for ages and perhaps even the descendants of the Stone Age men who were the first to inhabit this

11

country. But it is not the past of the Campanian people which is of interest today; what is important for the historian of Pompeii are the traditions which survived from these dim ages and which account for the development of the city. Although the Greeks, the Samnites, the Etruscans and the Romans successively left their mark on the aspect of the city and its vicinity, the Oscan language continued in current use until the period of the Social War in 90 B.C. This war, lasting two years, aligned the confederated peoples of the Roman republic against Rome, who denied them the freedom of the city and regarded them as subject peoples. Campania was involved in these hostilities, and Pompeii recruited for her defence troops levied from among various Italic groups. As divers inscriptions of that epoch testify, Oscan was the common tongue of this composite army, whether the force was constituted out of authentically Oscan tribes, or the necessities of leadership imposed a unity of language on soldiers of different peoples not therefore all speaking the same dialect.

The origin of the Oscans remains uncertain. Some historians would have it that Campania was their native region, but certain analogies of language make it a possible supposition that they came from Illyria and invaded Italy by crossing the Adriatic or the Julian Alps. Their conflicts with the Ligurians, Umbrians and Etruscans go beyond the scope of this work, as does the hypothesis that they may have constituted the original basis of the Roman people. If Pompeii already existed as a town at the period when properly speaking it was Oscan, nothing of that has remained. No trace of a genuinely Oscan civilization has come down to us, and it would seem that the endowing of these people with a culture worthy of the name was due to the Greeks, who very early on settled in this region.

It was in the eighth century B.C., in fact, that the first Ionian settlements appeared in Campania, by reason of the remarkable facilities which the Gulf of Naples offered to foreign navigators. The little cities which sprang up round the trading centres of Ionian merchants had for the most part Greek names: Naples itself is none other than the ancient Neapolis or 'new city'. Pompeii must already have been a settlement of some importance since she did not come in for re-baptizing and kept her Oscan name.

It is imagined that the district must have been cattle country, as some philologists derive the word 'Italy' from the Oscan term '*viteliu*' or 'calf'. I do not quite know what to make of this hypothesis, which is here set down for what it is worth. Be that as it may, the coastal lands of the Gulf of Naples had to cope with foreigners who were not content with coming to trade with the native populations. The situation of Pompeii in particular, by the sea, with the mouth of the Sarno offering a position favourable to maritime trade, and sited as she was on a height allowing of defence against aggression and surprise attack, soon marked her out to the Greek immigrants as an important strategic point which combined with the bases of Cumae, Dichaearchia (the present-day Pozzuoli) and Misenum, would command the entire Gulf, of which the headland of Sorrento, dedicated to Athena, was also a firm bastion.

As the Greeks were not brutal conquerors but shrewd merchants, they met no opposition on the part of the Oscans. Neighbourly relations were speedily established between the newcomers and the natives and, as always happens in such circumstances, it was the more civilized people, that is to say the Greeks, who imposed their culture. The Ionians, as is well known, always felt constricted in their own homeland and incessantly sought a foothold on Mediterranean shores; Sicily and southern Italy appeared to them as a land favoured by the gods, where it would be pleasant and profitable to establish colonies. Campania was rich in raw materials; using the coastal towns as a springboard, it would be easy to penetrate into the northern regions of Italy, Etruria in particular, which possessed abundant metal mines.

The sites of Pompeii and Herculaneum – the latter named after the tradition that Hercules, returning from Spain, had broken his journey and founded a city there, which the Greek historians of the fourth century B.C. called Heracleion – quite as much as those of Cumae, Pozzuoli and Naples, were to become the first nucleus of a prolonged Greek occupation of southern Italy. What had been initially a chain of coastal trade-centres where the Hellenic merchants came to sell their manufactured goods to the natives, exporting what the buyers gave them in exchange, became fairly rapidly a succession of flourishing towns which, like those of Sicily, mirrored Greek civilization, the latter having no difficulty in supplanting what Oscan civilization there may have been; and it can be affirmed that Pompeii and Herculaneum, from the

13

time they first entered into history, were placed under the ensign of the Hellenic spirit.

The immigrants had however to reckon with their Etruscan neighbours, who had considerable maritime power, who enjoyed an intensely busy trade, and who were animated by a determination to wield power that was as disturbing for the peoples bordering on them as it was remarkable. But the Etruscans could not have been powerful enough to establish a lasting hegemony over the towns of the Gulf of Naples, or even to mark these with their imprint. It seems that the Etruscans succeeded in dominating the area for scarcely half a century, since the Greeks fiercely opposed them and managed to wrest it from them definitively after the naval victory of 474 B.C. off Cumae. Forced to give up their ambition of possessing Campania, the Etruscans retreated into Tuscany, Umbria and Latium, and the Greeks re-established their control over the towns, which in fact they had never completely lost, so strongly had these places fallen under the influence of the Hellenic spirit.

This influence may be seen in the defence arrangements of Pompeii, which are of purely Greek type, and in the pristine structures which we shall encounter below in surveying the oldest part of the city, which is the Triangular Forum.

But it can sometimes happen that military strength – not to say brute force – will ultimately prevail over an opponent who is more highly civilized but less well equipped for war: this is what came to pass when the Greek and hellenized towns of Campania were exposed to the Samnite invasions.

The Samnites, said to have belonged to the Sabellian tribe, inhabited Samnium, the region north of Campania. In Roman history they have the reputation of hardy and formidable warriors; even though subject to Rome, they were never completely subdued and during the third and second centuries B.C. continued to vie with her for leadership of the Italic peoples. The Samnite soldiers depicted on an ancient Roman fresco were strong, tough, fierce highlanders, avid for military conquest. From the moment when they first had designs upon Campania, the hellenized Oscans and the Greeks could offer but feeble resistance to the invasion of these terrible campaigners who, as well as being dedicated to soldiering, were splendidly accoutred.

The Samnites' chief ambition, inspiring all their undertakings up to the time when they were definitively crushed by the Romans, was to set up a federation of the Italic peoples, of which they would naturally be the leader. This ambition clashed with that of Rome tending in the same direction, her policy being aimed at subjugating these same Italic peoples, including the Samnites. These latter, if they could annex Campania, would lay hands on flourishing towns and a fertile region, and acquire extremely strong strategic positions to facilitate the maritime expansion after which they were undoubtedly hankering, as their greed for conquest knew no bounds.

Having conquered Campania, they rebuilt Pompeii according to the formula specific to the Italic peoples, and the city still bears numerous traces of this: there are, for example, houses built after the Samnite type, utilizing the style and technique of this people, which are clearly distinguishable from the method of the Romans who were to come later. In the use of building materials two Samnite periods can be recognized: the first dating from the fourth and third centuries B.C. – they had acceded here around the end of the fifth – employing mainly volcanic substances; the second from 200 to 80 B.C. using tufa more. The *palaestra* known as the Samnite one is an excellent example of their architecture.

The Campanian towns were once again contained in the sphere of Italic civilization, but the Samnite power was not to be of long duration. The Samnite Wars, which took place between 343 and 290 B.C., began with the Samnite attack on Capua, which called Rome to its aid. It was during this war that the famous Roman heroes Decius Mus and Manlius Torquatus distinguished themselves. During the last period of the war, the Samnites having allied themselves with the Etruscans and Umbrians, the outlook for Rome seemed very precarious, but Curius Dentatus put an end to hostilities by systematically laying waste the Samnite country, thus finally overwhelming these people.

There was no reason for Pompeii to be involved in this war, apart from the fact that she had pledged her allegiance to the Samnites, but the Romans deemed it expedient to push their enemy as far back as Campania, which for them too was a fine prize. In 310 B.C. a Roman squadron appeared in the Gulf of Naples, making for the mouth of the Sarno, on whose shores rose the walls of Pompeii. Admiral Publius

Cornelius landed his soldiers, who began to devastate the country. Then it was that the Pompeiians, hitherto little concerned with the Samnite Wars, reacted forcefully against the insolence of the invader and fought off the Romans. Twenty years later, unhappily, the Italic republic was no more, and Rome replaced the Samnites as ruler of Pompeii, on which she imposed the status of ally (*socius*).

The allies retained a certain autonomy; their traditional institutions and their own language were left to them, but they had to acknowledge themselves subject to Rome, though without acquiring Roman citizenship; this constituted a rather humiliating dependency. In point of fact, however, Pompeii remained Samnite in custom and aspect. The control exercised by Rome was restrained and slight (as she was much absorbed in her struggle with Carthage, the suzerain hardly wished to antagonize her vassals), and Pompeii rested faithful to this allegiance, when other Italic peoples took their chance on regaining independence by backing Hannibal. *Carthago deleta*, the Pompeiians were repaid for not having broken faith with Rome.

But they were not quite without hope of throwing off the Roman yoke, and when the Social War broke out in 90 B.C., they too were enrolled under the banner of Judacilius and Pompedius Silo. Rome mobilized all her forces, under the command of her best generals, Sertorius, Marius, Sulla and Murena, to quell her rebellious allies whose federation constituted a powerful coalition. For about two years fortune favoured now one and now the other of the adversaries, but Sulla finished by overwhelming the Campanians. In 89 B.C. Herculaneum and Pompeii were taken after a long siege.

Stabiae had been completely razed to the ground; in the time of Pliny, all that remained of this city was a few villas. Such tactics did not encourage the Pompeiians to open their gates to Sulla, who was well known to be brutal, savage and implacable in his dealings with the vanquished, even when they yielded themselves up to his mercy. Pompeii therefore bore the siege, after having reinforced her garrison with Oscan tribesmen, to whom were allotted quarters in different parts of the city; and in these circumstances the walls were marked – as will be described below – with inscriptions in the Oscan tongues, to indicate the lay-out of the quarter in general and of various strategic points.

The city was saved, however, by a diversion created by Lucius

Cluentius, who tried to relieve her by bringing up an army of reinforcements; Sulla rushed to meet this army, pursued it to Nola where he massacred it and there imposed a peace. Apart from the devastations inflicted on several cities of the federation, the allies, though vanquished, carried the day, since Rome gave them what they wanted: that is, the status of Roman citizenship. But in order to avoid a recurrence of such events, she withdrew all the liberties which she had previously left them, and took the opportunity to establish in the conquered territories colonies of army veterans, among whom were distributed estates taken from the inhabitants.

A weighty and often hard infliction, these colonies of veterans, from whom a new class was to evolve, were highly detrimental to the people of the regions where they were established. These soldier-husbandmen in fact formed a kind of garrison to be mobilized at any time; and their relations with the people dispossessed in their favour were not always equable.

As regards Pompeii, Sulla did not resort to the harsh reprisals that he had inflicted on the Etruscan cities which had gone over to Marius; these had been razed to the ground by Sulla's order and their entire populations had been led into slavery. Dictator for life in 81, undisputed master of a Rome in which his reign was one of terror, he had the greatness of spirit to spare the Campanian cities which had held out against him in the Social War. He had a fondness for this region, and had a magnificent villa built for himself near Pozzuoli, and here in 78 he was to end his days.

Two years before his death, wishing to reward his old comrades of battle who had fought with him in Italy, Africa, Cappadocia and Greece, he established, after his victory over Mithridates, the colony which was to bear the name of Venus, already beloved of the Pompeiians: the Cornelia Veneria colony. Formed out of estates from which citizens who had been imprudent enough to side with the allies had been banished, and placed under the control of the dictator's nephew, Publius Sulla, this colony was the starting-point of the romanization of Campania.

Just as, some centuries before, Pompeii and Herculaneum had gladly accepted the Greek influence, so now of their own accord they submitted to Roman institutions. The two cities benefited, besides, from the

17

interest taken by the capital in a region with so many natural advantages. Many were the Romans who made a habit of coming to take their thermal cure in the hot springs of Pompeii as well as in those of Pozzuoli and who, prolonging their stay much beyond what was necessary for the cure, settled permanently or provisionally in Campania and had town houses and country villas built. This altered the aspect of the two cities and the future of their inhabitants; trade boomed, and the standard of living was transformed. The old Samnite cities, now become Roman watering-places, saw the upsurge of a new class, the bourgeoisie, who took the lead in municipal affairs. If Herculaneum was not much affected by this social evolution, Pompeii on the contrary was profoundly changed. Making good use of her substantial new prosperity, she expanded her luxury industries, her agricultural output and her trade with over-seas countries.

By the same token, she became a choice plum for the greed of the rebel slaves who, under the leadership of Spartacus, laid waste Campania in 73 B.C.[1] How a fugitive slave, a gladiator risen from the arena, could make all Italy tremble for several years, hold the Roman legions in check, and found a kind of revolutionary republic in the districts he had conquered, is like a romance of fiction. It was an extraordinary history, that of this young Thracian captured during the war waged by the Romans on his people, brought to Italy and devoted by his master to the profession of gladiator. Animated by a desire for revenge on those who had massacred his family and reduced him to slavery, aware of the enormous power inherent in the mass of slaves employed in town and country, Spartacus, endowed with the abilities and spirit of a ruler, determined to call his fellows into revolt.

Fired by the enthusiasm of a visionary harlot whose lover he was and who had told him he would gain the royal crown, he began by stirring up the gladiators attached like himself to the barracks of Capua. The Capuan gladiators defeated the small detachment of soldiers sent out to quell them – it had been imagined that a simple policing action would suffice – and the victors spread into the countryside, calling out the slaves in revolt. Their army kept growing all the time, well equipped with arms won from the defeated legions marshalled against them, until the men under Spartacus ultimately numbered more than 70,000, and the finest Roman generals could not prevail over them.

At the start of operations, Spartacus wished merely to get out of Italy and return to Thrace, where he would take his hereditary place as chieftain, but his lieutenants and his forces had a more immediate objective: to pillage Italy, make their masters expiate the sufferings and humiliations inflicted on the slaves, seize Rome and set up a government of this pitiful proletariat, which was what the servile condition amounted to. A slave was in fact a chattel completely at the master's disposal and, for all the mitigations of his lot in the course of centuries, was still a kind of sub-man powerless to control his own life, unless he managed to amass some money through which he could buy his freedom from his master and move up into the class of freedmen.

Ill-treatment was not spared the slave, even if monstrous owners like the notorious epicure who had disobedient or idle slaves thrown to the lampreys were rare;[2] all that prevented landed proprietors from abusing their human livestock was the fact that trained slaves, specializing in some particular work, were expensive. They were feared, they were mistrusted; and the old law which provided for the execution of all the slaves of a master who had been assassinated, on the supposition that they could all have been accomplices of the crime, guilty of having wished it if not carried it out and capable of rejoicing in it, was aimed also at preventing uprisings and quelling them with extreme savageness.

The inhabitants of Pompeii saw the gladiators and rebels pass before their walls when, hard-pressed by the legions of Crassus, Spartacus took the bold course of sheltering in the crater of Vesuvius. At that time, the volcano did not have the same aspect as today. Within the memory of man, there had not been an eruption. The mountain was covered with fields, vineyards, groves, even forests abounding in game. The situation of the slaves must, however, have been critical, for merely to encircle the base of the volcano sufficed to block any way out for the besieged. Threatened by starvation and drought, and ashamed at being caught in a trap like an animal, Spartacus succeeded in getting his troops out down a side of Vesuvius which the Romans had not thought to block, for it was very steep and appeared impassable. Spartacus had his soldiers contrive rope-ladders out of branches of the vines which grew abundantly here, and so managed to thwart the vigilance of his enemies, on whom he afterwards fell, taking them by surprise, as they thought him still dug in on the summit of the mountain. The Pompeiians escaped

19

with a good fright, and when the army of slaves moved on out of view, they gave thanks to Venus, their patroness, who had saved them. Crucified together with his last faithful adherents, Spartacus expiated his reckless ambition to free those men whom the social conditions of the time had inescapably condemned to slavery.

This scare over, life went on as before, easy and happy, in the Campanian cities, which had quite given up any claim to independence and adapted themselves all the better to Roman rule as they found it in their own interest. Accordingly as the Romans, attracted by the waters of Pompeii, became more numerous, the villas on the sea-shore and on the mountain slopes were seen to multiply.

The emperors themselves had a great fondness for this Gulf of Naples. Tiberius established his favourite residence on Capri, Caligula on Ischia, and the whole shoreline of the Gulf from Cumae to Sorrento was adorned with magnificent dwellings where the masters of the world, great court personages, the Roman aristocracy and the class of parvenus who thought to move up in the world by rubbing shoulders with the nobility, all lived in happy and voluptuous idleness. Very remote was Rome with her noisy plebs, her streets blocked with crowds, her tall buildings keeping out the daylight from the narrow alleys, her political quarrels and intrigues.

The advent of Spartacus's army, possibly only a stone's throw from the walls of Pompeii, had been the last threat of a warlike nature to have troubled the peace of her citizens. With the exception of some foreign campaigns, episodic and powerless to disturb the security of the Empire, no peril could shake the Romans. The reign of Augustus and the Pax Romana gave a considerable spur to trade, and Pompeii of course had her share. It was in that period that the houses of the wealthy inhabitants were rebuilt with a corresponding degree of luxury and taste.

Even more completely assimilated by the Romans than they had been by the Greeks, the Campanians could not imagine that their tranquillity would ever be troubled by some external happening; they placed their trust in the power of the legions and the wisdom of the emperors. It had not occurred to them that all peace is ephemeral, that any kind of well-being is open to terrible reversals. It was Vesuvius which was to bring home to the Pompeiians the cruel instability of fortune.

THE VOLCANO ROUSED

The Earthquake of the Year A.D. 62

FOR centuries Vesuvius had remained perfectly tranquil. Explosions of gas and eruptions of lava, which had once been frequent and had given the ground upon which Pompeii was built the features determining the lay-out of the city, had virtually ceased, within the memory of man. Neither the old Italic inhabitants, nor the Oscans, nor the Samnites had experienced the wrath of the volcano; the region, in past time often convulsed with earthquakes which had conferred on the Gulf of Naples the outline it retains today and had divided Ischia, Capri and Procida from the mainland, appeared to have nothing more to fear from this elemental fury. To look at Vesuvius, now green and covered with vineyards and fertile fields, it was scarcely conceivable that down its once-bare slopes had poured those torrents of fiery lava which, cooled off, had settled in dark beds, upon which the first inhabitants of Pompeii had built their humble dwellings.[3]

The taste of security is so strong with men that when a danger is once past they refuse to imagine that it might return. No kind of tradition of disaster had been handed down through the generations, no hazard had supposedly threatened the Campanians apart from that stemming inevitably from the ambition and greed of neighbouring peoples, tempted by this fortunate land. From the elements themselves, there was nothing to fear. The deep caverns in which the earth's fire still boiled and rumbled were so remote as to form no part of people's imaginings.

Thus it was a day like any other, with the usual round of work and pleasure, this 5th of February in the year A.D. 62 when, in spite of the winter being severe elsewhere, Campania was bathed in brilliant sunlight. It was midday. The people had interrupted their business talks, speechifying and bargaining, and had gone home for their meal. Taverns and hostelries rang with the demands of clients, and slaves were busying

21

themselves about the stoves, when there resounded a long, muffled roar, come from no one knew where. This ghastly noise was so extraordinary that no one could divine its origin or significance; nothing like it, as far back as could be remembered, had ever been heard. The sky was blue, the air calm, the breeze mild and fresh. Being superstitious and given to anxieties about having displeased a god by some omission in the worship due him, the Pompeiians thought that Jupiter must be vexed; then they fixed on Neptune as the one, since a suspect turbulence was heaving the sea, raising towering waves. Not till the moment when the rumblings and crackings could be heard underfoot did the Pompeiians guess the truth. Already large clefts divided slabs of the paving, and walls of houses reeled as if pushed by giant hands. Enormous columns, torn from their bases, smashed on to the temple mosaics with a horrible din, and tiles slipped from the roofs to shatter in the streets.

The inhabitants hurried from their houses, crying out and making for the open where they would not run the risk of being crushed by the collapse of houses and of the magnificent buildings that were the city's pride. Those who lived near the gates got out speedily into the country, which was hardly better off than the town. Unexpected chasms suddenly would yawn across the roads, swallowing up wretched people. Entire houses and orchards disappeared into gaping abysses. Those left behind in the city, however, were the worst off, for they did not know which way to escape, with all the streets blocked by heaps of rubble.

Floods soon added their havoc to that of the earthquake. The great reservoir situated near the Porta Vesuvio gave way, unleashing torrents through the city, and these waters swiftly joined the streams gushing from the bronze and lead pipes broken by underground heavings of rocks. The whole ingenious conduit system for catching, channelling and bringing the mountain springs into Pompeii – the system on which the aediles plumed themselves and which was constantly being improved and kept up at great expense – had been destroyed in a single instant.

The first tremor was of brief duration, however, and a moment later quiet was restored. Amidst the clouds of dust rising from stones and plaster, with the walls still trembling, the Pompeiians regained hope and assurance: the cataclysm was over. All ran for their houses, if the earthquake had found them away from home, to find out what had happened to their families and possessions; but scarcely an hour had passed when another roar and tremor revived all their fears, precipitating everyone once more into the streets. So it went on till evening: spaced out unpredictably at shorter or longer intervals, the spasms of the earth kept on recurring, but from the increasing faintness of the tremors it seemed as though the fury of the thing were abating. Nevertheless, the people hardly dared believe in their full deliverance from it, since throughout that afternoon the successive alternations of hope and despair had kept them panic-stricken.

Nightfall brought a return of security at last. But quite a number of columns, unsettled on their plinths, still fell, and tottering, broken walls folded up; and each time, the inhabitants of the quarter where the accident occurred would rush out of their houses, wailing and shrieking as if the wrath of the earthquake were once more upon them. Two valuable documents describing the cataclysm of 62 have come down to us. One is a letter of Seneca's, exactly reporting the happening which devastated southern Italy that year and which in all likelihood afflicted the whole shore-line of the Gulf of Naples.

With calm restored, the effects of the disaster could be reckoned at leisure. Yawning abysses riddled the ground, some of these so huge that in one a flock of six hundred sheep, as Seneca noted, had been swallowed up in a single instant. Magnificent country villas were so badly damaged as to be beyond repair: the owners could only abandon them. In the city itself, public buildings had been worse damaged than private houses, which were constructed of lighter materials. The temples had particularly suffered: the one dedicated to Isis, almost wholly destroyed; the Temple of Jupiter, where the columns had crashed to the ground, dragging down the gilded roof with its glittering acroteria; the Temple of Venus Pompeiana, who had sadly neglected her duties as watchful guardian and protectress of the city.

As regards that part of the city where the Forum was situated, we have the description of an eye-witness who was actually in the Forum at the moment of the cataclysm, and who wished to set down what he saw for the benefit of posterity. Later, in visiting the house of the banker Caecilius Jucundus, in the Via di Stabiae, we shall look at the shrine of the Lares, situated to the left of the entrance. On this, the banker had had placed two marble bas-reliefs depicting exactly what had happened on that 5th of February, 62, at the moment when Jucundus, strolling in the Forum, felt the ground heave and saw the columns of the Temple of Jupiter sloping perilously over him.

Jucundus was fortunate enough to escape the disaster and reach home safe and sound. He had attributed his rescue, as was fitting, to his Lares, who had protected him, and his first care was to decorate the shrine of these family gods with a representation of the event from which he had been delivered. The ex-voto dedicated by the banker to his Lares is no masterpiece, but its worth for us is the greater in that it constitutes a photographic, almost a cinematographic, document of what the man saw with his own eyes.

The first bas-relief depicts the north part of the Forum, towards which Jucundus's gaze was directed at the onset of the earthquake. We recognize very distinctly the two triumphal arches flanking the Temple of Jupiter to the right and to the left, the two equestrian statues set up on their high pedestals, and an altar. We can imagine Jucundus outlining with his fingertips, for the benefit of the sculptor who had not actually been at that scene of the catastrophe, how the statues were reeling on their bases, the columns falling sideways dragging down the architrave. The second bas-relief portrays what happened at the Porta Vesuvio, and what Jucundus saw at the end of the street on which his house fronted, when he finally got there.

The distance from the Forum to the banker's house is not very great, but he would have had to go by the Via di Nola before reaching the Via di Stabiae, and doubtless he ran into throngs of men and women rushing in all directions, vehicles with teams out of control, rubble piling up everywhere, and it must have taken him some time to go that short distance. It was probably when he reached the corner of the Via di Nola and the Via di Stabiae that, looking in the direction of the Porta Vesuvio, he saw the monuments near it collapsing in their turn. We can recognize very clearly the great *castellum* or reservoir, such as it was when discovered in 1902, and the three arches of the Gate itself, shaken by the earthquake; and what is even more striking in this depiction of the catastrophe is, in the street between the Gate and the reservoir, a chariot harnessed to two oxen, overturned by the earthquake, and smashed with the impact. All this is so exact and so vivid that a news photographer, arriving with his camera on the scene of the disaster, could not have rendered it more accurately.

24

The Eruption of A.D. 79

For seventeen years Pompeii was occupied with repairing the damage wrought by the earthquake. The citizens were eager to rebuild their houses more beautiful and luxurious and their temples even grander and more richly decorated than before. Peace and prosperity, the briskness of maritime trade and the safety of navigation finally obtained after the destruction of the nests of pirates that infested the Mediterranean, guaranteed the Campanian cities a long period of tranquillity and well-being. The political storms which sometimes stirred Rome reached the provincial cities only as a muffled, subdued echo. The life of the Pompeiians, between the two catastrophes, was without incident or disaster; memories of the terror which had been felt at the time of the earthquake had faded; there was no reason, it seemed, for such a calamity, unknown for so long, to recur; and regular and pious sacrifices assured the people of the gods' favour. The latter had just shown their good will once again to the Romans by giving the Empire a new master, so adored that he had been nicknamed the 'love and delight of mankind': Titus.

Despite the conjunction of these favourable omens, disturbing indications appeared at the beginning of August, A.D. 79. The ground again began to quake, but the tremors were so brief and the effects so tame that people were not much concerned. The damage was confined to some cracked walls and some statues unsettled on their bases. However, one portentous fact was recorded: springs ceased their flow and wells dried up. The people of antiquity were always disturbed by these unaccustomed events, interpreted as a mark of divine displeasure. Geologists could of course have explained that the disappearance of the earth's waters signified a considerable increase of vapours in the subterranean passages running into the crater of Vesuvius and an enormous rise in the pressure upon the stratum of lava which formed its cap.

The first weeks of August passed, nonetheless, in calmness and security; but on the 20th, grumblings and roars such as had preceded the earthquake of 62 were heard rising from the bowels of the earth. The ground was shaken, a cracking sounded, and out of the depths of the sea, normally so placid, alarmingly great billows were heaved up. This disturbance of the elements was communicated also to animals:

25

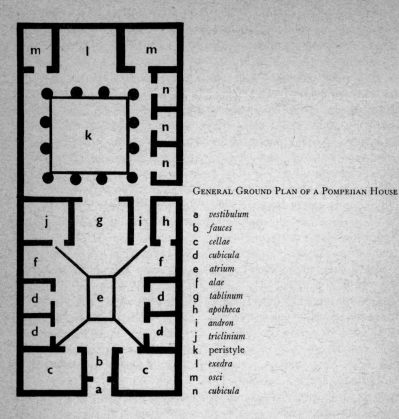

GENERAL GROUND PLAN OF A POMPEIIAN HOUSE

a   *vestibulum*
b   *fauces*
c   *cellae*
d   *cubicula*
e   *atrium*
f   *alae*
g   *tablinum*
h   *apotheca*
i   *andron*
j   *triclinium*
k   peristyle
l   *exedra*
m   *osci*
n   *cubicula*

horses, always so sensitive to anything unwonted, appeared uneasy and excited as if foreseeing, long before people could, what was going to happen. Cattle too snorted, bellowed and fought in their stables. Birds were flying away in every direction, silently, scaredly, as they do when a storm is imminent. Finally, the atmosphere held that terrible and weighty suspense which is commonly the prelude to catastrophe.

On the morning of August 24th, at last, a staggering, deafening crack, as if the earth had broken open in two, resounded from the volcano, while simultaneously the ground shook longer and more violently than on the previous days. Although there had been bright sunlight, the sky darkened suddenly, and birds stricken in full flight by an unknown malady fell to the ground. In this customary warmth of a Campanian high summer, something frightful and unbearable was rising from the earth, a heat comparable to that from a baker's oven, a foetid and burning blast.

Those brave enough to look towards Vesuvius were stupefied to see that the outline of the mountain had changed: the summit, which had been slightly convex, was now shivered and split, and presently nothing further could be seen, for out of this mouth torn open by fissures there suddenly gushed a mixture of smoke, flames, blazing mud and incandescent stones. In the darkness which had abruptly fallen, these fiery stones crossed the sky like shooting stars, but instead of being extinguished on reaching the ground, they set fires wherever they fell. Simultaneously the burning mud, overflowing to the surface in green and blue flashes, poured down the slopes of Vesuvius, carrying away the walls of villas, overwhelming farms, scorching vineyards and orchards, and rushing towards the sea, which itself was swollen and heaving in its bed, throwing up waves of boiling, sizzling water on to the banks. A kind of fearful struggle took place between the burning water and the flaming mire, which came together with an insane uproar. In certain places, the victorious seas swept the harbours, crushing galleons, pleasure-craft and heavy merchant ships: elsewhere the mud burst over the beach, forcing the waves so far back that today there can be seen, at a great distance from the shore, these deposits of lava fallen to the bottom of the sea and stretching out there.

According to what formation it encountered and the nature of the eruption, which varied among those places where the crater had opened up like the rind of a pomegranate, the torrent of lava mingled with a rain of ashes, flints and huge stones crashing down on the rooftops like ballistic missiles. Had it been possible to see through this atmosphere made impenetrable by the smoke, the solid rain of lapilli, and the mephitic gases that caught at the throat and made people's eyes water, they would have perceived that the outline of Vesuvius kept changing constantly as enormous fragments of the rock-face caved in and torrents of engulfing mud poured over the rims of shattered rock.

Towns and villages within a radius of some fifteen miles around Vesuvius fell victim to the disaster; more or less gravely afflicted according to their situation, all of them, including those farthest away, received

27

their share of scorching cinders and fiery stone. There was no means of defence against such a horror; flight itself offered no sure escape, for the torrents of burning mud moved as swiftly as a galloping horse, and no obstacle could stop them; the solidest walls were as nothing, metal dissolved in this furnace, and blocks of freestone were swept away like sandcastles.

In a matter of hours, these charming and prosperous towns disappeared under thick layers of burning matter which flattened the tall houses, poured in through the windows and split the roofs. Equestrian statues were seen floating like merest branches in solid mud; and constantly new surges of lava streaming down from the crater piled up on those which had already overrun and covered the afflicted cities, and which, cooling, formed a solid, indestructible crust over thirty feet thick.

Any calamity whatever, and however terrible its results, is always a windfall for the scholar who happens to be on the spot and who is fortunate enough to be able to observe its nature and development. Chance would have it that in that year the war fleet stationed at the Cape of Misenum was commanded by an officer who was also a distinguished naturalist: Pliny, called the Elder to distinguish him from his nephew Pliny the Younger.

At the onset of the eruption, the squadron commander thought first of all how fascinating it would be to observe the phenomenon at close quarters; and he boarded a galley, ordering the crew to row with all their might, as he wished to follow the development of events from nearer. He was so fascinated by the course of the disaster and so absorbed in noting down its process on his tablets, that he did not trouble about the risk he was running; he fell victim to his own scientific curiosity, and the precious tablets on which he had recorded his observations were lost.

Fortunately the letters written by his nephew Pliny the Younger to Tacitus have been preserved; for some days all Rome was discussing the calamity which had devastated those gilded cities in which, apart from all else, so many well-known Romans had been living. Tacitus, as an efficient historian, wished to know exactly what had happened and he asked Pliny for information. So it came about that, amidst his grief over the loss of his uncle, Pliny the Younger, himself an eye-witness and a keen one, sent his scholar friend a report of the catastrophe. This account is so real and vivid and detailed, and it re-creates so well the atmosphere of the event, that it is only fitting for it to be set down in full.

The Report of Pliny the Younger

'You ask me for an account of my uncle's death, so as to be able to hand down a more accurate report of it to posterity; thanks for this; I know that as related by you his death will immortalize his memory.

'He was at Misenum where he was commanding the fleet. On the ninth day before the Kalends of September, at about the seventh hour, my mother informed him that a cloud of extraordinary dimensions and appearance had been seen. He took his sun-bath, then a cold-water one and, after having eaten lying down, he set to work. Having called for his sandals, he climbed to a spot from which he had a better view of this remarkable phenomenon. The cloud was rising: onlookers could not tell, at a distance, from which mountain; later it was known to be Vesuvius. More than any other tree, the pine gives an idea of the shape and appearance of that cloud.[4] Projected into the air like an immense tree-trunk, as it were, it opened out into branches. I imagine that taken up by a sudden gust which then died down and left it, or defeated by its own weight, it scattered widely, now white, now dark and flecked, according to whether it bore along earth or ashes.

'A grandiose spectacle, worth a scientist's while to study at closer quarters. My uncle had one of his small craft got into trim and gave me the option of accompanying him. I answered that I would rather work; as it happened, he himself had given me something to annotate. As he was leaving the house, he received a note from Rectina, Caesius Bassus's wife, who, alarmed at the nearness of danger (for her villa was at the foot of the mountain and escape was possible only by ship), begged him to save her in this extremity. He changed his mind, and what he had begun for love of science, he now continued out of humanity. Having the quadriremes lowered, he took ship to rescue Rectina and many others as well, for this pleasant coast was extremely populous. He hurried to the places from which others were fleeing; he steered eastwards, directing course straight into the danger, and was so immune from fear that he dictated or noted down all the changing phenomena that he observed.

'Already ashes were falling on the boat, hotter and more thickly in proportion as it drew nearer; and also pumice-stones, black, ashen flints shattered by the fire. The sea, driven back, was no longer deep enough; rubble from the mountain made the shore inaccessible. Momentarily my uncle considered turning back, and his pilot urged him to do so. But "Fortune favours the brave," he said then. "Make for Pomponianus."

'Pomponianus lived in Stabiae, a town isolated by a cove where little by little the sea is thrusting into the curve of the shore-line. Here the danger was not yet immediate, but terrible all the same, and near at hand, what with its inexorable advance. Pomponianus, resolved to sail as soon as the opposing wind died down, had loaded all his movables on to ships. Favoured by this same wind, my uncle got to him, found him overwrought, but embraced and cheered and encouraged him, and to reassure him with his own confidence went to bathe. After that he sat down at table and ate with gusto or – which would be no less admirable – with the appearance of gusto.

'However, on several points of Mt. Vesuvius could be seen shining great flames, huge conflagrations, their brilliance and clarity enhanced by the night. And my uncle, to allay his companions' fears, told them that this was only country houses, abandoned by terrified rustics to the consuming fire, and empty. Then he lay down and slept a proper sleep, for those who stayed near the door heard the sound of his breathing, a big man's strong, resonant sound. Meanwhile the court on which his room abutted was filling up with ashes and pumice-stones, heaped to such a level that if he had waited any longer it would have been impossible to get out. Wakened, he went to rejoin Pomponianus and the others, who had not been resting. They took counsel. Should they stay in the house or range into the country? Houses, shaken by frequent and prolonged tremors, and as if torn from their foundations, tilted to the right, to the left, then resumed their original positions. In the open, there was the danger of the falling pumice-stones, though these were charred and light. Between these two hazards, it was the latter that they chose, my uncle giving in to the best policy, his companions replacing one fear with another. With towels they fixed pillows to their heads, as protection against the falling stones.

'Elsewhere the dawn had come but here it was night, the blackest

30

and thickest of nights, though counteracted by numerous torches and lights of every kind. They went back to the shore, to see from nearer at hand if the sea would allow of an attempt; it was still tumultuous and adverse. There my uncle laid himself down on a cloth spread out for him and twice called for cold water and drank it. Presently the flames and the sulphureous odour heralding their approach put everyone to flight, forcing my uncle to get up. Leaning on two young slaves, he rose and immediately fell down dead. I suppose that the thick smoke must have impeded his breathing and closed the respiratory passages, which in his case were naturally weak and narrow, often making him winded. When light returned, three days after my uncle had seen it for the last time, his body was found intact without any injury, and his clothing not in the least disarrayed; he looked more like a man asleep than like a dead one.'

This letter, with its sober brevity of a report, sets down exactly the impressions of a young man – he was eighteen – in the presence of a frightful cataclysm, and one who had himself come under the rain of volcanic matter. But another letter from Pliny the Younger, also written to Tacitus, supplements the one just cited, since, as already noted, the young man had declined to accompany his uncle and had stayed at Misenum, reading a volume of Titus Livius and, in keeping with his practice as a student, taking notes.

This second letter – probably an answer to one from Tacitus who, after having thanked him for his account of the circumstances surrounding Pliny the Elder's death, asked the nephew to tell him what he himself had noted and experienced – is full of striking images; and again, the considerable distance between Misenum and the towns immediately stricken by the eruption must not be forgotten.

Despite the hardihood which he showed, and which perhaps he assumed with a youthful bravado, in not wanting to interrupt his reading, Pliny the Younger nonetheless decided to quit the house, with the danger imminent. But he did so only after the pleas and reproaches of one of his uncle's friends, lately arrived from Spain, who, astonished by their unconcern, begged him and his mother to leave as quickly as possible. And at the very moment when they crossed their threshold, we find them caught up in the herd of fugitives:

'It was the first hour of the day, however the light appeared to us still faint and uncertain. The buildings around us were so unsettled that, in this place which was open, to be sure, but narrow, the collapse of walls, seeming a certainty, became a great menace. We decided to get out of the town. The panic-stricken crowds followed us, obeying that instinct of fear which makes it seem prudent to go the way of others; in a long, close tide they harassed and jostled us. Once clear of the houses, we stopped, and there encountered fresh prodigies and terrors. The chariots which we had taken were, though on level ground, knocked about in every direction and even with stones could not be kept steady. The sea appeared to have shrunk into itself, as if pushed back by the tremors of the earth. At all events, the banks had widened, and many sea-creatures were beached on the sand. In the other direction gaped a horrible black cloud torn by sudden bursts of fire in snake-like flashes, revealing elongated flames similar to lightning but larger.

'And now came the ashes, though as yet sparsely. I turned round. Ominous behind us, a thick smoke spreading over the earth like a flood followed us. "Let us get into the fields while we can still see the way," I told my mother, for fear of our being crushed by the mob around us on the road in the midst of this darkness. We had scarcely agreed on this when we were enveloped in night, not a moonless night or one dimmed by cloud, but the darkness of a sealed room without lights. Only the shrill cries of women, the wailing of children, the shouting of men were to be heard. Some were calling to their parents, others to their children, others to their wives, knowing one another only by voice. Some wept for themselves, others for their relations. There were those who, in their very fear of death, invoked it. Many lifted up their hands to the gods, but a great number believed that there were no more gods and that this night was the world's last, eternal one. Some, with their false or illusory terrors, added to the real danger: "In Misenum," they would say, "such and such a building has collapsed, and some other is in flames." This might not be true, but it was believed.

'A certain clearing appeared to us not as daylight but as a sign of the approaching fire. It left off some distance from us, however. Once more, darkness and the ashes, thick and heavy. From time to time we had to get up and shake them off for fear of being actually buried and crushed under their weight. I can boast of not having uttered a single lamentation, not a single word that might have been a sign of weakness, in so

32

1. Corpse of a Pompeian struck down in flight from the city. Pompeii Antiquarium.

2. Temple of Apollo at Pompeii. The great court with the statue of the god.

3. The narrow lane today called the Vico Storto, at Pompeii.

4. The great Palaestra at Pompeii. View of the west colonnade.

5. The Amphitheatre at Pompeii. A general view of the *cavea* and part of the tiers.

6.   Temple of Apollo at Pompeii. Columns bearing an inscription.

7. House of the Vettii, Pompeii. Painting in the lararium representing the domestic spirits and the guardian serpent of the hearth.

8. Forum Thermae at Pompeii. Statues of Atlantes supporting the cornice in the tepidarium.

great a danger. I imagined that one with all and all with one were going to perish – a wretched but strong consolation in my dying. But this darkness lightened and then like smoke or cloud dissolved away. Finally a genuine daylight came, the sun even shone, but pallidly, as in an eclipse. And then before our still-stricken gaze, everything appeared changed and covered, as by an abundant snowfall, with a thick layer of ashes.'

This letter of Pliny the Younger plainly re-creates the factual and psychological atmosphere of the catastrophe and its effect on that Italian population, fiery, sensitive to the least stir, often reacting excessively to the emotions that seized hold of them. The idea that the gods had abandoned them or were dead, and that night was extending its sway over the entire world, is that certainly of a panic-stricken crowd, driven from their homes by an unprecedented disaster. What made this calamity even more frightful was its extent and its duration. Despite the great distance from the Gulf of Naples to Rome, ashes and lapilli fell on the Romans themselves and on various other Italian cities far removed from Campania. An enormous number of towns and villages had been destroyed, totally or partly. The psychological shock was immense, and there were echoes of it a century afterwards, at the time when Dion Cassius heard tell of the end of Pompeii and of the fearful prodigies that had first heralded it and then marked it.

In such cases, the popular imagination is given free rein. It was not sufficient to blame Vesuvius: legends were recalled according to which giants, immured in the chasms under volcanoes, exhaled pestilential fumes in breathing, and set off earthquakes when returning to their millennial sleep. Certain individuals claimed to have seen these giants, released by the explosion, flying in the sky or walking about the earth. Others believed that the stars had come unfixed from the sky and rained upon the cities. As for the person unknown who wrote on a wall of Pompeii "*Sodom, Gomorrah*," he was probably a Jew, or perhaps even a Christian, who in the horrors of the disaster still had time to recall the abominable cities destroyed by the fire of heaven and buried under the waters of the Dead Sea.[5]

The Last Day of Pompeii

The number of dead in Pompeii during the eruption is estimated at about two thousand: a tenth of the population, in fact. The suddenness and fierceness of the disaster were such that it seems astonishing that so many of the citizens were able to flee in time to reach safety. It is true that among those two thousand there are not counted all the un-numbered dead who, taking ship, were wrecked in the boiling waves, or those who died in the fields where ashes crushed and buried them. A very great number, lastly, were asphyxiated by the gases breathed up from the ground, less deadly in the open country than in towns, but inescapably and fatally poisoning those smitten with them.

What was the first spontaneous reaction of the Pompeiians when the initial rain of fire began? It must not be forgotten that for four days ominous symptoms had multiplied, recalling those which had been experienced seventeen years before at the time of the earthquake, and which many of the inhabitants had not forgotten. It may therefore be supposed that as early as August 20th, when the first cracklings were heard, all those people who could conveniently leave their business and the city had already departed. Some took refuge in their villas, believing themselves safer here than in their houses where the earthquake had done greater havoc than in the country. But they made the mistake of judging the present by the past; an earthquake alone had devastated the city in 62, while in 79 the earthquake was only an accessory to the real disaster: the eruption. In this latter case, country residences were even more exposed, in all probability, than the cities.

The inhabitants who had stayed in Pompeii were surprised by the first showers of ashes and got away as quickly as possible. Luckily this happened during the morning at a time when most of the people had left their houses and were attending to business or pleasure in the Forum, the Palaestra or the Thermae. If the event had occurred during the night, the number of dead would certainly have been greater.

It is interesting for present-day man, rediscovering the city as it was on that 24th of August, 79, to put it to himself what he would have done in such circumstances and which escape route he would have thought advisable. The instinctive reaction of the individual in the face of imminent danger is flight: to flee as far as possible from the source of peril is an immediate and spontaneous act, where reflection does not intervene. That is what most of the Pompeiians did; and so as to get away the more swiftly they brought horses and beasts of burden out of the stables and sheds, mounted them and urged them to a gallop. It is doubtless for this reason – that anything which could be ridden was put to use – that corpses of animals, except dogs, have not been found in the ruins.[6]

There is evidence of this frenzy to get hold of anything ridable in the chariot laden with amphorae which has been discovered in front of the 'tradesmen's entrance' of the House of Menander; the vehicle is ready to go, but the draught animals had been hastily unharnessed and mounted. The very haste with which the throng jostling in the streets or urging and pressing on their mounts made for the gates, caused the weird bottle-neck entailing so many accidents. The narrowness of the gates, of which some had only a single arch, could not provide outlet for such an unlikely crush of panic-stricken fugitives.

To avoid being trampled by this frenzied throng, in which everyone was thinking only of his own safety and took little heed of anyone else, certain people thought it prudent not to be in too much of a hurry and to wait on events: experience shows, certainly, that in some cases panic causes more deaths than an actual catastrophe itself. The incurable optimists who always claim that 'everything will work out,' the aged and infirm, and their near and dear ones who did not want to leave them, stayed behind until the time when flight was no longer possible. There were also those who were anxious to take away with them money, valuables or objects with a sentimental or religious value, and who wasted much time in getting together their bundles.

Another instinctive reaction, finally, was that of those unfortunates who thought themselves secure in sealed rooms where they supposed that ashes and poisonous vapours could not get at them, or who could not make up their minds to leave their homes until such time as the streets were already impassable. Knowing from the letter of Pliny the Younger that at Misenum it was necessary to keep constantly on the move and to shake one's garments so as not to be suffocated and crushed under the weight of hot ashes, we can picture what must have happened in Pompeii, situated as it was directly at the foot of the vol-cano. With the thickness of the mineral deposit covering the city up to a height of over thirty feet, we may realize the speed with which the fugitives were crushed under collapsing roofs and walls, or buried under the fiery shower of lapilli. They would swiftly be made oblivious of what was happening by the mephitic vapours accompanying the deluge of ashes and asphyxiating the victims.

Not only Pompeii and Herculaneum disappeared under the torrents of lava, but also Stabiae and places whose names we know today but whose exact locality will probably always be unknown, as they were so totally wiped out. Where was Leucopaetra? Where are we to look for the remains of Taurania? Will Oplontis be brought again to light one day, as Pompeii and Herculaneum have been?

They were dead cities, emptied of their inhabitants and already unrecognizable beneath their crust of ashes and lava, on which for three days still the fiery substances belched forth by Vesuvius continued to fall, as if the elements were relentlessly pursuing the men of whom none, during the first hours of the cataclysm, had been spared out of all those it had overtaken. Pompeii had become a vast necropolis containing two thousand corpses, the sight of which was destined to give the first searchers of the ruins, and us today, an impression of infernal horror.

When the unfortunates who had not been able or had not wished to flee were surprised by death, if they were sheltered from the mineral downpour their bodies were reduced to skeletons, but more often they were covered by the masses of liquid and miry lava which little by little hardened and cooled to form a kind of stony shell in which the body decomposed ˙normally. Their corpses exist therefore, in the rocky magma, within the mould of a void which preserves the shape of the body.

Thus it is that what could be called moulds of these corpses are still frequently encountered in the excavations, and more will doubtless be discovered in the areas not as yet cleared. The most recent corpses are those of a man and woman and an old beggar who were caught by the explosion when they had just left the city by the Porta di Nuceria, and whose age, station and physical peculiarities, persons and clothing are now known, thanks to the process invented by Fiorelli.

Later, in describing the advances made during the last century in the work of unearthing and reconstituting Pompeii, we shall speak of the eminent place held by Fiorelli in the line of archaeologists of this site. For the moment, it will suffice to describe how he obtained casts of the disintegrated corpses, the shape of which had been preserved, inside, by the shell. He worked this with his 'lost wax' process, in the same way as a sculptor casting a statue. It having been ascertained that the imprint of the victims had left a space in which there remained only some trifling bony fragments – for example, the skull of the man found in 1956 at the Porta di Nuceria – the space was filled with liquid plaster, and when this had cooled and hardened, the casting was stripped of its shell of clay, it being necessary to proceed with great caution, as this crust of ashes nearly two thousand years old was as hard as stone.

What could reveal more truly or dramatically the last agonies of Pompeii than these frightful remains, some of which are displayed to the curiosity and pity of visitors in the Antiquarium? Obviously the most striking and spectacular have been kept to interest the tourists, but what is more important is the value to archaeologists of knowing how the inhabitants were dressed at the moment of the eruption and what objects they were carrying away with them. We learn thus that the beggar of the Porta di Nuceria had received of public charity sandals of very good quality and in excellent condition, and that he was carrying a sack into which he thrust the alms in kind that were given him.

It is a disturbing sight, to encounter these bodies tormented with suffering, anguish and fear, and petrified by suffocation in their appalling postures, each of which reveals the pangs of an agony individually lived through, the horror of a death swift or slow as the case varied, but inexorable. In the gladiators' barracks situated behind the Great Theatre there had been a moment of panic when the eruption began, but these rugged creatures got out all together, and it can be imagined how with their fists and swords they must have cleared a way for themselves through the crowd. In their headlong flight they forgot two of their number, undergoing punishment for some misdemeanour or other, who were locked up, their wrists manacled, in the room which served as prison cell. In another room of this barracks, among a heap of skeletons, the corpse of a woman wearing magnificent jewels has been discovered, her presence at variance with such a place.

An explanation appears, however, in the fact that, harshly treated as they were in their barracks, the gladiators were permitted to receive periodic visits, especially from prostitutes, whose attentions were allowed to be indispensable for the appeasement of their carnal appetites.

But the gladiators consorted not only with courtesans; these heroes of the arena enjoyed, throughout the city and in every class of society, an enormous popularity, to which the graffiti, as we shall see, bear witness. Ladies of rank and of loose morals often competed for their favours, and it is possible that the 'woman with the jewels' was one of those rich, distinguished Pompeiian women, who had chosen this fine summer morning for paying a visit to her lover in the barracks, where the sentry would complaisantly look the other way.

It was also a woman, the mother of a family, this one, who was escaping by the Porta Ercolano in the direction of the Villa of Diomedes; she had a baby clasped to her breast, and two little girls ran beside her, holding on to her garments. Some distance from the spot where this unfortunate family was struck down, in front of the gate to the Villa of Diomedes, was found lying a man holding by the halter a common goat, with a bell suspended from its collar; he had been struggling to drag it along with him. Elsewhere, in the House of Orpheus, there was a dog whom no one had thought of untying when they all fled, and who struggled fearfully, trying to dig his way through the ashes piling up on him. Still another dog in the House of the Vestals, but this one was found trapped together with his master, and neither died instantaneously nor was even asphyxiated: examination of the man's bones shows in fact that they were gnawed by the dog, after his master, the first to die of starvation, had been devoured by the animal, mad with terror and hunger.

Among the corpses piled in the so-called Vico degli Scheletri (Skeleton Alley), each reveals the manner in which that particular individual died, in keeping with his character, his psychology and perhaps also the belief which he might have had in the possibility of a joyful after-life. A woman was lying on her side, her head leant on her arms, as if asleep, the whole aspect of her body suggesting the tranquillity of slumber, a calm passing, without any struggle or agony. Beside her, a young girl who had put on her beautiful embroidered sandals that day had fallen with a gesture of despair and suffocated, while their servant, as he probably was, a colossus of a figure, struggled against asphyxiation and the rain of ashes with the furious and powerless resistance of an athlete who, maddened to feel his strength useless, contorted his arms and legs in a last effort to stay upright.

The priests of the Temple of Isis, situated between the Palaestra and the Temple of Jupiter Melichios behind the tiers of the Theatre, were having a meal when the eruption began; they were eating eggs and fish, which have been found nearly intact on the tables of their triclinium. These men, accustomed as they were to a spiritual existence in which their thoughts were directed to the hereafter, and assured of an after-life by their knowledge of the mysteries, did not show an unseemly haste to save their own lives: there were more valuable things to be protected.

They began by getting out the holy objects, the statues of Isis, plates and vessels on which the goddess's image was sometimes linked with that of Bacchus, and lastly the temple treasure; all this was thrown pell-mell into a sack of coarse cloth which the strongest among them hoisted over his shoulder. The vicissitudes of their flight and death are self-evident: it suffices to follow the Isiacs' trail and to mark their fall, one after another. The one carrying the sack was the first to give way; his companions rallied round to pick him up and gather together those objects which had been scattered. They were setting out together once again across the Triangular Forum, when a row of columns forming a portico toppled down, crushing several of them, while the golden plates slipped from their hands. The survivors took shelter in a house where they were trapped by streams of ashes and mud, and one after another they died there; the last had found a hatchet and succeeded in breaking through several partitions in his efforts to regain the street, but he was faced with a solid wall which withstood his hatchet, and behind him the burning mire kept steadily mounting, and so he died, still standing, wielding his hatchet.

In a tomb of the Necropolis of the Porta Ercolano, within the precincts of the *pomerium*, the descendants of someone deceased were celebrating a funeral feast-day, perhaps the anniversary of their relation's death. They were banqueting, in keeping with the custom, in a beautiful chapel painted with frescoes; but their ancestor's tomb was also their own, for the lava blocked up the bronze door and, to eternity, immured the living with the dead.[7]

Everywhere corpses, in this blasted city: corpses of young women, having stripped off their garments so as to run more swiftly, past caring about displaying their bodies; corpses of irresolute folk who made up their minds to get out only at the moment when their doors and windows were completely choked with mud; the corpse of a young girl who had lost one of her shoes; the corpse of a pregnant woman weighed down with the infant moving inside her; the mingled corpses of a family who, dying of asphyxiation, opened a window before which was a wall of fiery ashes; the corpse of a scrupulous house-keeper who was unwilling to be parted from her keys and her two vessels of silver; the corpses of the owners of the House of the Faun who, too much attached to the things of this world, lost time which might have saved their lives in emptying their jewel coffers, their caskets of gold and their sideboards full of silver dishes, and who, ascertaining too late that the house was already surrounded with lava and covered with a roofing of ashes, came back into their tablinum, to die there.

Certain ones we know by name. It is Tegetus who, unwilling to be parted from his beautiful bronze ephebus, died beside the marvellous statue in which he so delighted; it is the children of Paquius Proculus who were killed in their playroom on the first floor of their parents' luxurious house; it is Pansa who stayed behind to pack up his works of art carefully; it is Rufus who breathed his last in a terrible effort to inhale one more mouthful of air.

In some cases these life-casts reveal a whole story, such as that of the steward Erotus, who in his master's absence administered the property. At the onset of the eruption he ordered the slaves to stay in their rooms, but when the ash falling through the impluvium into the atrium reached the height of a man, he told them to make for the upper storeys and get out by the windows or by breaking through the roof. Some, emerging precipitately, fell into the lava, which immediately swallowed them up. As for the steward, he shut himself up in his little room by the entrance, made his little girl lie down on her pallet, and stoically waited for death, clasping in his hand the purse which had been entrusted to him, and his insignia of office, his master's seal.

What we see today of this Pompeii which disappeared in A.D. 79, nearly twenty centuries ago, is the history of a city and a people, but it is also – as these corpses show – the history of a great number of individual destinies; the tragic end of these men and women who in the face of danger and imminent death acted on a moment's impulse but also according to the dictates of their character. The casts after Fiorelli's method give us their physical details, from which can be deduced their age, strength and occupations; the features of their faces, imprinted in the tufa, reveal their mental state at the moment when the lava hardened their death-mask: the rebellion of the sensualist, the calmness of lovers or married couples who fell together, side by side, mingling their last breath, the serenity of the Orphic or the Pythagorean who believed in the next world and knew that nothing dies.

Infinitely varied are the lessons to be drawn from these ghastly remains, these pallid bodies, made immortal in grotesque, terrifying attitudes; the real lesson gleaned from a past re-created by archaeologists: the intimate secrets of the life of each being, dashed into a collective fate but never ceasing to be unique and different from all others.

THE DEAD CITIES REVIVED

LET us imagine a foreign traveller – a Greek, a Gaul or an Iberian – whom business or pleasure has brought periodically to Campania, and who in the last days of August, 79, draws near these charming cities which he is used to finding so enjoyable. We are supposing that he knows nothing of the disasters that have just occurred, and that he is unaware of all the tragic changes which have befallen the region. On horseback he follows the coast road, coming from Naples, and suddenly he stops, stupefied, before the landscape of desolation stretching ahead of him. The air is still tinged with an acrid smell, and although the sky has again become a clear blue, grey particles still float here and there.

If he lifts his eyes towards the summit of Vesuvius, he sees a yawning rent, jagged as a mouth of hell, and cavities out of which thick vapours rise. It is as if gigantic hands have roughly opened that mouth and separated the two jaws of the volcano. The mountain slopes covered with woods, vineyards and gardens a month ago now display nothing more than bare earth, sombrely grey, hollowed in deep grooves. Brown cliffs standing up from the ground at regular intervals are billows of hardened lava.

Who could believe that rich orchards and fine fields had been here? This arid, loathsome crust is reminiscent of hell, and the traveller might well believe himself passed without intermedium from the world of the living to that of the dead. If he looks for familiar villages, he perceives nothing more in this ghastly and silent desert than layers of sharp flints vomited forth by the volcano, and of ashes mingled with mire. No more trees, no more houses. The naked earth, sinister and sterile, unfolds in its dismal waves uninterruptedly from the mouth of the volcano to the road; and soon echoes of underground chasms covered by lava resound under the horse's hooves. The passers-by whom the traveller encounters bow their heads, cover their faces, avert their eyes when they enter the blasted region

This entire district now is unrecognizable. The vast villas, luxurious and splendid, which formerly dotted the countryside, with their rounded pines and tall cypresses, their silvery olive-trees and their pomegranate-trees flashing red fire: all have vanished without trace. Vanished too are the graceful cities extending their terraces along the sea. Not a farm, not a village remains. Only silence, horror and death. The traveller tries to distinguish the roof of Herculaneum, the temples of Pompeii, which stood out so splendidly in relief against the sky. Everywhere the same blackish mud, hardened, scarcely cool, out of which not a single column emerges. Who could say whether those famous and magnificent cities, whose beauties were extolled by mariners in every Mediterranean port, had been here or farther on?

In a few weeks, when the aura of superstitious dread round the places struck by the fire of heaven has subsided, when fear of another eruption has abated, when an atmosphere of dismal permanency has spread over the lava fields, some refugees will return to look for traces of their homes. By what indications are they to recognize that at such a spot in the crust of lava a familiar house had existed? They bring implements with them, and vigorously attack the mass of broken stone under which the cities are buried. By strenuous efforts they manage to dig pits and hollow out tunnels, and they enter the darkness which still stinks of mephitic gases. They are searching for remains of their parents or children lost in the catastrophe, for valuables, money, the tools worn to their use. This dangerous, killing labour – for the foolhardy searchers re-ascend half-asphyxiated by the *mofeta* – proves useless. Tremendous efforts gain them only a meagre result; death holds tightly to what it has taken.[8]

The survivors, settled in neighbouring cities spared by the eruption, grow accustomed to the new living-conditions provided them. Why return to that infernal desert? What is there to be got out of that immense necropolis buried under fathoms of tufa? Of what use to return, even in imagination, to a past totally finished?

Years pass. Old people recount to the young ones the disaster which devastated the region. Those who still remember the sites of the cities point them out from afar, but under that uniform desolation it is impossible to distinguish the spot where a town had been, or a field. Centuries pass. The contemporaries of the event have long since rejoined their ancestors in the shades. The deep-rooted memory of the eruption is gradually transformed into a vague, uncertain tradition. The legend, according to which there were once cities in that place, is recalled. What cities? This is no longer known. It is not even certain that the legend is true: how are these reports of the ancients to be verified? The names of Herculaneum and Pompeii have been obliterated from the memory of the people whose ancestors formerly lived there; when still, at long intervals, allying this remembrance to the almost mythical greed for fabulous treasure, people speak of one of these dead cities, they say simply 'the City': '*la Città*'.

La Città

It is under this name that Pompeii, invisible and undiscoverable, nonetheless survived. The rumour of buried treasures was handed on from generation to generation. Bold men ventured to descend into the shafts dug by the Pompeiians on their return after the catastrophe, but they ran against impassable masses of stones. They encountered fearful skeletons of men who had struggled violently against death before sinking into the burning, reeking mud. They found no treasure and at each step they took in these stinking tunnels, fear of landslips which would despatch them to join the corpses of former times speedily interrupted their explorations. The most intrepid gave up such searches, dangerous as they were and bringing in only slender takings. And then, as the centuries passed, new ideas, new customs like grains of sand in an hourglass came into being in the country. A new religion and a new society swept before them everything recalling the past. The Barbarians established themselves in Italy, the Saracens constructed their forts and *souks* there, the peoples of the North dreamed of conquering the peninsula. The Germans, Angevins and Spaniards contested southern Italy. Less and less did anyone think of '*la Città*', and even people's curiosity about it died away.

In the fifteenth century, however, the Renaissance spreading through all Italy was manifested in a dual movement and aspiration: a complete renovation of ideas, manners and customs to an authentically modern spirit, and also an almost fanatical passion for antiquity. Everything ancient was considered to be excellent and perfect. Every time the torso of a statue, a fragment of bas-relief, a piece of architrave bearing some words of an inscription, was found, it was proclaimed a masterpiece. Roman patricians dug in their vineyards and gardens in search of ancient works of art, and when they found any, they decorated their *palazzi* with them. The demand became so great that dealing in antiquities constituted a lucrative business. Ingenious forgers then took to manufacturing 'antiquities' for the ill-informed collector, and Michelangelo himself sculpted a sham antique which he sold as genuinely Roman in order to expose the blind predilection of those amateurs who had no interest in the genius of artists of their own time, but on the other hand squabbled over the merest scrap of marble dug from the ground.

History contains extraordinary resurgences. While the memory of *la Città* had remained almost completely obliterated during the Middle Ages, it seems that the Renaissance gave it a revival of interest. This exclusive passion for antiquity, this fervour brought to bear on seeking out evidence and on digging the ground in pursuit of remains of temples, palaces or basilicas, rekindled the interest of scholars and artists in that southern Italy where once had been flourishing cities. At Baia, Cumae, Pozzuoli, extremely interesting ruins were brought to light; why not also on the other side of the Gulf, beyond Naples?

This name, *la Città*, occurring at long intervals in legend and hearsay, piqued the curiosity of the humanists, who had pondered Martial's epigram, the forty-fourth of the fourth book: 'And here, Vesuvius, but yesterday shaded with green vines; its far-famed grapes were pressed in the moist vats; here, its hills, dearer to Bacchus than those of Nysa. Long since, on this mountain, the satyrs would lead out their choruses. It was a dwelling sweeter to Venus than Lacedaemon; by the name of Hercules this spot was dignified. And all was consumed in the flames, all covered with the grey ash, and the gods themselves would that they had not such power.'

But the view presented to the fifteenth-century traveller no longer corresponded to Martial's description. Woods and gardens, consolidated by centuries of security, had resumed possession of Vesuvius. Villages had been built, some even growing to the stature of small towns. The volcano was so peaceful, henceforth, that its slopes could without uneasiness be planted and built upon. If it happened that someone digging a well or laying the foundation of a house came upon ancient remains, he would call to mind *la Città*, but would not linger over this memory.

However, chance, which is often the Providence of archaeologists, willed it that in 1594 Count Muzzio Tuttavilla should have the idea of diverting the water of the Sarno to his beautiful villa of Torre Annunziata; with this intention, he ordered an underground channel to be dug. It so happened that the shortest route which this channel could take exactly crossed the ruins of Pompeii, entering what had been the city on the side of the Amphitheatre, then extending along the Temple of Isis and the Forum, and crossing the Necropolis of the Porta Ercolano, cutting through Pompeii's longest side.

The workmen digging the channel were not archaeologists, and the foremen directing them took little notice of the ruins encountered underground in their route. They chanced to bring to light inscriptions which, if only their curiosity could have been roused, might have led to the most immense discoveries. They even turned up a document which contained the answer to it all. In one of these inscriptions, which were rare and mostly inexplicit, there were two key words: '*decurio Pompeis*'. This concerned a Pompeiian magistrate, a decurion; and any people less heedless would have seen a remarkably valuable clue here. However, it was briskly concluded that a villa of Pompey had been accidentally stumbled upon; and then, the channel completed and the water streaming into the handsome fountains of the Tuttavilla estate, the matter was quietly forgotten.

While for so many centuries no one had ever thought about Pompeii, the humanists, avid readers of Latin texts, had come across the letters written by Pliny the Younger to Tacitus; they had read in Dion Cassius the description of the eruption. The fame of the martyred cities, the Sodom and Gomorrah of Campania, reappeared from time to time in the ancient authors, and the moderns began to muse about it, for it was an extraordinary and exciting thing, the history of these cities buried by an eruption and vanished without trace from the surface of the earth. Perotto spoke of it in his *Cornucopia*, Sannazzaro in his *Arcadia*, and it even came to pass that by some extraordinary intuition, gleaned mysteriously and inexplicably, the topographer Ambrogio Leone inscribed on a map of Campania the name '*Herculanum Oppidum*', not actually on the site of the real Herculaneum, but on that of Portici. This was in 1503.

It seems scarcely possible when the channel from the Sarno to Torre Annunziata, which was six years in the completing and was directed by an eminent architect, Domenico Fontano, crossed Pompeii through its entire length, that no one thought to establish a connexion of ideas between the tradition of *la Città*, the rare allusions of ancient texts, the findings of the workmen digging the channel, and the fact of the existence of the dead city of former times. This casualness can be explained in only one way: as the channel was being cut through the surface layer of the crust covering the buildings, the workmen mostly passed above these, without suspecting that a city of 163 acres was spread out below them.

The channel had already been completed for thirty years when a German humanist archaeologist, Holstenius, visited Naples and its environs and became passionately absorbed in the question of *la Città*. For him – and it is not exactly known on what data he based this assertion – *la Città* and Pompeii were one and the same. In 1651 Camillo Pellegrino supported the hypothesis laid down by the German in 1637, but still without furnishing proofs; however, in a less arbitrary fashion than Holstenius, he suggested the possibility that Pompeii was at least situated on the place denoted traditionally under the name of *la Città*.

The events bringing to light the remains of the Campanian dead cities were to come precipitately. On the occasion of a well being dug on the site of *la Città*, a controversy arose between the architect Picchetti and the historian Bianchini, concerning fresh inscriptions found by the well-diggers, inscriptions in which recurred the name encountered by Fontano's workmen a century before, at the time of the channel digging. Was this to do with Pompey or Pompeii? The architect opted for the Roman General, Bianchini inclined to the city. As public opinion was not roused by this debate, and as the disputants supported their theories in books read only by specialists, the matter rested there.

But happily the impetus had been given, and the numbers of connoisseurs interested in the Pompeii question became greater, and the research more active. Four years after the boring of Picchetti's well,

Macrini returned to the site, in 1693, descended into the tunnels, noted ruins of ramparts and columns and the rubble of houses, and expounded the idea that if Pompeii was not to be confused with *la Città*, at least excavations to find it should be undertaken in this region. It was not, however, Pompeii which was first discovered, but Herculaneum and, as usual, by a remarkable combination of circumstances.

The Treasure Hunt

Once again it was the question of a well that caused a peasant from Resina to go down into the ruins of what had been Herculaneum. Resina had in fact been built on the stratum of stone and ash covering that ancient city. The peasant's well having dried up, he wanted to deepen it so as to tap another level of water, but to his great disappointment the water continued elusive. Examining the earth that he removed, he saw that blocks of marble were contained in it. This was a windfall, since sculptors paid well for marble of such quality.

Now it happened that in 1710, through the vicissitudes of war and politics, Italy fell into the power of the Austrians; and a Colonel bearing the grand name of Maurice de Lorraine, Prince of Elbeuf, having married an Italian princess of the house of Salsa, contracted for a magnificent villa to be built for him in the neighbourhood of Portici, not far away. He brought over a French artisan who had invented the technique of manufacturing, from a mixture of stone and powdered marble, a cement as brilliant and hard as marble itself. The find of the peasant from Resina having reached the ears of the Prince of Elbeuf, the latter inspected the haul and at once realized that these splendid marbles could come only from ancient buildings of grandeur and distinction. Troubling no longer about the cement needed for the villa, he bought all those ancient marbles that were still in the peasant's possession and then bought the land, and hired workmen to set about excavations directed by himself.

The Prince of Elbeuf, it may be supposed, was not, initially at least, inspired by any archaeological passion; what he wanted was the wherewithal to decorate his new villa magnificently, and he was not much concerned about learning and scientifically establishing the origins of these precious bits of column and of sculptured architrave, of which he began to make a collection. Starting from the well, horizontal passages

48

were bored which blundered across the ruins of Herculaneum and opened out in the very midst of the Theatre. Knowing what marvels were contained in the theatre of an ancient city, we can imagine how an archaeologist would have been beside himself with joy at such a find. Faced with precious marbles, decorated with columns, profusely adorned with statues, vases, candelabra, the steps of the Theatre constituted in ancient times a veritable museum. And for the first time in history, an ancient theatre was discovered intact, in its actual state for the beginning of a performance, that is to say with its stage fittings, its machinery for making the gods and demons appear, its scenery, its accessories, its performers' dressing-rooms.

There was nothing like it in Rome or in the other cities of Greece or Italy, whose theatres have come down to us in a ruined state. In that of Herculaneum, on the contrary, apart from the masses of ash and lava which had infiltrated, a filthy torrent, everywhere, each object, each stone was still in place. Unhappily the Prince of Elbeuf was to destroy all that. As precious marbles and statues were taken from the Theatre, which the Prince believed to be the Temple of Hercules, they went to embellish the villa at Portici, which thus became the first nucleus of today's great archaeological museum of Naples. In every direction his workmen deepened these tunnels, called *cuniculi*, sunk in the tufa, and extracted everything movable, without taking the trouble to note down meticulously, as archaeologists do, the placing of objects and the succession of strata in which they were discovered.

Whatever the discretion imposed by the Prince on his assistants, the splendid, opulent findings made at Resina were bruited about, the report getting to Rome and disquieting the Pope. It was also discovered that the three most beautiful statues found in the Theatre had been transported to Vienna, Elbeuf having presented them as a gift to Prince Eugène. To the displeasure of the people, who saw themselves cheated of their subterranean treasures, were added the protests of scholars and art-lovers who wished an interdiction placed on the export of objects from excavations. It may be, too, that having stripped the Theatre of everything of financial interest, the Prince had been alarmed by the outlay required for carrying on the work. Chance had led him to happen upon the finest building in Herculaneum, at the first stroke of the spade, but around that building, he imagined, there were probably only houses of little consequence which could not be worth the trouble expended on investigating them.

The work was therefore suspended, Elbeuf returned to Austria, and Herculaneum relapsed into oblivion. The opportunity had been lost of clearing the ruins methodically and scientifically; but it must be remembered that no one, or scarcely anyone, conceived of what was later to be the ethic of archaeological investigation, nor the principles with which these excavations would be conducted, such as disturbing the earth as little as possible and leaving objects in place for as long as the site had not yielded up all the information expected of it.

Several eruptions, between 1717 and 1737, having occurred in the region, it seemed inexpedient to undertake these difficult, dangerous and costly labours in places still threatened by the fury of the volcano. The treasure-hunt began once more when Charles III ordered the Prince's excavations to be continued in the Theatre, which again began to yield up marvels: a bronze quadriga, great statues of emperors, jewels and magnificent frescoes, immediately transported to the villa at Portici, which served as museum, and rousing cries of admiration from artists who declared these paintings to be 'splendid, of a striking verity, and superior even to those of Raphael'.

Unfortunately the direction of the excavations fell to a Colonel of Engineers in the Neapolitan Army, Alcubierre, who committed monumental blunders and went as far as having bronze letters encrusted in a marble slab torn away without first reading the inscription formed by them. Managed thus by a soldier turned archaeologist by favour of the king, the clearing operations in the Theatre and surrounding buildings proceeded with the same disorder, the same incoherence, the same greed for valuables as in the time of the Prince of Elbeuf.

People of this time, even cultivated ones, would have been very surprised to learn that for an archaeologist a shapeless piece of brick, a potsherd, could be more precious than the richest vase or most beautiful statue, since the former open the way to the disclosure of an unknown civilization. As soon as the excavations of Herculaneum ceased to yield up an abundant harvest of treasures, Alcubierre acted as Elbeuf had done: he stopped the investigations at Resina.

He did not, however, remain inactive. A scholarly Neapolitan, Martorelli, had just been put on the trail of Pompeii by findings made by peasants in the locality of *la Città*; he advised the Colonel to give up at Resina and move over to the so-called *Città*, where there seemed to be ruins of considerable importance, more easily accessible than those of Herculaneum. Alcubierre studied the position, went over to Martorelli's way of thinking, and enrolled twenty-four diggers, including twelve convicts. On March 23rd, 1748, the first spade cuts were made in a spot which, providentially, was above the ruins of the Temple of the Fortuna Augusta. If the men had chanced to dig down initially into a part of the city poor in works of art, it is almost certain that the investigations would have been abandoned, as had occurred at Herculaneum as soon as the work was no longer productive.

Alcubierre's technique was bungling, disastrous for the ruins themselves and void of all scientific method. He had his men dig anywhere, at random; the earth taken from the shafts they threw where it pleased them, and they haphazardly blocked up the openings that had not led to any spoils. Today archaeologists clear a buried city methodically, down to virgin soil; in the time of Alcubierre, tunnels were bored in a happy-go-lucky way, frescoes were torn from the walls that they adorned, weapons, vases, coins were swept up, and all removed without any question of the state or place in which they had been found. The museum was the be-all and end-all of excavations, which had no other object than to amass in the rooms of this museum the greatest possible number of notable objects.

So it went on, alternating from Pompeii to Herculaneum and back again to Pompeii, just as a mine-shaft is abandoned when the mineral in it is becoming exhausted so that the working of it no longer provides an income. Disappointed at having set his convicts to work for a scant return or even none at all, Alcubierre left *la Città* and returned to Resina. He now had with him a Swiss engineer, Karl Weber, who for the first time in the history of the Campanian excavations conceived of archaeological pursuits as other than a treasure-hunt. There was still no question of scientific method in the class of that applied today, but Weber's technique was infinitely superior in every way to the erratic procedures of his predecessors, and it is to this that is owing the progress that was made, from Weber's entering on his duties, in the clearing, preservation and setting to rights of the discovered ruins.

With Weber begins that research method which could be called the 'disciplined treasure-hunt'. The Swiss realized that it was not enough, in exploring the remains of ancient cities, to get together sufficient objects to fill a museum, and that it was necessary also to collect the maximum possible data on the civilization which these cities evidenced and embodied. He was among the first to understand what 'live archaeology' must be, and the immense body of knowledge that could be gleaned by it. Instead of extending random tunnels into the immense space of the great Theatre of Herculaneum, he undertook the task which, considering the modest resources at his disposal, was admirable and colossal, of clearing the site.

In order properly to evaluate Weber's work, we must remember that his workmen toiled in underground passages, where the air was faulty, and lit by feeble lamps. To establish, even approximately, the plan of a building in this rocky mass pierced by narrow galleries, and to set about an actual clearing comparable to that which can be performed in a city in the open air, was a remarkably bold undertaking. With only a small number of workmen at his disposal and with modest finances, Weber plunged recklessly into the adventure, and his initiative was not long in earning him the hostility of his chief, Alcubierre. Jealous of his underling's successes, Alcubierre accused him of ignorance and incompetence, subverted his diggers, and had the propping of the galleries – similar to mine-shafts and supported in the same way – removed, so that they would cave in.

The rich booty brought out of the Theatre of Herculaneum had wakened a discovery-fever among the inhabitants of Resina. The fact that this town had been built on the very site of ancient Herculaneum, and that the latter could not be reached and cleared without a prior demolition of the modern town – which even today makes the excavations here so difficult and complicated – divided public opinion. In the town itself, the tunnellings, endangering the safety of modern dwellings, were regarded with suspicion and, as has continued to our day, Resina with a stubborn determination impeded the revival of Herculaneum.

In the countryside, the situation had a rather different aspect. The peasant who found valuable objects in his field was amply compensated for any inconvenience to his farm, orchard or crops. Thus the countryman fortunate enough to live above the villa known today as that of the Papyri hastened to inform Alcubierre and Weber that he had just discovered, while digging a well, marble columns and precious paving.

Engineers and diggers went down into this well, broadened and deepened it, opened out lateral passages, and soon encountered a dazzling profusion of bronze statues and extremely beautiful marbles, and the remains of a sumptuous villa which had undoubtedly belonged to an eminent Herculanean. What must have been the wonder or fear of the labourers on seeing emerge from the tufa these great bronze dancers with scintillating eyes staring with a menacing contempt? As spade and shovel hewed away blocks of lava, which had the consistency of granite, heads crowned with laurel emerged, overwhelmingly vivid portraits, sleeping fauns, animals portrayed with a naturalistic verisimilitude so perfect that they might be alive. All this went on in the toxic atmosphere of carbonic acid, its heavy gases seeping through the passages and choking the workmen.

In this villa, which Maiuri has rightly observed to be 'the most valuable and the richest villa of the ancient world', a discovery almost as splendid as that of its museum of statues was soon to draw the excited interest of the European scholarly world. It will be seen in a later chapter how the library of this villa and the magnificent papyri contained therein held the clue to the one-time owner's identity. The story of the discovery of the papyri, and of their unrolling and deciphering, will be related. For the moment it must suffice, since now we are concerned only with the history of the excavations, to emphasize that the exhumation of these ruins literally riddled with masterpieces served to give a new impetus to the spirit of research animating King Charles III and his Queen. The Neapolitan sovereigns, through their reading of books on antiquity and their study, under the direction of scholars, of the objects amassed in the Villa of Portici, ended by acquiring a very decent archaeological culture, as extensive as anyone other than a specialist could have in that era.

Despite these signal successes, or perhaps because of the credit they would bring to Weber, Alcubierre continued to impede his assistant's work. Repeatedly he alleged that *mofeta*, the carbonic gas, was deadly to the men working in the tunnels of Herculaneum, and he proposed to the King to turn his efforts to Pompeii. Charles III agreed to this, and the discovery of Cicero's villa, also to be described below, convinced the ruler of the advantage of opening up new works in that quarter.

Unhappily this success was without a sequel, for in that region round the villa – which certainly is not very far from the Porta Ercolano, but in a scantily populated quarter chiefly taken up by the Necropolis, the villa of Diomedes being rather distant – the presence of so rich and important a residence was quite exceptional. Alcubierre thus lost a good deal of time digging here to little purpose; discouraged, he gave up this line.

That was in 1749. For five years Pompeii was left alone, and Herculaneum was the exclusive object of the work; then, one December day in 1754, repair work on the road passing to the south of the city, in what had been the region of the Porta di Nuceria, brought to light tombs (which will be described in the chapter on the necropoles) and some remains of a house. Alcubierre rushed with Weber to the spot, and they went at the digging again furiously, and above all with an impetus that nothing was to interrupt to this day. They were still unaware, however, that this was Pompeii, the experts not being agreed as to the identity of *la Città*. It was only in 1763, on the 20th of August, that these doubts were cleared away and a certainty established by the unearthing of an inscription on which was plainly cited: '*res publica Pompeianorum*', 'the commonwealth of Pompeiians'.

It may be noted in passing that though the interested public was of course not so numerous as today's, there were nonetheless a considerable number of persons who took an interest in these dead cities so recently revived and who wanted to see them. The King never omitted to take his distinguished guests to examine the works, and the custom was established, in order to flatter these noble amateurs, of laying on for their benefit the staging of a 'discovery'. Discoveries being extremely rare and unpredictable and never occurring at the actual moment which would have been wished, the 'find', in a pre-determined spot, was organized in advance. At the appointed hour, the strolling dignitaries would approach the pit where workmen were digging. After a few minutes the workmen would utter cries of astonishment and joy, meanwhile lifting up out of the ground a small statue, a vase or a coin which had been planted there on the previous day. The object was passed from hand to hand, duly admired, then given over to the director of excavations, who took it along to the museum while the visitors went away extolling the wonderful riches of this site and the fascination provided by the technique of excavation.

With a small team of workmen the labours thus continued, regularly but still unmethodically. Still the digging was done at random, extending the investigations in a quarter where the spoils had been profitable, and abandoning the work where it seemed to be yielding no return. Not always were statues or 'treasures' happened upon; however, a new interest arose, pertaining to important buildings. Thus in 1764 the Great Theatre was discovered, in 1766 the gladiators' barracks, in 1767 the Temple of Isis, in 1771 the Villa of Diomedes. Progress was rather slow, and did not always encompass spectacular results, or financially attractive ones; but the principle was henceforth adopted that the work was not to be interrupted save by main force. Up to the present this has remained a guiding principle of archaeologists directing the clearing of Pompeii, which goes on unceasingly.

Among the instances of 'main force' is one to which, to their sorrow, the inhabitants of this region are always vulnerable: the periodic wakenings of Vesuvius. There were several of these during the seventeenth and eighteenth centuries; that of 1631 buried for a second time a large part of Herculaneum, and in 1759 a very serious eruption occurred. Another instance, no more escapable, is war. The war did not spare Pompeii any more than other cities, and in 1943, despite the reverence which civilized people are supposed to have for works of art, squadrons of planes several times bombed the restored city, causing it irreparable damage.

Pompeii Through the Fortunes of War

The expeditions made into Italy by the armies of the Directory, of the Consulate and of the Empire, turned the state of the peninsula topsy-turvy, creating republics and breaking up kingdoms and principalities. The Kingdom of Naples became, at the stroke of a pen, the Parthenopaean Republic, and the Bourbons took the road of exile. A French General replaced them in the government of the city: this was Championnet, who took office in 1798. The change-over of régime was accomplished without too much disturbance; there were only a few brawls when the French regiments entered Naples and established themselves there.

In leaving his capital, the King had taken with him only the portable works of art of his museum; the rest was exposed to the hazards of war, and in fact French artillery, intervening to calm the turbulent Neapolitans, shot off the head of an equestrian statue, that of Marcus Nonius, discovered at Herculaneum. This was the only casualty of the day; and the damaged head was repaired with great care and that remarkable skill which is the prerogative of Italian restorers.

As soon as he was settled into his position as Governor, Championnet took an interest in the dead cities. In France as in England, in these last years of the eighteenth century, there was a revival of Classicism. Bonaparte's campaign in Egypt had set off a violent craze for everything antique. A new period began in the history of art: the works of Winckelmann, who had long studied the Campanian antiquities, created an extremely inquiring intellectual atmosphere, and the Revolution itself had glorified the Roman virtues.

The success of the excavations at Pompeii thus came at a moment which, despite the war, was highly favourable; just as had been the case during the Renaissance, when the French invasions of Italy fostered the discovery of the cult of antiquity and its establishment in France, so at the end of the eighteenth century the Italian campaign was to influence, in a striking and most characteristic way, the modes of furniture, fashion, public taste, sensibility and the intellectual climate itself. Officers posted to Naples were therefore delighted at being able to admire, on the spot, this antique style to which the revival of Classicism had already acclimatized Paris. And it was the same in England, where Nelson's staff and the personnel of Sir William Hamilton's Embassy, on returning from Italy, in like fashion spread the new mode, as represented by Wedgwood and his famous pottery, Etruria.

With the departure of the Bourbons had ended the deposits of money for paying the diggers at Pompeii, and these workmen dispersed; but Championnet, who had visited the site and was interested in the ruins, wanted the excavations got under way again at once. He declared himself quite ready to defray the expenses of this, and commissioned a scholarly archaeologist-priest, Padre Zarelli, to take charge of the work.

However, King Ferdinand, acceding to the throne after the departure of the French, began by stopping all subsidies to the excavations; he dismissed the workmen and despite the objections of La Vega, who was in charge of the work and emphasized the dangers of interrupting it, ordered the closing of the work-sites at Herculaneum and Pompeii.

In the disturbance created by the European war and amidst the havoc wrought by it, it seemed to him futile indeed to use his money for clearing demolished houses, whatever knowledge could be gleaned from them by historians, archaeologists and philologists. Paradoxically it needed the return of the French and the reign of Joseph Bonaparte, brother of the Emperor, for Pompeii once again to be awakened by the echo of the diggers' spades. The new King frequently visited the ruins, where from 1806 about fifty workmen attacked successively the Basilica, the Temple of the Fortuna Augusta and the House of Sallust. While during previous years all the reports put before Ferdinand had been discouraging, repeating always 'nothing new, nothing new' (for the good reason that the workmen, for lack of pay, had left Pompeii, and that only the most desultory work could be done on such ungrateful soil), Joseph Bonaparte's engineers vied with one another in zeal. He had them work clearly defined zones, not giving up in any one quarter before it was completely cleared.

He was not fortunate enough to witness the success of his projects; it was Murat, his successor to the throne of Naples, who managed to bring off the purchase of lands. There were at that time one hundred and fifty labourers in the two work-sites, who, when the work in each region was finished, would join up. The enthusiasm shown by Queen Caroline for the excavations spurred on the workers. She came to inspect the sites, asked to be shown the newly discovered objects, and on her advice fountains and water-jets were restored in the gardens of exhumed houses; for this, it sufficed to repair the ancient pipings and connect them with the springs which had supplied them of old, to hear once again the music of stream and cascade in the *nymphaea*.

A fine soldier but a mediocre statesman, Murat had one outstanding virtue which Napoleon knew how to appreciate and reward: he had breadth of vision. Not satisfied to consider the clearing of the entire city, he thought as well of completely restoring it. La Vega, used to the slothful calm of Ferdinand's reign, rather lost his head, what with the impetuosity of Murat, who thought to carry out the excavations like a cavalry charge. Aware of the need for a large working force, the fiery Marshal had required that five hundred labourers should be employed. Instead of the six hundred ducats monthly consigned to the investiga-

57

tions, the Queen gave two thousand. She had secured her husband's agreement to the assigning of officers to supervise the work, and to a company of Neapolitan soldiers being added to the civilian workmen. Out of her own pocket, she contributed to the publication of François Mazois's monumental work on the ruins of Pompeii, and would hand out munificent tips when she visited the site.

It was still endeavoured to reserve sensational and spectacular finds for her visits, as she was so delighted to see these made before her own eyes. She enthused over the beauty of the jewellery and works of art, and was moved at the sight of skeletons, which crumbled to dust at the first contact with air, for in that era the preserving methods since invented by archaeologists – especially the paraffin wrapping – were not yet known. She would not have the least discovery kept from her: informed about everything, surveying it all, she tripped briskly among the streets of Pompeii, questioning the works directors, and with much regret taking the road back to Naples, once again to resume the weary duties of official life. She so adored Pompeii that it became necessary to fit up a small apartment for her where she could stay when the fancy took her to come and spend several days amidst her beloved ruins.

When the Kingdom of Naples collapsed in 1815, Caroline was desolated at leaving forever these houses and temples, picturesque and moving as they were, where she had passed such happy days. She retired to Florence (where she survived until 1839), and never returned, after her husband's death, to Naples: it would have been too wretched to walk, as a mere visitor, those excavation grounds which once she had brightened with her eager curiosity and her royal largesse.

Pompeii had lost much in losing Murat. In 1815 Ferdinand returned once more to the throne, and once again inflicted his stinginess on the excavation directors. This same year saw the death of La Vega. Works published in the period of Joseph and Murat, *Il Teatro di Ercolano* of Giovanni Francesco Piranesi and *Les Ruines de Pompeii dessinées et mesurées* of Charles François Mazois the architect, had admirably continued the work of Winckelmann, who at the end of the eighteenth century had directed society towards an exact knowledge of both the forms and the spirit of antiquity.

For some years, virtually until 1860, the excavations were continued rather desultorily, and were often interrupted or slowed down. Also

King Ferdinand's whims had to be complied with: he regarded Pompeii as a curiosity to which he would drive his distinguished visitors. As the flagstones placed athwart the streets to allow pedestrians to cross without muddying their feet impeded the Royal carriages, he had the stones removed; happily, they have since been replaced, and are in fact one of the special features of Pompeiian urbanization, as they did not exist in Herculaneum, where the traffic of vehicles was less excessive.

Ferdinand I was succeeded by his intelligent, cultivated son François, who bothered hardly at all about administration of the State, but who on the other hand displayed an active sympathy with Pompeii, where he loved to walk of an evening in the moonlight, as a sign of his Romantic temperament. He likewise ordered a resumption of digging at Herculaneum; and in consideration of the difficulty presented by the houses of modern Resina, he elected to explore completely that part of the ancient city not covered by the present-day town, and to clear the ruins in such a fashion as to bring all possible discoveries to the light of day, in accordance with the principle of working in the open observed with such success at Pompeii. At Herculaneum it was in fact first necessary to divest the ruins of their enormous thick crust, hard as stone, representing the appalling flow of liquid mire that had seeped into all the houses.

At a depth which, according to the district, varied from forty to nearly sixty feet, this muddy lava, semi-liquid, had been amalgamated into the buildings, often leaving the walls and upper storeys of houses quite intact; whereas at Pompeii the upper portions collapsed under the heavy deluge of stone and ash. It might be said that Pompeii was crushed from above by the vertical fall of burning, heavy matter, while Herculaneum was invaded horizontally by a river of lava which rose progressively as more and more enormous torrents burst from the mouth of Vesuvius. More pliant than the mixture of ashes and lapilli collapsing everything in their path, this Herculanean mud as it piled up left standing the walls against which it mounted and the roofs it covered. The task of the archaeologists was quite different therefore in the two cities. But the prodigious masses of hardened lava which had to be broken, shifted and removed abated the zeal of archaeologists and works directors, who got on very slowly until about 1860 or 1870 when activity in the work-sites revived at Herculaneum as well as at Pompeii.

The fact that the excavations were not very extensive maintained these Campanian ruins in their character of 'dead cities', thus the more deeply to move the Romantic heart and mind. Travellers' accounts record how in these remains of the past they sought, according to their nature and temperament, either instruction or emotion. For those who desire to be informed, a Pompeii completely cleared and restored as she is today to her pre-eruption state, with her gardens and trees, fountains and statues and shops where the fuller's vat, the baker's oven or the wine-merchant's jugs are again within reach of a prospective customer, is of much greater interest than the often formless remains seen in the engravings of Piranesi and Mazois.

From a study of the documentary engravings of Piranesi's *Antichità Romane* – this is the elder Piranesi, father of the one who published the *Antiquités d'Herculanum* for Queen Caroline – can be discerned the poetic feeling imbuing these buildings overgrown with vegetation and living as it were their life of ruins, which is much intenser and more authentic than in the careful, painstaking restorations of today's archaeologists. To what extent is *reconstitution* quite distinct from *restoration*? This is extremely difficult to say. Between the informative, educative ruin and that which moves the emotions, there is not only a variance of degree in the conducting of more or less extensive restorations, but above all a difference of conception in the actual method applied to dead cities in their revival. The criticisms levelled at Evans, when he restored the Minoan palaces of Knossos, arose from these contrasting views, all moreover equally valid, between partisans of affecting ruins and those of instructive ones.

It must also be remarked that the astonishment and disappointment of visitors to Greece and Sicily would be very great if, in place of admirable marbles given a patina by wind and sun and light-receptive to the point of appearing lit from within, they saw before them temples bedaubed with vivid colours, touched up with gold and silver, such as the ancient Greeks themselves saw. An intact Parthenon would doubtless 'say' much less than the one we have, however tremendous otherwise might be the interest of studying it in all those details effaced by time.

It was not, as it happened, a sovereign, but a revolutionary leader who had the whim of choosing as director of antiquities at Naples and

60

head of the archaeological excavations a man who appeared the least possible suited to fill that post: the novelist Alexandre Dumas. Dumas showed much imagination in his writings, and that quality is not amiss in archaeology either; but it cannot be said that he was eminently qualified for this delicate task for which nothing had prepared him. To explain this surprising nomination, it is necessary to go back to the onset of relations established between Dumas and Garibaldi.

When the leader of the Red Shirts organized the famous Expedition of the Thousand, he gained the support of foreign liberals, who helped him to set up his small army, to equip and arm it. Dumas was one of those who with money and enthusiasm assisted this liberation movement; attracted by the dare-devil side of the venture, the author of *The Three Musketeers* offered to participate in it. For him, however, it was not a case of disembarking at Genoa and firing on Austrian troops but his help, though far-removed from the field of battle, was highly effective: so much so that it procured him in return the appointment by Garibaldi to the directorship of the Naples Museum and of the excavations at Pompeii and Herculaneum.

It is a curious story, that of the short-lived authority wielded by the novelist over the staff of the excavations. Dumas incurred the hostility of his subordinates because he had announced the advent of French archaeologists who were to have worked side by side with the Italian ones. This project was regarded with as much disfavour as that of Waldstein half a century later who was imprudent enough to propose an international collaboration. The heads of the work accused Dumas of ignorance – which was probably just, though he had set himself energetically to studying – and of extravagance: he squandered the excavation funds, they claimed, on his own pleasures and the luxuries of his household.

Become *persona non grata*, the novelist therefore withdrew; and it was then that King Victor Emmanuel called in the distinguished person who was to give an unprecedented impetus to the excavations and, more, was to pursue them according to a genuine scientific method.

The Scientific Excavations

Not to denigrate the worth, zeal and abilities of his predecessors, perhaps even of Alexandre Dumas, a considerable change in the spirit and technique of the Pompeiian excavations can be distinguished from the time when Giuseppe Fiorelli took on their direction. The talent and diligence of this man, already well-known for his numismatic and archaeological work, were outstanding, and in addition he was fortunate in being attended by circumstances which showed themselves extremely favourable.

From the political point of view, firstly, he arrived at a moment when the Italy of the Risorgimento, impatient to gain recognition as a great independent nation, was developing everything that could make her national patrimony more widely known and admired. Very justifiably Italy has always gloried in her prodigious artistic heritage, and the new King, intent on encouraging all intellectual movements, undertook to give a great lustre to the excavations of Pompeii and Herculaneum. In this favourable atmosphere, the conjunction of Fiorelli and Victor Emmanuel took place.

Fiorelli had in fact been a victim of absolutism and Austrian tyranny. Notorious to the Imperial police for his liberal sentiments, and perhaps too for his belonging to a cell of *carbonari*, he had been imprisoned in 1848. It is said that colleagues jealous of his work and of his first successes had taken care to inform the Austrian police of his underground activities and of the overwhelming proofs that could be mustered against him. He had been released, however, but on his emergence from prison found himself without work, and was going about in search of a position when the brother of King François II summoned him to examine a curious finding that had just been made at Cumae near Naples and had been offered for sale to the King's brother.

This comprised several corpses dating from antiquity, discovered in some necropolis, and extraordinarily well preserved. The faces retained an astounding freshness, a life-like resilience and a regularity of feature, as if miraculously kept from putrefaction. A large sum was being asked for them, but the thing was so strange and rare that the Count of Syracuse, the King's brother, would have concluded the purchase if he had not had a slight suspicion. So as to settle the matter, he sent for Fiorelli, the specialist in antiques, to come to the palace, despite the man's bad reputation politically. Fiorelli examined the heads and perceived that they had been very skilfully modelled round the skulls with wax and were nothing more than a very clever but outrageous swindle.

The Count of Syracuse asked the archaeologist what reward he wanted. 'Give me the means to excavate,' answered the scholar. It would not be Pompeii or Herculaneum, which already had a director, but Fiorelli knew several sites where it would be of interest to dig. With the support of his aristocratic protector, and henceforth shielded from police molestation, he investigated some sites of secondary importance. He obtained no sensational result but acquired invaluable experience and was able to put his system of scientific diggings into practice up to the time when the Count's death exposed him anew to the hostilities of his colleagues, the King's somewhat malevolent indifference, and the suspicions of the monarchists who saw in him a dangerous revolutionary both on the political level and in the field of archaeology.

This reputation as a revolutionary which thus dogged him and which, true or false, proved harmful to him until the Risorgimento, served him providentially after the expulsion of the Bourbons and the Austrians. Victor Emmanuel knew about the work written by Fiorelli on the history of the Pompeiian antiquities – *Pompeianorum antiquitatum historia* – which came out in Naples in 1860, the year also in which The Thousand, setting out from Sicily, triumphantly went up through Italy which, carried away by their ardour, was united in a liberating enthusiasm. The King heaped on Fiorelli all the titles and offices that he could receive; he made him director of the excavations, curator of the museum and Professor of Archaeology at Naples University. He promised him that a sufficient number of labourers to do effective work would be at the sites, under his orders, and that the necessary funds would not be lacking; it only remained to get down to the task, and all would go well.

In fact, all did go well. In December, five hundred workmen took up spade and shovel, and the wagons, brought over by the contractor who held the commission for earth disposal, stood by. In January of 1861 Pompeii showed an activity such as had never been seen there, even in the time of Murat. If spectacular findings were perhaps less frequent and less vaunted, this was because Fiorelli adopted a severe, almost ascetic discipline, to which none of his predecessors could have submitted, even supposing that they had been personally so minded, for it was in complete opposition to the old ways of treasure-hunting.

In what did the novelty of the method applied by Fiorelli consist?

This method was carried into various spheres. It was firstly the establishing of the indispensable journal of excavations; up to now a kind of diary had been kept, chiefly recording the visits of distinguished guests, and of value doubtless to the historian but of little interest to the archaeologist. Fiorelli substituted for these accounts of royal outings descriptions of the objects found in a given site, their position, their situation in the strata of ground, with the conclusions to be drawn from these various data. Such is in fact the first requirement of modern scientific archaeology: the placing of the object, and its situation in relation to other objects, are sometimes more important than the thing itself. This is why today such great care is taken to photograph meticulously each stage in the clearance of a site, and nothing is touched before the general arrangement of a tomb, for example, and the position of each object has been fixed, described and set down.

To continue by taking a tomb as our example, the manner in which the corpse was buried, whether stretched out or in a bent posture, facing towards one of the cardinal points or another, is profoundly informative about religious beliefs, magical practice, burial rites and faith in the after-life. Should a skeleton be handled without precautions, it might never be known that an arrow piercing the skull caused the death of this man, or that a stake had been driven into his chest to prevent his resurrection in the form of a vampire.

The burial furnishings are also highly instructive, and it is important to know which objects have been found near the head of the corpse or near his feet, and how they were disposed. The least haste, the least clumsiness, a premature movement caused by impatience or zeal, could be disastrous, unwittingly destroying an irreplaceable source of information. Heretofore, as we have seen, it was considered that the object of the digging was the valuable article, the work of art, and that all the rest must be negligible; in the nineteenth century, every detail was seen to be important in archaeology, so that often even something appearing less valuable, and in the eye of the layman quite lacking in interest, was more so.

Fiorelli was fortunate in coming into archaeology at an era when that science, still quite young, was already beginning to make tremendous progress and to establish its ethic. Synchronization of the New Excavations at Pompeii and Herculaneum and of researches carried out

1 House of Neptune and Amphitrite at Herculaneum. View of the nymphaeum with its decoration of masks and paintings.

2 Temple of Isis and Pompeii. A small chancel and altar.

3 House of the Bas-relief of Orestes, at Herculaneum. View of the atrium with its painted columns.

4   Detail from bronze statue of Dionysos. Pompeii Antiquarium.

5   A decoration using inlaid polychromatic marbles. Naples Museum.

6   Fresco at Pompeii depicting Mars and Venus.

7   Weight of bronze scales. Naples Museum.

8   Glass jug with a blue handle. Naples Museum.

in Egypt, Mesopotamia, Iran and Greece was to be effected. The second half of the nineteenth century, despite all its uncertainty and errors, which have to be acknowledged, was the golden age of archaeology: the clearing of Pompeii and Herculaneum, far from being an isolated phenomenon, was in fact part of a vast whole, a wave of active research which spread across three continents.

This takes away nothing from Fiorelli's achievement – quite the reverse – but only shows how enlightened circles, connoisseurs and even amateur archaeologists would henceforth regard the technique and ethic of excavations. The passion for precious materials, admiration for the beauties of works of art, ambition to fill a museum, ceased to be the stimuli which they had hitherto and almost exclusively been. The scholar as it were had replaced the artist on the site of the excavation although the archaeologist is often both. It will be seen that there is, in this aspect, little difference between the geologist studying a terrain and the archaeologist unearthing a dead city: for questions of pre-history and often even of proto-history, the presence of a geologist is usually necessary.

Fiorelli now dealt with the problem of rubble disposal. Pompeii before 1860 can be pictured as a confused mass of pits and heaps of matter, scattered in all directions over the whole surface of the city. Hardly any streets were completely cleared for the visitor, and everywhere was this rubble, its piles always shifted rather than removed. Having identified and pinpointed, on the plan worked out by himself, those portions already explored, Fiorelli undertook to dig between those, so as to join uninterruptedly all the work-sites in progress. The topography of the *insulae* thus took shape, with the large principal streets, the *decumanus* and the *cardo*, the transverse streets and the small lanes connecting them.

With the earth removed and carted away from the city, the streets resumed their pristine appearance. Earlier procedures had consisted of first clearing the streets and then, these being open, entering the houses by the ground floor; these had had the drawback of making the walls fragile, and as a result many had in fact collapsed during the work. Fiorelli adopted an opposite method: he began by drilling down to establish the plan of the streets and then, instead of digging outside the houses, he attacked the interiors. Penetrating by the roof, he would

65

thus empty the building of all its encumbering matter; then, having located and shielded paintings, furnishings and other objects, and having propped the walls from inside, he would finish the clearing of the street.

On the plan devised by himself, and divided into *regions*, the latter subdivided into *insulae* (corresponding to our 'blocks' of buildings), the original aspect of Pompeii reappeared bit by bit. Fiorelli tirelessly saw to everything himself, and would keep an eye on the merest rubble taken from the ruins.

He exerted a stricter watch on the labourers, most of whom certainly were honest, but there could always be among them the few less scrupulous individuals who on occasion might conceal part of their findings so as to sell them to antiquarians. The money which Queen Caroline had lavishly bestowed when some beautiful object was brought her had taught the diggers the commercial value of certain pieces. However carefully the work-sites were watched, leakages could not be altogether prevented. Collectors and antique-dealers readily making themselves the accomplices and receivers of these thieves, it was necessary to keep a guard on the ruins at night so as to prevent inroads by clandestine diggers, and during the day so as to ensure that some workman was not misappropriating a precious vase, a piece of jewellery or a coin, which when his job was done he would sell in Naples.

One of Fiorelli's great principles, lastly, which became likewise an article of belief with his successors, was that wherever possible objects should be left in the place where they had been found, on condition of course that they were not running the risk of theft or damage. For portable and valuable objects there was a considerable risk, but when it was a question of marble tables, basins, fountains, altars to the Lares, jars, even statues, the danger was less. As to mural paintings, above all, Fiorelli's directive was explicit: they were not to leave the walls that they adorned. It was proper, of course, to take every precaution against their being damaged; after all, the technique of the painters of former times was so perfect that their works had spanned two thousand years without losing anything of their brilliance and freshness.

Until the period of scientific excavations, it was imagined that the only way of safeguarding these mural paintings was to detach them from the wall and take them away to museums. In the eighteenth century

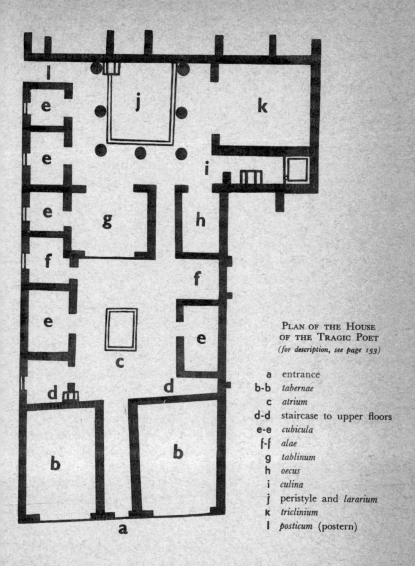

PLAN OF THE HOUSE
OF THE TRAGIC POET
(for description, see page 153)

a	entrance
b-b	*tabernae*
c	*atrium*
d-d	staircase to upper floors
e-e	*cubicula*
f-f	*alae*
g	*tablinum*
h	*oecus*
i	*culina*
j	peristyle and *lararium*
k	*triclinium*
l	*posticum* (postern)

Morriconi prescribed varnishing them before their removal, so as to prevent their peeling and fading; but this precaution did not prevent numerous frescoes from falling to bits in the course of that delicate operation, or while in transit to the museum, and the ones which we admire today at Naples and in various European galleries such as the Louvre are only a part of all those so transferred at their peril.

To leave objects *in situ* is not altogether without disadvantages – several houses were for instance destroyed in the air-raid of 1943 – but it is still the best policy and the most generally observed at all excavations where it is applicable. Thanks to this method, the museum can be considered superseded here. Pompeii in its entirety has become a museum, but one with all the charm of life and all the picturesqueness of day-to-day familiarity with things in current use.

Not that the frescoes are exposed to much danger, for at the time when they were painted it was already the practice to insulate them from the wall to prevent the humidity from damaging them. To this end, a kind of ledge was interposed between the wall itself and the painted surface, keeping the latter away from the surface of bricks; or else a layer of perforated bricks, sometimes even sheets of lead, were slipped between. Today certain ones have been detached from the wall and then replaced after a coat of cement proof against humidity has been spread over the wall. In some houses, where the paintings might have been harmed by the touch of careless or feckless visitors, they have been glassed-over. Similarly every effective precaution has been taken to obviate too strong rays of the sun which could fade the colours.

It is now exactly a century since Fiorelli began work in the ruins of Pompeii. He formulated, for the benefit of generations of directors of the work who have succeeded him and finely carried on his task, the ethic of excavation, and adapted to it effective processes for uncovering everything but leaving it in its pristine state. Reconstitution of the things found, as fast as they are discovered; restoration of the ancient city in appearance and spirit as these are revealed; re-creation of both essentials and accessories in such a way as to make today's city a perfect replica of that of former times; the avoiding of conjectural or excessive restoration while at the same time carrying out the aim of providing 1960's visitor with the completest possible revelation of the Pompeii of

79: such were Fiorelli's guiding principles, which his successors have continually improved upon.

The traveller returning periodically to Pompeii notices constant changes, not only in the presentation of newly cleared insulae, but also in the arrangement of those long known. The devoted care accorded to the buildings and gardens, the exquisite taste governing alike the placing of works of art and of trees, perpetually create unexpected and charming improvements.

Pompeii and Herculaneum are in a state comparable to that of no other ancient cities. Among the dead cities of past millennia, a number were devastated by invasions or burnt to such an extent that, of some, not so much as two consecutive stones have remained. Others have been progressively transformed in the course of centuries, the destruction of the ancient buildings prefacing the construction of new ones.

Instances, so frequent even today, of wanton and criminal destruction of ancient buildings which with a modicum of trouble, intelligence and decency might have been preserved, reveal how governments and public bodies pay no heed to the representations or pleas of archaeologists. As against ancient cities razed to the ground so that their very *corpus* has disappeared, and those which have died by degrees and are still so doing, Pompeii and Herculaneum occupy a quite exceptional place.

It is not easy to determine at what moment began the democratization of Pompeii, a democratization which Herculaneum never attained – thus explaining the very great difference in aspect of the two cities. But the evolution was far advanced if not completed in 79, and not the least surprising fact which strikes today's visitor is the contrast between the aristocratic elegance of certain dwellings and the vulgarity of the trades or businesses established in them.

This social phenomenon arose from the increasing wealth of the business class as a result of the thriving trade, operating through the medium of the port of Pompeii, between northern Italy, Greece and the countries of the East. The Sarno was at this time a navigable river up which ships of respectable tonnage could proceed quite far, and its large estuary contained the harbour installations. This commercial prosperity had raised men of the lower-middle class, often freedmen who through their ability and intelligence had made fortunes, to administrative positions and the status of eminent citizens. These erstwhile slaves came from a wide range of nations, since Rome was in the habit of recruiting her slaves everywhere, from Brittany to North Africa, from Spain to Asia Minor.

The social history of Pompeii reveals, simultaneous with the rise of these new-rich proletarians, the decline of the aristocracy, which did not enter into trade or business. Thus there came about, at the moment when these freedmen were greatly expanding their trading activities, an exodus of the upper class, who left a city which had become noisy, vulgar and over-run by *nouveaux-riches*, and retired to the country, where they devoted themselves to the cultivation of their lands, in which they achieved considerable progress. Before quitting Pompeii, they made over their elegant mansions to merchants and artisans, who set themselves up without ceremony. Hence, the wonder of today's visitors at the sight of fullers' vats set out in atria or gardens created once for the delight of some gentleman of leisure.

Space being at a premium in this city whose walls prevented her from expanding in proportion to the growing need, it was essential that works and shops should be established wherever possible. The great business street called the Via dell'Abbondanza gives an idea of Pompeii's unforeseen development through this remarkable upsurge of the mercantile and artisan class. These artisans and merchants had to find premises; thus they first rented a few ground-floor rooms in an aristocratic house and soon it became evident that the gentry and the old-established great merchant families could not co-exist with such pullulating tenants. Crowded out by these, the original owners withdrew to the first floor, but the quiet that they sought was no more to be found there. It was then that, giving up city life, which was no longer to their taste, they retired to the peace and quiet of their villas.

The problem therefore presented to archaeologists by the vigorous social revolution in Pompeii was this: ought aristocratic houses taken over by trades and businesses to be left in the state in which the eruption had found them, or should they rather be restored to their original condition of before the democratization? The care taken by directors of the work since Fiorelli to respect entirely the state of things at the moment of the eruption has impelled them to leave everything in place, handsome statues and frescoes juxtaposed with dye vats; this extraordinary arrangement, moreover, makes it evident how workmen and shop-assistants were for the most part careful of the beautiful environments in which they toiled.

The division of vast private mansions into dwellings of the people has frequently embarrassed the archaeologists, who find themselves confronted with extraordinary alterations inexplicable without reference to this subject of social history, and without which we can scarcely understand the composite character of a city where the elegant neighbourhoods and the business streets were not distinct, as is normally the case in modern cities, but intermingled. Doubtless, without the eruption of 79 this process of democratization would have been still further developed and accentuated in proportion with Pompeii's ever-growing importance as a centre of commerce and industry.

For us today to see the dye vats of the fuller Ubonius in a charming garden is no more shocking than the sight of the kitchen range and its great bronze vessels in the House of the Vettii, or the blacksmith's tools in the workshop of Verus, or in the Via degli Augustali the baker Modestus's oven from which the bread of the daily baking had not yet been taken when the ashes of Vesuvius began to fall. It is all so intact that we can work the olive-press at the oil merchant's in the Via degli Augustali or the little corn-mill at the baker's in the Vico Storto.

The visitor of 1960 sometimes has the disturbing sensation of intruding in a house where he is not expected and where he is disturbing the privacy of the occupants. The cloth is laid on the *triclinium* table in the House of the Philosopher, where the host is to receive his friends and discuss philosophy with them while drinking an old Campanian wine out of silver cups already set out at the guests' places. The great bronze doors of the House of Loreius Tiburtinus have been left open so that close friends can come in without troubling the porter or sending in their name. Marble benches are set out at intervals for the relaxation of the house's occupants and visitors; and it seems almost surprising not to see in the little kiosk serving as a chapel to the Lares and situated in a corner of the atrium the flowers, wine or incense which the visitor, before anything else, would offer to the family's guardian spirits.

The gardens too have been reconstructed in their original beauty, with the graceful pattern of lawn and flower-bed. The basins and fountains and murmuring streams re-create the cool, soothing atmosphere of the

71

nymphaea, where minute waves play a thousand reflections on multi-coloured mosaics of the chapels dedicated to the nymphs. The affluence of vegetation, verdant still and fresh, gives an impression in these gardens of time standing still.

POMPEII FORMERLY AND TODAY

To understand the old Pompeii through that of today will be the object of our tour of this city which, more than any other in the world, allows of our divining the way of life, private and official, great and humble, in these provinces subject to Rome at that epoch when the ancient world was to be profoundly stirred by the advent of Christianity. Elsewhere, at Rome or in Athens, the monuments of antiquity are mingled with contemporary houses, the centuries adding on, like geological strata in the land, what each has contributed. Here, between the first century A.D. and us, nothing has intervened, no foreign element has been introduced into what is, so essentially, the life of antiquity. Between the day of the eruption and that when we walk through the streets of Pompeii (and what is said here of Pompeii applies equally to Herculaneum) nothing has arisen to alter the aspect of things. It seems to us as though we are walking in the very footsteps of the men who passed here some moments before the catastrophe.

Fully to realize this acquaintance with the past, we must first of all survey Pompeii in its entirety, noting the general arrangement of districts and public buildings; we must look out the lie of the land, then delve into the intimacies of individual lives, enter shops and private dwellings, mix, in imagination, in the existence of these men who in the last analysis were not very different from us, who were animated by the same emotions, the same interests and the same cares. But before embarking on these questions of detail, let us get a panoramic view of the city.

Surveying Pompeii from an aeroplane, at a sufficient altitude to have at a single glance a bird's eye view of the entire city, but low enough to distinguish the lay-out of the different quarters and the placing of the chief monuments, we notice with surprise how irregular is the outline of the walls, contrary to what is usually seen in the plan of Roman cities and of the Etruscan ones which probably served as their model.

This irregularity is explained by the fact that Pompeii was not built all at once or according to a set plan, but grew and was altered over centuries; the one hundred and sixty-three acres which composed the area of the city proper on the eve of the eruption of 79 were attained only in the course of slow development up to the Imperial era – let us say, the last years of the Republic, when the general lay-out was fixed once for all. But as the city enclosure did not allow for unlimited expansion, it was in the direction of the suburbs and the surrounding countryside that Pompeii grew. The crush of people in overcrowded streets, a continual population increase which, for lack of accommodation, obliged house-owners to divide their premises to contain a larger number of tenants, the desire to escape the noise and bustle, inspired more and more well-to-do citizens to retire to their villas. They were then near enough to the city to be able to look after their businesses, if they had retained these, or to attend theatres and circuses, and at the same time they found amidst gardens and fields that tranquil felicity to which Virgil aspired and which made so many Romans sigh with nostalgia.[10]

Those aware of the principles governing the founding of Roman cities, their strict regularity, their proportions laid down by tradition and determined by religious or occult beliefs, would expect to find at Pompeii the regular rectangle, divided into streets intersecting at right angles, in emulation of a military camp, of which the site and dimensions were decided, by priests, after consulting the omens, and established in accordance with very old and very strict ritual. In ancient Rome the moat bounding the enclosure of a city was sacred and, it is related, Romulus had killed his brother Remus because the latter, on the day of the solemn founding of Rome, had either mockingly or as a joke leapt over the furrow which his brother had just dug with a plough and which marked out the shape of the future city.

The moats, walls and gates were invested with a sacred character and governed by tabus which could not be infringed under pain of death, even if the offender were otherwise an excellent citizen, a victorious soldier, or an eminent magistrate. But, it must not be forgotten, Pompeii was not founded by the Romans: the latter were newcomers in the history of the city, which, well before their advent, had already attained a high degree of power and wealth.

Yet another reason than the relatively late intervention of Rome

74

accounts for the irregular profile of the city: the fact that the citizens were obliged, in whatever period, to respect the nature of the terrain on which the first foundations of Pompeii had been laid. This terrain is not uniformly even: it has differences of level resulting from the ground itself being irregular and broken. The city's situation, on the slopes of Vesuvius, was splendid in that it offered the inhabitants the pleasure of exceptionally lovely vistas. The drawback was the volcanic nature of the land, shaken by numerous eruptions that had taken place before the first human settlement here. The billows of lava and beds of tufa, product of these eruptions, overlapped, leaving between them deep grooves and rocky protuberances which no mechanical means in that era could level: it was with shovel and spade that Pompeii was built, and it is an open question whether steam-shovels or bulldozers could have done the job better.

A rather marked slope on the north side; rocky cliffs formed by the abrupt stop and successive hardening and cooling of the lava flow, to the south; the bed of the Sarno: all inscribing fairly nearly the shape of an irregular basin, at the bottom of which lay the Forum and its surrounding buildings. The ground on which the houses and public buildings were erected is quite even, and it is clear that the architects and planners turned the slightest advantage to good account; this is why, relinquishing the idea of giving their city an arbitrary symmetry which would not have conformed with the actual nature of the ground, they built the walls thus, permanently fixing the city's lay-out, and making the best use of the ledges of the terrain. The vague rectangle thus drawn presents quite a clean line to the sea, but the short side at the opposite end is as if flattened, crushed by the Porta di Sarno, as the irregularities of ground require.

Clever and judicious restorations have re-established the walls and gates of the city in their original state of before 79. The actual composition of the walls had been greatly modified, according to circumstance, as was made necessary by the uninterrupted development of a city which from the moment of her growing rich in money and prestige, and playing an important part in Mediterranean trade, was exposed to the envy and greed of her neighbours as well as of foreign peoples.

In order to defend themselves against attack by land or sea, though it might be only the pirates who infested the Mediterranean and comprised small commonwealths strong enough to worry Rome and withstand the attacks of her fleet, the Pompeiians had built ramparts. These fortifications were altered in accordance with the city itself: simple earth embankments as long as there was only a primitive township to be protected, they were raised to high, thick walls when the citizens had amassed public and private treasures enough to need such guarding.

It happened also that during the long periods of peace when tranquillity seemed assured, the ramparts were left to crumble; at the first threat of attack, the people hastened to rebuild them, each one bringing his stone to the rampart, with an urgency spurred on by fear. Surveying technically the formation of these ramparts, we descry there, in the same way as the geologist reading the history of the earth in strata of soil, the chronicle of Pompeii's vicissitudes.

Under Roman domination, the future of the Campanian cities was completely altered; the power of the Republic, then of the Empire, kept the Pax Romana reigning over the western world. Just as truly strong individuals have no need to prepare means of defence, since no one will be imprudent enough to attack them, so powerful nations are assured of their impunity, their reputation of invincibility sufficing to surround them with spiritual ramparts imposing fear, respect and subservience. From the time of Pompeii's becoming Roman, she had no further need of fortifications, the very name of Rome being her effective safeguard.

What can today be studied of the pre-Roman ramparts here, shows what precautions the Pompeiians took against land or sea attack. These fortifications consisted essentially of two parallel walls separated by a space of some twenty feet; the walls were made of chunks of tufa or large blocks from the Sarno, and the space between them was filled with a mixture of earth and stones. Stout buttresses, covered over with earth, made these ramparts unshakable. Some twenty-five to thirty-three feet high, according to the nature of the ground on which they were built, they were topped by crenels behind which archers and slingers lay in wait on the part facing over the country; on the reverse, the wall overlooking the interior was six feet higher so as to prevent enemy projectiles from falling into the city, and to enable the defenders to gather these up and hurl them back on to the attacker, so making good use of the enemy's own munitions.

At stated intervals, towers reinforced the walls. At the time of the siege by Sulla, there were twelve of these; we know their number and names thanks to inscriptions marked up during the siege to enable the soldiers, if they got lost, more readily to locate the place where their company was stationed. These inscriptions, again, were in Oscan, the language understood and spoken most probably by the whole of the native and foreign troops in the service of Pompeii.

The tower situated at the northern end of the Via di Mercurio – Tower XI according to the military enumeration of that time – has been carefully restored and gives a complete idea of what siege architecture was like in the time of Sulla, about 89 B.C. This date is rather conveniently furnished by the scrawl of a soldier, probably bored during his watch, who to amuse himself wrote beside the loophole of the tower where he was on guard the name of the Roman General besieging the city. The Pompeiians made their towers square, contrary to the logical and functional principle laid down by Vitruvius, who recommended circular towers so as to avoid the corners which made the masonry more vulnerable to battering-rams and the projectiles of the *ballistae*. In keeping with the custom of that period, the towers had three storeys; the bottom one was provided with a small door opening out on to the moat and enabling a sortie to be made to set fire to the enemy war-machines or to repulse the attacker at the moment when the force of the assault began to decline. The two upper storeys had loopholes where the marksmen lay in wait.

The number and placing of the towers had been fixed in consideration of the vulnerability afforded by the city's natural situation. There are three of them between the Porta Ercolano and the Porta Vesuvio, one only between the Porta di Nola and the Porta di Sarno, two by the Porta Marina, and the others reinforced the fortifications of the city gates.

Eight gates gave access to the city; they were cut in the ramparts and carefully fortified to avoid their being seized by an enemy approaching by stealth and evading the vigilance of the watchmen. In keeping with ancient usage, they were shut every evening, and each day the morning opening and the evening shutting of the gates of Pompeii comprised a little ceremony. But it was not only a question of scaring off or discouraging a possible assault; the gate had also to be beautiful, imposing and majestic, so as to impress the stranger at the moment of his entry with the city's power and prosperity. It was hence lavishly decorated and adorned with statues of divinities presiding over the fate of the city; people arriving, whether or not they were citizens, would pay their respects to these statues, addressing a prayer to them while passing through, and petitioning for the success of their business and journey, as did the inhabitants of Italian cities of the Middle Ages to images of the Virgin placed at street corners. Although Venus was the official protectress of Pompeii and naturally recognized as such by a people much inclined to the pleasures of love, it was most often a statue of Minerva which watched over the gates; doubtless it was supposed that this chaste, sober goddess was more suitable for a function as important as guarding the city.

Approached from the sea, Pompeii was entered by the Porta Marina with its two arches, one reserved for pedestrians, the other for chariots and beasts of burden; this latter would not seem to have been as frequently used as the other gates, for heavily-laden vehicles avoided it on account of the steep gradient of the road leading to it. Moreover, once past the gate, the street became narrower inside it, so that traffic was impeded and blockages more frequent; its only advantage was that it emerged almost directly on to the Forum, thus shortening the way for pedestrians hurrying there on business.

Following the walls round towards the north-west, we find ourselves at the Porta Ercolano, formerly called the 'Salt Gate' (Porta Salinensis) because the yield of the salt-mines came in here. Rebuilt during the Roman era, probably towards the end of the first century A.D., it no longer had any military function, the Pax Romana allowing the Pompeiians to enjoy a well-earned security, but its bases hark back to the time when there was still a need for protection against possible attack. Larger and more majestic than the Porta Marina, because it was one of the most used entrances, it had three arches, the central one, very high and large, serving as right-of-way to vehicles, and those opening to right and left of it being narrower and used by pedestrians. As the ramparts had ceased to have a function at the time when this gate was renovated, a portion of the walls was freely demolished to enlarge the street.

Farther east, in the northern part of the city, opens the Porta Vesuvio, destroyed during the earthquake of 62. Jucundus's curious bas-relief (see page 24) depicts this structure in the act of collapsing

78

under the earthquake; arches are giving way or tottering, and yawning vaults and splitting pillars can be seen. The condition in which the gate was discovered by modern archaeologists shows that it had not been completely rebuilt by 79, but was still, like so many houses in Pompeii, undergoing reconstruction. Traffic having become much heavier on the great road that completely traversed the city to the Porta di Stabiae – this road, formerly called the *cardo*, today being the Via di Stabiae – it was necessary to provide broader and freer passage to the press of vehicles and pedestrians using this entrance.

Of the Porta di Capua, next in the circuit of the city, not a great deal is as yet known, for there is much digging still to be done in this only partly cleared area of Regions V and VI. Let us then proceed straight on to the Porta di Nola, which is at the end of the large street called the Via di Nola. This gate is one of the most interesting, for traces of different restorations which it had undergone in the course of centuries have been found. A sculptured head of Minerva, as keystone, dominates the entrance arch on the side facing the city, and there is an Oscan inscription recording that a certain Popidius had undertaken, at some moment of its history, maintenance and repair works. His repairs were carried out, it would seem, without much regard for blending the different periods of the constructions, since parts are of brick, others of limestone and others still of volcanic rock.

The Porta di Sarno faces, at the opposite end of the city, the Porta Marina; between these runs the *decumanus major* of antiquity, Pompeii's longest street (about 1200 yards), today called the Via dell'Abbondanza. From what remains of this gate, it would seem to have contained a single arch, used by vehicles and pedestrians alike, but it is difficult to make out exactly the design and method of construction, as it was grievously damaged by the two cataclysms and by pillagers who stripped it of its handsome facing of limestone slabs to use these in the building of their own houses. Beside the entranceway was situated a little kiosk which must have served as guard post for the soldiers watching over the security of the city or for the revenue officers who collected the duty on taxable merchandise.

Despite occasional disputes, like that which set the Nucerines and Pompeiians against one another during a ceremony of games in the circus – a brawl which led to the closing of the Amphitheatre for ten

79

years, after the magistrates had pronounced sentence – an unbroken traffic of commercial exchange existed between Nuceria and Pompeii. The gate, called the Porta di Nuceria, through which this trade passed, forms part of the New Excavations; it was rather narrow, built of great blocks of stone, and the road leading to it had a steep gradient. Its arch is in a good state of preservation, and in its masonry can still be read, as in the Porta di Nola, the history of various periods of repair and conversions carried out from the Samnites to the Romans.

Concluding this outer tour of the city is the eighth gate, the Porta di Stabiae. This latter is one of the most interesting, because less extensively repaired than the others, thus giving an accurate idea of a fortified gate before the installation of the Pax Romana. It pertains, evidently, to a primitive era, with its single, heavy and massive arch, its enormous blocks of limestone so contrived as to repel the force of war-machines; it is very much the entrance to a fortified city, and pedestrians, obliged to use the same right-of-way as vehicles, horsemen, beasts of burden and flocks, had only the expedient of the footways, placed at the sides for their benefit, when they were too hard pressed by the wheels, horses or oxen. We can still see the niche in which undoubtedly stood the statue of Minerva, protectress of the ramparts, and some inscriptions: one enumerating in Oscan the various routes inside the city, and probably, again, meant for the Campanian troups who came to reinforce Pompeii's garrison at the time of the Social War; another one perpetuating the merits and bounty of the duumviri Avianus and Spedius, who applied themselves to re-making the road and who perhaps even paid the paving expenses out of their own pockets. These costs must have been rather considerable, for the Roman tradition required durable building, and the necessities of trade as well as those of war demanded rapid, unimpeded circulation on well-kept roads.

The Romans' remarkable attentiveness to maintenance of their roads, which rayed out in all directions from Rome, has always been and will always remain a source of wonder, even for us who have benefited by the advances of science and mechanics. As is well known, there still exist in the English and French countryside sections of these roads once followed by the legions and chariots laden with various products, and these segments are in as fair condition as they were at the moment when the contractor of public works laid the last limestone slab above the several layers of stones, cement, rock and earth which comprised the foundation of the road itself, which was thus in no danger of giving way or disintegrating.

Finding in part some of the routes that led travellers of former times into Pompeii, we are especially interested in the streets: the state in which they have remained, from the eruption of 79 to today, gives the visitor an excellent idea of the way in which the various quarters of the city were divided and connected by a system of communications reproducing, as we have noted, the traditional plan of a military camp. Thus the city is spanned, on its east-west axis, by the *decumanus major*

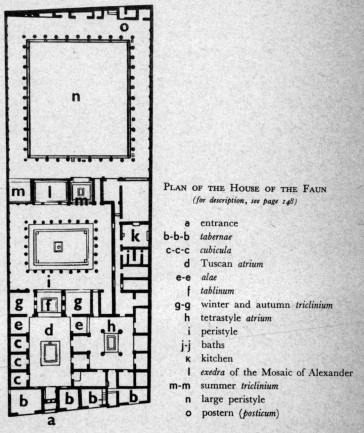

PLAN OF THE HOUSE OF THE FAUN
(for description, see page 148)

a	entrance
b-b-b	*tabernae*
c-c-c	*cubicula*
d	Tuscan *atrium*
e-e	*alae*
f	*tablinum*
g-g	winter and autumn *triclinium*
h	tetrastyle *atrium*
i	peristyle
j-j	baths
k	kitchen
l	*exedra* of the Mosaic of Alexander
m-m	summer *triclinium*
n	large peristyle
o	postern (*posticum*)

and the *decumanus minor* which intersect the *cardo* at right angles. Laid out in rectangles bounded by these main roads, the various quarters were crossed by greater or lesser streets, also intersecting one another at right angles. A glance at the plan of Pompeii shows that if the lay-out rather closely resembles that of a modern American city, it is the antithesis of a mediaeval one, which was generally rolled in on itself like a seashell with the winding streets rarely displaying a right angle.

How did strangers and the inhabitants of the city themselves distinguish the different streets, when these did not bear names, or numbers as in American cities? In none of them have any of those sign-plates, so efficient today, been found, and when quite exceptionally a marked indication has been discovered, it dates from the Social War, the period when those auxiliary units installed in Pompeii, ignorant of the turnings familiar to the locals, needed to be shown the way.

None of the designations, so picturesque and convenient to the present-day visitor, existed in former times; there was no question of the Street of the Mask, the Street of Skeletons, the Street of the Brothel, the Street of the Hanging Balcony, the Apothecary's Street. Modern archaeologists have seen fit to baptize the streets accordingly as they were cleared, just as they marked off regions, up to nine in number, and insulae: the region, as we have seen, being a neighbourhood, the insula a block of houses. With this arrangement it is easy to get rapidly and without complications to any house, by knowing the number of the region and that of the insula.[11]

The dimensions of the streets vary greatly: just as in a modern city, their proportions can be those of an avenue or a boulevard or a lane. Among the avenues firstly must be cited the above-mentioned *decumanus major*, today's Via dell'Abbondanza, with its width of about twenty-eight feet, exceeding the twenty-six feet of the *decumanus minor*, the Via di Nola. Ordinary streets were from ten feet to about sixteen in width. Traffic being as heavy as it was in Pompeii, certain streets had been made one-way, obviating collisions and clashes of wheels between vehicles pounding along at full gallop. The ruts and the deep furrows worn in the stepping-stones, good solid ones of volcanic trachyte or limestone, are evidence of their long usage. To keep pedestrians out of the way of vehicles, footways had been laid out on either side of the road, and the stepping-stones were placed at stated intervals athwart the street – from one to five stones according to the street's width – to make crossing easier from one footway to the other. Southern Italy, though not a wet region, is subject to sudden storms, involving heavy downpours; on such occasions a deluge would beat down on the city, streams gushing down the streets, and the passer-by who ran for shelter under the roof of a house or in a shop could conveniently, without wetting his feet, cross the roadway in a few skips, whereas without these useful stones he would have floundered into water up to his knees. Doubtless too the slaves or convicts employed in cleaning the streets washed them in plenty of water, to sweep away the ordure; at such times also the stepping-stones would have been a godsend to pedestrians.

The problem of the water-supply and its distribution were always among the Roman's chief preoccupations. They needed a great deal to supply the pools, baths and fountains of private houses, and more still for the thermae, which used enormous quantities. There were also numerous fountains at street-corners and cross-roads, where housewives came to fill their jugs, or where animals were watered. This water, so precious and needed in such abundance, had come originally from household cisterns situated in each dwelling, the impluvium serving to divert the rain-water that fell on the roof into casks provided to catch the moisture. Water was also drawn from wells often sunk very deep, up to more than a hundred feet, through the layers of volcanic lava. During the periods when Pompeii was Oscan and Samnite, these were the usual means of getting water and they seem to have sufficed.

They sufficed at all events until the advent of the Romans, under whom the city developed considerably, the population grew enormously, and from the second century B.C., the Romans' habit of spending a great part of their day in the thermae (not the whole time in the baths, of course, since physical-culture gymnasia, libraries and rooms for discussion and recitals were also attached) called for increased means of water adduction. What the Romans had done in their capital was now accomplished here: the waters of the neighbouring mountains were brought in by aqueduct and underground pipes, and as certain of these waters, being of volcanic origin, were mineral, cure establishments treating various ailments were then effectively set up. It was

83

owing to these curative springs, diverted to special thermae, or to certain special rooms in ordinary thermae, that Pompeii acquired a substantial reputation as a watering-place, and that many visitors came periodically for their season there, as today at Vichy, Carlsbad or Montecatini.

So as to assure a regular water supply and avoid droughts resulting from lack of rainfall or drying-up of springs, enormous reservoirs or *castella* were built and employed as well in distribution of the water into the various quarters and for filtration. The remains of the two principal reservoirs can be seen today, one in the upper part of the city so that the pipes would have the necessary down-grade, the other near the Porta Vesuvio, just by the Forum Thermae. By dint of the pressure steadily maintained in the centres of water distribution, water was freely supplied to houses, through an ingenious system of pipes which it has not been difficult to restore to working order and which today as formerly supplies the pools, fountains, kitchens and bathrooms of distinguished houses.

For those who did not have water in their homes, there were fountains, conveniently placed, and decorated with bas-reliefs and statues. For a sociable people like the Italians the fountain was not only a place to fill pitchers and buckets, but also a sort of popular club where they got together to chat, exchange the latest news, public and private, weave their idylls, discuss the merits of actors and gladiators, ridicule officials and magistrates. Around the basin, made of marble or travertine, idlers and busier folk readily assembled for conversations varying in length according to how much time they had to spare. They would lean familiarly on the figure of the god or goddess, Mercury or the Concordia Augusta (mistakenly interpreted as an allegory of Abundance because of the horn of plenty on its shoulder), from the mouth of which spouted a jet of clear and singing water. We can imagine these corner fountains, at which today's visitor barely throws a passing glance, as they once were, centres of interminable gossip, often of quarrels over right of priority, and of whispered courting-sessions between serving-maids and loafers.

There were also altars at street-corners, but these were much less frequented than the fountains, although dedicated to the Compitales Lares, who were the city's guardian spirits. Very simply made of stones or bricks, decorated with impressive serpents, allegorical bas-reliefs or pictures of the ceremonies usually performed there under the aegis of the 'street officials', the *vicomagistri*, they received the sacrifices of priests allocated to that duty, as well as the offerings of believers who were supplicating the Lares for, perhaps, the success of their business.[12] During the unearthing of the altar situated near a fountain in the New Excavations of the Via dell'Abbondanza, it was seen that this altar still held the remains of the sacrifice that had just been made or was perhaps even in progress at the moment when the eruption put priests, congregation and curious onlookers to flight.

This profusion of altars even in the streets, some being only a kind of cubic pedestal, others more elaborate kiosks, shows that religious life in Pompeii was intense. It was all the more so, perhaps, because to that need which all men have for supernatural protection was added for the Pompeiians the ever-threatening presence of an enemy whose rages were not frequent but whose awakening must always be dreaded.

Though frequent in the prehistoric period, the eruptions had become more and more rare, and the inhabitants of Pompeii had grown used to living next-door to a volcano which appeared peaceful enough, covered as it was with vegetation and vines yielding an excellent wine, called perhaps then as now by the name of the vineyard from which it comes, *Vesuvio*. Vesuvius had not been directly responsible for the cataclysm of 62, but the internal stirring of the lava and the expansion of gases in the entrails of the volcano had certainly been not unconnected with the earthquake, fearful as it was. The damage caused in the city by this tremor, the fear it had awakened in those who had witnessed it or been among its many victims, had probably increased the piety of the Pompeiians and their alacrity in religious ceremony and sacrifice, in the hope of appeasing the dangerous and hostile powers well-known to be capable of harming men in every way.

Be that as it may, Pompeii was a religious city, judging at any rate by the number of temples which had been built and chapels consecrated, more or less officially and openly, to oriental sects and to the mysteries which had taken root there.[13] One of the first questions that comes to mind on the subject of the Pompeiians' religious life is whether Christianity had penetrated here and gained initiates. It is known that St. Paul had journeyed in the south of Italy around A.D. 60, that is to say even before the earthquake, and it is probable that his preachings had accomplished some conversions. It was supposedly a Christian, probably revolted by the immorality rampant in Pompeii, who marked on a wall that furious inscription which has come to light: 'Sodom and Gomorrah'. The man who called down the wrath of heaven on these Campanian cities, compared here with a good deal of exaggeration to the abominable ones of Palestine, was familiar with the Bible, but that would not necessarily make him a Christian: Jews were not lacking in Campania, favourable as it was to speculation and business, where, however, no trace of a synagogue has been found among the religious buildings registered by the archaeologists.

On the other hand, a sensational discovery made in February 1939 at Herculaneum – in a house of the fifth insula – affords the possibility that, if there is no proof of St. Paul's proselytizing in Campania having borne fruit in Pompeii, Herculaneum contained a number of Christians. Was this 'room with the sign of the Cross' a small chapel designed for the prayers of a scanty congregation, or was it a place of private worship? It is impossible to say; moreover, the controversy is not yet resolved between partisans of a Herculanean Christianity and their opponents who refuse to allow that the imprint of the Cross, found in the House of the Bicentenary of the fifth insula, has any religious significance.

We shall not pretend to decide on so delicate a problem, which must be referred to the authors who have debated it. It will suffice here to describe the 'little room of the Christian' – let us so call it – and leave the reader to form what opinion he will, after having provided him with the facts of the case.

While workmen were clearing the upper storey of the house known as that of the Bicentenary, which had formerly been an aristocratic one until the reign of Claudius, and then was converted into apartments rented out in all probability to humble folk, they noticed in a room scarcely more than ten feet long, and windowless, a sort of wooden cupboard placed on a podium against the wall facing the door. This cupboard, which can also be interpreted as an extremely simple altar, almost a *prie-dieu*, is topped by a cross marked on the wall: or to be more precise, what is seen today is the place where a wooden cross, fixed with nails, had been; around the arms of this cross, a section of wall had been whitened with lime, as if to provide a frame and background for the sacred sign. The cross having been removed, for some unknown reason, the shape of the arms shows bare.

What has become of the cross itself? Did the man who had contrived this humble chapel detach the sign from the wall during one of the numerous persecutions attacking the Christians? Or did he hurriedly remove it when the roar of the eruption began, and flee clasping it to his breast in the belief that the holy sign would protect him? Be that as it may, there existed in this lodging-house at Herculaneum an individual or a family or a small group of believers, who placed the image of the Cross on the wall of their room. The theory refuting the arguments of those who hold that it could have been any object whatsoever in the form of a cross, is reinforced by actual examination of the wall. The cross must have been concealed from notice in a sort of framework with wooden shutters which could be opened and closed as necessary; closed to hide from prying eyes an object which could cause anyone unwise enough to display it to be sent to the rack, this little cupboard would open only to the fervent gaze of the Herculanean Christians. These cupboard doors might also have had a similar function to the so-called 'tsar's door' in the iconostases of Russian churches, behind which is concealed a portion of the celebration of the Mass.

Another and more definitive comparison is available: the 'altar' of the Herculanean Christian greatly resembles a number of altars to the Lares in that city and Pompeii. An obvious analogy exists between the closed cupboard in which was hidden the statue or sacred painting of the pagans, and the wall-cupboard in the room with the cross. The objects found on the floor of this little room are hardly conclusive; they are extremely simple vessels and flagons such as the occupant of this modest dwelling would have owned. It is permissible to suppose that, in the Campanian cities as at Rome, the Christian evangelization occurred first among humble people, who were doubtless attracted, more than others, by a religion promising eternal beatitude to the poor and the lowly. It must therefore have been a Christian belonging to the lower classes, perhaps even a slave, who had nailed to his wall the large wooden cross at which he worshipped.[14]

Was Mass celebrated in this humble corner of the House of the Bicentenary? Quite possibly. The sacred vessels and accessories of the ceremony have not been found; the Christian would have removed them hastily, after having torn the cross from the wall. The lower part of the cupboard, could, in any case, have secreted the articles necessary to the cult. Chapel or not, this room is one of the most moving places in the dead cities.

Some would see another proof of the presence before 79 of Christian communities in Campania, in the 'magic square' traced on a column of the west portico of the Palaestra at Pompeii. There has been a great deal of discussion about the mysterious significance of this square composed of five words placed one upon another – *'rotas, opera, tenet, arepo, sator'* – which have the idiosyncrasy of being readable vertically as well as horizontally. The most recent and decisive pronouncements on this subject, which remains violently controversial, are those of M. Jérôme Carcopino. I therefore refer the reader to the book in which he gives the last word on this question.[15]

If it seems certain that the Herculanean cross does prove the presence of Christians in that city, the 'magic square' is far from being an equal proof, though Grosser and Della Corte have interpreted this riddle as a convenient way of evoking, in disguised form, the words *pater noster*. One scholar so interprets these occult words as to produce, in English, something like: *God is the creator and keeper of all things.* Another sees it as: *God has held the works of man in His hand since the beginning of the existence of things.*

The magic square of Pompeii would be considered merely an oddity were it not also found elsewhere, and were it not the case that supernatural powers continued to be attributed to it in the Middle Ages. Finally, there is the question of whether the ingenious and mysterious arrangement of words could not be the work of a follower of some gnostic sect. It is impossible at all events, to attribute it to an adherent of one of the oriental religions whose activity has been proven at Pompeii and Herculaneum. Gnostic? Christian? The controversy is not closed, and keen cryptographers will continue to offer new interpretations of the magic square with the same conviction that others bring to locating Atlantis or unveiling the secret of the Great Pyramid.

The Temples

Not to leave the sphere of the concrete and positive, we must confine ourselves to surveying what the Pompeiian remains unequivocally reveal of the religion of the Campanian peoples before 79: the temples. These temples are, however, of various kinds. Some are dedicated to the great divinities of the Roman pantheon, Jupiter, Apollo or Venus; others to a goddess imported from Egypt who enjoyed a great reputation at Rome and had numerous and wealthy adherents in Pompeii: Isis. The suburban temple consecrated to the worship of Bacchus, and the 'sacred room' of the Villa of the Mysteries, can be regarded as minor temples, or chapels of a sect.

Pompeii had an extremely cosmopolitan population, comparable to that found today in Alexandria, Singapore or Hong Kong, and such as was met with, at the period when Pompeii was most flourishing, in the Roman settlements, described in the *periplus* of Ptolemy[16], all along the coasts from the Red Sea to the present-day Indo-China. Extremely busy trading centres, these settlements were built up in the Roman fashion and comprised everything essential to Romans living abroad: thermae, palaestrae, circuses and theatres where acts brought out from Rome were staged, touring the coasts from Alexandria to China. All peoples and races came together in these busy commercial cities, each bringing his own customs and ways, and his own religion.

Thus, after unimaginable peregrinations, an ivory statuette of the Hindu goddess Lakshmi found its way to Pompeii, where it was discovered in 1938 by Professor Maiuri in the house called that of the Four Styles because of its assembling in the same décor the four successive styles of Pompeiian painting. To whom could that beautiful and voluptuous and rather indecent image of the goddess of love, who is the Indian equivalent of Venus, have belonged? Possibly to a traveller who brought it back as a curiosity from one of his expeditions to India; or to a merchant dealing in exotic art-objects. There is known to have been considerable trade between Rome and India, where, among other things, was made that light, transparent stuff called mousseline, of which a factory has been discovered, dating from the Roman era, at Arikamedu near Pondicherry. Possibly there were connoisseurs of Far Eastern art at Pompeii who had similar objects, perhaps also

Chinese bronzes, in their collections? Future discoveries – with two houses out of five being still unexplored – may throw further light on these matters.

The boldest but also the most probable hypothesis to explain the presence of this enchanting ivory figure in the House of the Four Styles would be the supposition that there were Indians living in Campania – perhaps engaged in the mousseline trade – one of whom might have had a particular devotion for the consort of Vishnu.

As is only fitting, the temples are the first buildings that catch the traveller's eye on his entry into Pompeii by the Porta Marina. To the south, there are the ruins of the Temple of Venus, of which not much remains, as it was heavily damaged by the earthquake of 62 and the work of restoration had not been finished at the time of the eruption. Blocks of stone and marble, with which the masons and sculptors were working when they were interrupted by the catastrophe, are still to be seen scattered on the ground. It is a quirk of fate that one of the most heavily damaged sanctuaries was precisely that of the goddess whom the inhabitants considered the protectress of individuals and of the aggregate, and to whom they did honour in chapels both public and private. Empty and desolate is the promenade where once stood magnificent statues and smoking altars, and which commanded an admirable view over the sea and the port enlivened by incessant comings-and-goings of ships; here Sulla, who believed that he owed his military victories and political successes to this goddess, had established a cult for her and commended her to the worship of his soldiers, the ones whom he was installing as colonists in the city which, in addition to her old name of Pompeii, was to bear this new name: Veneris. Thus, through the dictator's predilection, the city was pledged to *Venus physica pompeiana*, whose image, nude in a sea-shell or chastely clothed in blue and crowned with laurel, was endlessly perpetuated in aristocratic houses, taverns and shops. As she had been born from the waters, believers who looked towards the sea imagined her carried in state upon each wave, attended by nereids, cherubs and dolphins. Because she was especially beloved of mariners, who in the peristyle of her temple would implore the sea to be merciful, she was frequently depicted as leaning on the rudder of a boat.[17]

There was no class of society which did not offer homage and prayers to her. The gladiators sought her protection in the arena; candidates for office charged her with enlightening the electors' minds, or, in other words, swaying the vote in their own favour. 'Vote for me, and Venus of Pompeii will make all your undertakings prosper,' many graffiti proclaim; and anyone intending harm to some devotee, either in his person or in his property, was denounced to her just wrath. She was so greatly loved that certain archaeologists believe the temple to have been undergoing restorations, on the eve of the cataclysm, not so much because the earthquake had demolished it as because the citizens' piety wished to raise to her a monument still greater and more magnificent. The enormous basements of masonry, arched with colossal freestones and still further reinforced by cramp-irons, were to serve as a platform for the erection of colonnades and halls worthy of her whom the entire people adored with such fervour. Such as it appears today, the Temple of Venus is more like a work-yard which the labourers have just left for the evening and to which they will be returning in the morning, than like ruins.

The two other principal divinities await the traveller when, having passed before the Temple of Venus, he stops on the other side of the street in front of the Temple of Apollo. This latter is in a much better state of preservation with its portico of forty-eight columns surrounding the great court and its raised podium crowned with Corinthian columns. This actual place of worship is one of the most ancient, since in the sixth century B.C. an earlier sanctuary of the sun god existed on the site; but of this latter nothing is left, since the oldest remains date from the Samnite era. In the time of Nero, a work of enlargement and decoration, which was to continue uninterrupted, was put in hand, each important citizen contributing his offering to Apollo, in the shape of altars, statues or ex-votos; and as the worshippers would want to know the time either to go to their devotions or to return to business, the duumviri Erennius and Sepunius had a sun-dial, made after the Greek fashion, suspended from a column of marble specially imported from Phrygia.

In the intense sunlight bathing the court of the temple, on a pedestal propped against a column, stands the statue of the god. He is naked except for a light cloth, a sort of scarf thrown over his arms, which does not impede his running nor prevent him from launching his arrow against the serpent Python. The bow has disappeared, but the gesture is strikingly vivid, giving a sense of all the power of the body rising from the lower limbs and gathering in the arm which is to shoot the murderous dart at the monster.

The *cella*, raised on the podium, surrounded by columns and painted and stucco-coated, still contains the oval-shaped stone called Omphalos, which in Greece, where it is likewise found at Delphi, was a symbol of Apollo; *omphalos* means 'navel', and this curious image is closely linked to the mythology of this god, for reasons which we lack space here to develop.

The Hellenic and Roman divinities were not jealous of their prestige, and gladly welcomed other gods or goddesses into their temples; on condition of like return, of course. Thus, in the sanctuary of Apollo, in addition to his own statue, pedestals and altars consecrated to his sister Diana may be seen, and also even some to Mercury, and, what is more astonishing, in a room of the temple's outbuildings, at the northern end of the portico, are paintings portraying Bacchus-Dionysos brandishing the thyrsus and pouring wine from his cup on to a leopard lying at his feet.

The Temple of Apollo is adjacent to the Forum and, as it is supposed, may actually have communicated with it. The Forum, in Pompeii as in all Italian cities, functioned as the centre of the people's life, the meeting-place of all those coming together on business and of all the idlers who could be sure here of encountering others of their own ilk with whom they could gossip for hours on end; the equivalent, in sum, of today's Piazza del Mercato or Piazza del Municipio, buzzing like a hive all day and far into the night with conversations, in the towns, whether large or small, of northern or southern Italy.

Occupying an entire short side of this long rectangle which is the Forum and which measures some 160 yards in length by 36 in width, stands the Temple of Jupiter, splendid and majestic as befits the dwelling of the king of gods, and dominated by the smoky mass of Vesuvius. Contrary to the case with the other sanctuaries, which have been restored according to what remains there were, we have a very exact reproduction of the Temple of Jupiter, as it was at the moment of the earthquake, in that bas-relief which the banker Jucundus had placed

92

on the altar of the Lares in his home. The sculptor of this ex-voto was scrupulous about portraying it all exactly as it had appeared on that day in the Temple court, so that we can give full credence to the documentary truth of this representation: with the exception, however, of one amusing detail, one rather grotesque error made by him. 'When it came to sculpting the two equestrian statues flanking the temple, being unable to copy them since they had collapsed, he portrayed, in his naiveté, instead of the crumbling of the statues the fall of the riders. It is thus not a little surprising to see these marble or bronze figures making prodigious efforts to keep their balance amidst all the confusion.' (Thédenat, I).

The Temple of Jupiter, being the city's capitol, shared by the king of gods with Juno and Minerva, had to be the greatest and most magnificent; elevated on a basement more than ten feet high, with its columns at once imposing and shapely, it must have dumbfounded with admiration and piety the visitors who thronged there for religious reasons or out of curiosity, by the extraordinary profusion of works of art collected in it. We cannot today have any idea of the luxury and beauty of these ancient temples, enriched as they were with colour, with gold and silver, with ivory, paintings and polychromatic stuccos, as seen by the Pompeiians of pre-62 – not afterwards, since the entire building, like the Temple of Minerva, was undergoing reconstruction. The remains were probably very unstable, for during the eruption of 79 a column fell on one of the workmen there, whose bones were discovered, when the ruins were cleared, crushed under the marble tambours. The statue of Jupiter itself was still in a crypt of the cella, where it had been left until the moment when it would be reinstalled in state in the rebuilt and magnificently decorated cella.

Another temple to Jupiter existed in the city, but dedicated to a personality of his other than the Capitoline: Jupiter Melichios – that is, the bestower of abundance on the crops, and the farmers' patron. The sanctuary of Jupiter Melichios is in the theatre district, at the corner of the Via d'Iside and the Via di Stabiae. It is supposed that throughout the period between the earthquake and the eruption, this temple replaced the forum's Capitoline one, which could hardly be used any longer. In this way the modest sanctuary of the rustic Jupiter, dear to the countryman and dedicated to agricultural toil, received two statues of Jupiter and Juno and a bust of Minerva, the presence of these sufficing to make of this humble district chapel a temporary Capitolium.

In all houses of a certain standard there was an altar dedicated to the Lares;[18] each family had its own Lares, under whose protection it was placed. There were probably neighbourhood Lares as well, and there were also those which presided over the aggregate destiny, no longer of such and such a financier or merchant, but of Pompeii as a whole; their temple was therefore situated at the hub of the city's activity, the Forum, between the Macellum and the Temple of Vespasian.

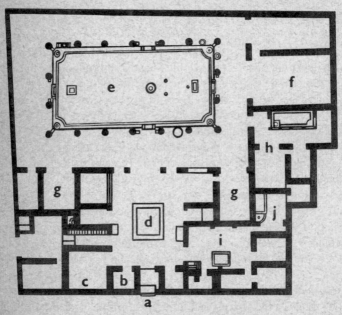

PLAN OF THE HOUSE OF THE VETTII
(for description, see page 158)

a	entrance	f	large *triclinium*	
b	*cella*	g-g	*oeci* of the peristyle	
c	*oecus* of the *atrium*	h	women's quarters	
d	*atrium*	i	small *atrium* with *lararium*	
e	peristyle	j	kitchen	

Such as they appear today, the remains of the Temple of the Lares are the remnant of the building constructed after the earthquake, partly to appease the household gods, who were thought to have been incensed by some remissness in the worship accorded them, partly to evince the inhabitants' gratitude that the whole city had not been demolished. Such were the guardian genii of antiquity: at once homely and formidable, bountiful and touchy, and capable of expressing their anger through such calamities. They had to be conciliated with prayer and sacrifice, and if some mishap occurred despite every precaution taken to satisfy their exigence, their anger must hastily be appeased with offerings prescribed by ritual.

With the advent of the Empire, a new cult had been installed in all the cities where the Roman authority made itself felt, a cult as demanding and uncompromising as that of the ancient gods: the cult of the Emperor himself, who was divine. Augustus, however, had been circumspect enough not to proclaim his divinity openly, but he achieved it through association with the Lares and by instituting in the last years of the first century B.C. – between 14 and 7, to be precise – profound alterations in the worship accorded the Lares and in the ceremonies addressed to them. He began by associating his personal 'genius' with that of these household and civic spirits; the *Lares publici* took the name of *Lares Augusti*, and the ruler's image was insinuated among those of the Lares. While thus rejecting, with a real or feigned indignation, the idea that he could be worshipped, Augustus wormed his way cleverly into the family of these gods, minor gods perhaps, but gods all the same. In the Forum of Pompeii, therefore, worshippers passed directly from the Temple of the Lares into the Temple of Vespasian, which was attached, without that conjunction scandalizing or even surprising the people.

Of the Temple of Vespasian, where the Emperor's godhead was worshipped – god terrestrial, visible and present – there remains, among the rubble, one of the most interesting and informative documents on religious life in Italy at that period when Christianity was just being born: the sacrificial altar has survived intact, despite the collapse of the buildings which crumbled around it. Less important than the *Ara Pacis* of Augustus, the altar of Vespasian shows us however on bas-reliefs the trappings of sacrifice and the sacrifice itself. As for the divinity to whom this sacrifice was offered, the actual statue of Vespasian has disappeared; only the altar remains, with the bull, the sacrificial victim, the sacrificers armed with their clubs and knives, the priests in long robes, the young officiating priests of the temple, and the flute-players who accompanied the hymns sung by the choirs.

The memory of Augustus himself is honoured in two buildings. One, situated in the Forum, beside the Temple of Vespasian, was dedicated by the priestess Eumachia, directress of the corporation of dyers, to two 'imperial divinities', the Concordia Augusta and the Pietas Livia, Livia being Augustus's wife; but this is not a temple properly speaking. The other, the Temple of the Fortuna Augusta, is located in Region VII – that is, in the very centre of the city, in one of the most populous and busy neighbourhoods. This temple was specially built in 3 B.C. for the Imperial cult by the duumvir Marcus Tullius on land belonging to him and at his own expense. The devotion of the Pompeiian magistrate to this 'father of his country', as Augustus is described in the votive inscription, is evidenced by the noble dimensions of the building and the beauty of its decorations, also by the pomp of the ceremonies performed there. We even know, from an inscription dating from the foundation, the names of the priests who ministered to the Imperial cult: Numitor, Suavis, Pothus, Agathemerus. In spite of this, the Temple of the Fortuna Augusta, whatever the bounties of the generous donor, seems like a mere local chapel compared with the temples of the Forum and the curious sanctuary, located in the theatre district, which is consecrated to a foreign divinity, but one powerfully established amidst the native gods in the Empire: the Egyptian Isis, wife of the unhappy god Osiris, who, according to the mythology of the Nile, is cut to pieces and devoured by his adversary, the evil god Seth.[19]

Before examining the temple itself we have to ask – for it is a very curious psychological problem – how Isis came to be one of the most popular and widely revered divinities in all the Roman pantheon. For this, we must go back to the actual springs of religious life in ancient Rome. What do we see there? A formalism in which the relations between men and gods are determined according to a fixed ceremonial to which it is necessary to defer if the gods are to be kept in a benevolent frame of mind. Each one has his precise function in the administration of the universe, and in the family home itself are encountered a number of lesser divinities presiding over the childbed, the kitchen and the threshold. A fair meed of respect, prayers and sacrifices maintains harmony between the world of men and that of the gods.

The metaphysic of such a religion is especially destitute; it is quite lacking in any mystique. For a long time, however, the Romans deemed it sufficient to arrange fair and advantageous relations between heaven and earth. The gods, on the whole, were functionaries on a higher level, to whom were entrusted the protection of the State, of the family hearth and of various social activities; for a long time, too, the Romans were content with these official cults to which came to be added, in the country, remnants of very ancient ritual religions, of the gloomy mysteries of the Etruscans, and of peasant superstitions which most often survived all conversions.

Disquiet, which is of the very nature of man, demanded more than this deferential and fearful politeness in respect of the gods. When Rome came in contact with peoples of the Orient, she was impressed at finding there pathetic religions, religions founded on sorrow and salvation. While Jupiter and Apollo were magistrates of the highest order, Adonis, Osiris, Atys, Mithra appeared as supernatural, fantastic personages who died and were reborn, and who promised their believers – that is, those individuals who had been initiated into their mysteries – eternal life.[20]

This survival – on the significance and range of which the Romans, accepting without question the traditional beliefs, had not seriously questioned themselves – now came to the forefront of their intellectual and spiritual preoccupations. If there really existed a life after death, what was it, and how could it be ensured? The ritual passage through the labyrinth where the torch of Orpheus and Demeter was seen shining, the baptism of blood flowing in the crypt of the *mythraeum*, the teaching of Osiris's daily resurrection with the sun and his annual rebirth with the new corn, the frenzied dances of the Bacchanals in which Dionysos died in the form of the grape trampled underfoot and was reborn in the joyous froth of wine: all these singular and fascinating things awakened in the most rational Romans philosophic thoughts of a strange, splendid nature. Whether or not to their advantage, disquiet began to trouble their consciousness, to the point of making them find the old official beliefs banal, prosaic and poor in feeling.

Rome hesitated to accept the introduction within her boundaries of these religions which many judged bizarre, extravagant and even unhealthy; but her policy of expansion, embracing the ambition of conquering all the known world, knew the usefulness of leaving to conquered peoples their faiths and cults. To add their gods to the customary divinities was also an excellent instrument of propaganda and domination. In annexing her vassals' gods, even if it was the Black Stone of Syria or the Diana of Ephesus with a hundred breasts, the Empire was making a profitable transaction.

Thus no obstacle was placed in the way of practising exotic religions, since policy and philosophical thought alike found this beneficial. On condition that the exercise of these cults caused no scandal and did no harm to the cult of the Emperor – which is where the Christians refused – they were willingly accepted, and freedom of the city was granted to the Great Mother of Syria alongside Venus and Minerva. So it is that Isis, in her turn, penetrated into Italy, with her retinue of brown and beardless priests, *sistrum* players and masked dancers.

This implanting of an Egyptian religion in the old Italian soil was not, however, accomplished without strife; and Isiaism did not, any more than Christianity, have an easy start. Initially the Isiacs were obliged to make do with clandestine ceremonies, and the right of assemblage was denied them. Sulla exercised tolerance in their favour, and they ventured to establish brotherhoods and build temples. Each emperor, according to his whim, authorized or forbade their public worship; Tiberius persecuted them and had their sanctuaries razed to the ground, Caligula shut his eyes to their activities, Nero approved. The vast dimensions of the Temple of Isis at Pompeii, and of the Temple of Serapis (another Egyptian cult) at Pozzuoli not far from Naples, show that there was an important community of Isiacs, whether Egyptians or Romans, in these two cities. Caesar's liaison with Cleopatra, the visit of the celebrated Egyptian queen to Rome where she was triumphally received, her identification with the goddess Isis, and, snobbery and fashion taking a hand, the Roman's eagerness to flatter the visitor by adopting her faith, aided in this firm integration of a belief which had no rapport with the old Roman spirit.

It is indeed a source of the greatest astonishment how a rationalistic people could show so much favour to forms of thought which initially could not but baffle and offend them, and with which they were at first incapable of communicating. It was above all by the social aspect of its teaching that Christianity attracted to itself first of all the poor and unhappy; the metaphysical conjunction probably came later. Then, this adoption – whether enthusiastic or moderate is of little account – of oriental religions would appear to be the result of a weakening of the old Roman religion, as we have noted above. Unappeased souls required something else. And so Mithra, Jesus, Osiris and Adonis had their chance. The fascination of the marvellous, the miracles and prodigies of these non-European gods, the spectacular rites with which they were celebrated, the mysteries themselves, so attractive by reason of the secrecy shrouding them and the initiates' agreeable conviction of belonging to a real and chosen élite, accomplished the rest.

The Temple of Isis had one great advantage over those of the other gods; instead of its being open only on holy-days, each day there were services that could be attended, one at dawn and the other in the afternoon. At the morning service the all-powerful divinity the Sun was honoured, with its daily rebirth out of the waves of the sea, to which the resurrection of Osiris corresponded. The afternoon one was consecrated to the benediction and offering of the water, bountiful and fecund element from which life had sprung and in which it is renewed and perpetuated.

The Isiac rites are quite well known to us, as they were frequently depicted in the paintings of public temples or of private sanctuaries which certain believers had in their houses. In this way a fresco from Herculaneum portrays a ceremony of the water with its ritual concomitants of music, chants and burning of incense. But people's imaginations were much more struck with the great festivals of Isis, the Isia, and the Procession of the Boat. This Isia, lasting three days, from the 12th to the 14th of November, commemorated the grief of Isis in her search for the body of her spouse dismembered by Seth, and her joy when having put together the dear remains she restored life into them.

The Procession of the Boat took place on March 5th, and ushered in the period favourable to navigation. The sacred boat was borne in state from the temple to the harbour, in a procession in which the priests and believers took part wearing strange, splendid costumes, and the

99

boat was then launched. But this ceremony had another meaning and a more powerful function: the vessel also represented symbolically the bark on which nightly the sun crossed the subterranean world to re-emerge at dawn; it was on a bark that the dead made their voyage into the underworld up to the point where they were reborn. It cannot surprise us to find in Egypt and in the Isiac religious allegory of Italy this boat which is also the symbol of human existence crossing the sea of destiny; and we shall come upon it again in the funeral sculptures of a tomb on which an eminent Pompeiian expressly had had engraved this allegorical image relating to the wish for survival.

The Temple of Isis at Pompeii suffered less from the eruption of 79 than did temples of the other gods, and it thus presents a suite of public and occult rooms in accordance with the various aspects of the cult. A mosaic serving as pavement in a great hall recalls to Isis the generosity of Numerius Ampliatus, who had this temple built at his own expense and in the name of his son, Numerius Popidius Celsius, who was then aged five; the fact that these donors bear Roman names shows that it was not a case of Egyptian merchants settled on business in Pompeii, but of Pompeiian converts who wished to manifest their devotion to the foreign divinity.

This temple is an elegant structure of perfect proportions, rendered majestic without being overpowering. The stuccos which still decorate the walls are in exquisite taste and give today's visitor an idea of what this sanctuary must have been in the era when frescoes in the Egyptian or Egyptianesque style adorned the walls with their symbolic representations, or reproduced scenes of the ritual and liturgy together with mystic episodes from the life of Isis and Osiris.

The trappings and instruments of the cult, which have been found in place, evince by their artistic beauty and richness of material the wealth of the Isiac brotherhood who served in this temple. It is easy to picture these priests and acolytes, tall and thin, clothed in white robes meticulously arranged, swinging bronze *situlae* filled with lustral waters, similar to those discovered, jumbled with candelabra, *sistra* and a portable fountain for ablution, in the ruins.

We are even familiar with the menu of these officiating priests, for in the kitchen of the outbuildings, as we have previously noted, there were still eggs and fish on the stove. Behind that kitchen was discovered, at the clearing of the temple, the skeleton of a man who had been caught unawares by the rain of ashes and trapped on a narrow staircase; near him lay the iron mace he had used in trying to break through the ever-thickening wall that immured him.

Other priests had been more fortunate than he, but – as mentioned in the chapter describing the eruption – had not been able to get very far, and their corpses mark out their route of escape. Some, carrying a statue of Isis, a sistrum, a silver plaque on which Bacchus was depicted beside the goddess, and a magnificent silver situla on which were shown the holy rites, had reached the Triangular Forum, but were crushed by columns. Other had fallen, still convulsively clasping to their chests ceremonial vessels, statuettes, rings and precious *paterae*; and the temple bursar, even in the moment of being asphyxiated, had not let go the cloth sack full of gold coins which had been entrusted to his vigilance and which he would not relinquish.

The great halls of the Temple of Isis were devoted to public cere-monies, but there were others, small and recondite like crypts, for the performance of the mysteries of Osiris and for initiation trials of which the tradition and ritual have survived into Freemasonry and such manifestations as in Mozart's *Magic Flute*. The stucco bas-reliefs decorating these halls are most lovely; in them are recounted various episodes of Greek mythology which relate more or less directly to the belief in an after-life attained through the good offices of the initiation. In style and sometimes also in subject they approximate to the stuccos in the Roman Basilica Pythagorica of the Porta Maggiore, this basilica likewise having been the place of meeting and worship for a sect of mysteries. The myth of Andromeda and Perseus relates to the doctrine of salvation proclaimed in the Eastern religions; Perseus figured here as the god or guardian-spirit who snatched Andromeda, likened to the human soul, from the clutches and jaws of the monster personifying death.

It need not surprise us to find worship of Bacchus linked to that of Isis in the latter's temple. Bacchus, a god of Eastern origin, was likewise one of suffering. Did he possess his own temple at Pompeii? This will be known when all the city's quarters have been cleared; but beyond the city on the Hill of Sant'Abbondio a curious sanctuary dedicated to him was discovered in 1947: a highly interesting evidence of this Dionysiac cult which the Roman Senate had tried to prohibit in that famous *senatus-consultus* entitled *De Bacchanalibus*.

The Roman decrees had probably lost much of their severity and strict application by the time they reached Pompeii, for the sanctuary of Sant'Abbondio is proved to have remained in use from the third century B.C., its date of construction, up to the catastrophe. Perhaps it was owing to its situation outside the city, which allowed of secret access to it, that it spanned with impunity the period – beginning in 186 B.C., date of the *senatus-consultus* – of persecution of the Bacchants.

This rather unpretentious temple was built, as is shown by an inscription in Oscan engraved on the altar, by Maras Atiniis, aedile of the Pompeii constituency: his name is Samnite, not Roman. The most interesting find made in this suburban temple is today in the Antiquarium at Pompeii: it is a bas-relief carved out of tufa portraying the divine couple of Bacchus and Ariadne; the fronton being very low, the two figures are seated; beside Bacchus are a panther and a satyr, and an Eros and a swan are beside Ariadne. We may recall the episode of Greek mythology representing Bacchus as a saviour god. Ariadne having been abandoned by Theseus after with her help he had slain the Minotaur in the Cretan labyrinth, she had remained alone on the island of Naxos and was in an enchanted sleep when Bacchus, risen from the sea, woke her and carried her off to share his own divinity.

There was also, in the city's environs, another sanctuary devoted to the Dionysiac cult: the famous Villa of the Mysteries, discovered in 1930, which is not only one of the most magnificent dwellings in a city which had so many splendid ones, and very characteristic of what the Pompeiians sought when they settled in the country, but also one of the keys to the mysteries, for the frescoes in one hall reproduce the various stages of the Bacchic rite and the initiation ceremony.

Our present-day knowledge of the development and import of the mysteries owes much to the discovery of this villa, which will be described in a later section. In this country retreat, the initiates could assemble without attracting as much attention as they would have done in the city; but in the actual hall where the orgiastic ceremony was portrayed, was found a statue of the Empress Livia who seems to preside over these strange and cruel revels: which shows that, even if he did not approve, the Emperor Augustus turned a blind eye to this cult.

102

BUSINESS, WORK AND RECREATION

The Forum

RECKONING, according to the usual and most probable estimation, that Pompeii numbered about twenty thousand inhabitants, the Forum appears exactly accommodated to the political, commercial and social activities of a population of that scale, bearing in mind that the whole of the citizenry would have comprised only a small percentage of these twenty thousand, since slaves constituted here as elsewhere the great majority. It would thus appear that a small minority of rich and influential citizens administered municipal affairs, moulding to their will, in the approved manner of politicians, the mass of common people, artisans and shopkeepers of free or freed status.

When we walk today in this vast empty space in which but a few incomplete rows of columns are still standing, and only a few walls indicate the shape and dimensions of public buildings, we find it difficult to picture this place as it formerly was, filled with a noisy, bustling throng, cluttered with open-air shops and the flat-baskets of pedlars, with vendors of pottery, tools, footwear, vegetables and cakes. On the walls were painted notices announcing the circus games, summoning buyers to an auction, vaunting the merits of candidates for municipal office; and all these daubed in vivid colours and large letters, the better to draw attention.

People walking through the Forum did not need to worry about traffic: this square was enclosed within boundaries preventing the entry of vehicles, and at the place where streets ran into it traces have been found of gates and grilles which could be bolted so as completely to prevent access on certain occasions. On every side rose statues, dedicated to gods, emperors or citizens who had deserved well of their country by their exploits or generosity and whose memory was thus perpetuated. Augustus had expressly laid down that his effigies and those of the

103

generals who had fashioned Rome's greatness and prosperity should be erected in the most frequented places so that the people might have before their eyes, as he put it, 'models enabling them to judge of himself in his lifetime, and afterwards of the rulers of subsequent ages'. To humour the Emperor, much zeal was shown in setting up the likenesses of notables in his dynasty, not omitting to go back as far as Aeneas who, so the well-known tradition would have it, had come to settle in Italy after the fall of Troy and had founded the family of the Juliuses. After the statue of Aeneas came that of Romulus who had built the walls of Rome, those of the Alban kings, and so on down to Augustus.

Unhappily the pedestals are empty today; the earthquake and the eruption sadly devastated the Forum and caused irreparable damage. The Forum had held, however, in emulation of the Roman one, some forty statues, several of which were equestrian; but a scant few of these had been restored or re-made after the earthquake.

In its plan and general aspect, it corresponded fairly exactly to the description of the ideal forum as formulated by Vitruvius in his treatise on architecture. 'The forums of the Greeks,' he wrote, 'are square, surrounded by double and spacious porticoes in which close columns support stone and marble architraves surmounted by galleries. The forums of Italian cities should not be so constructed, because our ancestors handed down to us the custom of holding gladiatorial combats there; the columns must therefore be more widely spaced, to allow of a good view. Under the porticoes, the money-changers' stalls, and above, the galleries, will be laid out in the most convenient way for the business transacted there and for collecting the tariff. The dimensions of the forum must be proportionate to the size of the population, otherwise there will be a shortage of space, or the forum, too scantily filled, will look empty. The width will be two-thirds the length, the shape thus being rectangular, a more convenient proportion for shows. The columns of the upper storey will be one-third less in height than those below, which being more heavily laden must be stronger.'

The architects of Pompeii conformed, in the main lines, with Vitruvius's injunctions, but with the exception that as the Forum measures some 160 yards in length by 36 in width, the ideal proportions were not altogether heeded. Moreover, renovations in the course of centuries modified the original plan; the buildings themselves reveal the history

104

of the Forum, not only in their style but also by the materials used. The materials are, in general, Sarno stone formed by the river's alluvia, Nucerine tufa, lava, volcanic pumice-stone, limestone and tufa. In the primitive era known as the pre-Samnite (sixth to fifth centuries B.C.) the construction was of limestone; the Samnite period is divided into two parts, the first (sixth to third centuries B.C.) combining volcanic stone with limestone, and the second (200 to 80 B.C.) with tufa the dominant material. With the Romans, from 80 B.C., there appeared brick and cement-faced brick. Examination of the Forum portico, for example, clearly shows the distinction between what remains of the Samnite construction and of the Roman, since the first is of tufa and the second of a beautiful white limestone, smooth and shining, giving the illusion of marble. It was the Samnites who built the first two-storeyed portico, in the Doric style and from Nucerine stone, of which there are important elements still extant today; this bent demonstrates the influence of the Hellenistic civilization with which the Samnites, as has already been noted, had been impregnated and which gave the city as a whole its first striking aspect.

To have a precise idea of this portico, at the period of Pompeii's grandeur, we must reconstruct mentally the second storey, where offices and stalls were fitted up, and paint in strong colours these columns which today are white. It troubles us to admit – because this does not appear concurrent with what we imagine to be the flavour of antiquity – that the buildings and statues were vividly and variously coloured; we praise the purity and pallor of the marble, though formerly it was covered with a fine coat of wax on which was spread a polychrome which today would be called 'loud'.

Certainly this polychromy was the product of an aesthetic choice, and of a disputable aesthetic, but above all it answered a practical purpose. In these sunny countries, such as Egypt, Greece, southern Italy and Sicily, where the light for the greater part of the year is dazzling, the volume and outline of monuments would have been 'killed' by the light and rendered almost invisible, had they not been accentuated, stressed by warm highlights of colour. The polychromy of the structures, at Pompeii as in the whole Mediterranean basin, stems from this functional necessity, and in addition it satisfied the predilection of the southern peoples for colours that 'sing', and sing strongly. Similarly orators who harangued the people in the Forum had to have a powerful voice and winning eloquence, for they needed to dominate the hubbub of conversations and the cries of sellers; on the southern side of the square, in front of the portico, there has been discovered among a row of statue pedestals a large and massive rostrum, of greater dimensions than the usual stands, which is today thought to be the *suggestum*, from the top of which public-criers announced news, and where politicians followed one another, eager to win the electors' votes with those beautiful, fulsome phrases which, on all rostra in every age, have resounded almost unchanged.

To enter the long side of the Forum facing south, from the Via Marina,[21] the street ascending from the port, is to be confronted with a very large building whose function has long been disputed and which is today called the Building of Eumachia. This building has, virtually, the dimensions and lay-out of a temple, and it did in fact have a certain religious character, since it had been dedicated, as already mentioned, to the Concordia Augusta and the Pietas Livia, by a woman whose statue still adorns the building: Eumachia. This statue, on which still can be seen some traces of polychrome, represents a woman, of an aspect at once mild and majestic, severely shrouded in solemn draperies. She performed priestly duties – we do not know in which temple – and probably also enjoyed a great fortune and public authority, for the building of these handsome-columned porticoes, certainly peopled with statues and almost entirely covered over with precious marbles, must have cost the generous Eumachia very dear. She offered it up, so affirms the votive inscription, in her own name and that of her son, Numistaeius Fronto.

This was not, however, a temple, despite the dedication to the deity of the Emperor and Empress, but quite simply the corporative or syndical building of the most active and important group of workers in Pompeii: the fullers. It was the fullers who, on the base of Eumachia's statue, claimed the honour and merit of having had that statue made to show their proper gratitude to the woman offering them this magnificent building. We can better understand its nature and function if we compare it with the Venetian *scuole*, palaces belonging to corporative groups or neighbourhood councils; they comprised a chapel adjoined to their meeting-halls and placed under the guardianship of a patron saint

106

(St. Roch, St. Mark, St. George) just as Eumachia's building was dedicated to the Emperor's divinity.

Why would Eumachia have taken so great an interest in the fullers, that is to say in the cloth-makers and -dyers, to the point of offering them this splendid, spacious guild-hall, if not because she was most probably the owner of fullers' workshops or president of their syndicate?[22] The corporative building was so constructed as to harmonize with the whole of the Forum's monuments; and its own portico, with the double row of columns, called *chalcidicum* in the votive inscription, went very well with the Forum portico. It would appear that if this building is reminiscent of a Venetian *scuola*, it also had the function of what is still called a *fondaco* in Venice: *fondaco* of Turks, *fondaco* of Germans, in other words a building combining stores for merchandise, meeting-halls and work-rooms, perhaps even lodgings for guests in transit. In the courtyard there were probably shops and stands where the fullers sold the products of their industry; it was in fact the woollen market, and in the covered gallery were heaped bales of merchandise.

If we marvel at still finding here so many decorations sculpted with exquisite art, so many rare marbles which Eumachia had had imported from Africa, Greece and Asia Minor, as well as numerous statues now vanished and frescoes almost entirely obliterated, we must remember that the Venetian *scuole* and the *fondachi* also were adorned with frescoes by Carpaccio, Titian, Giorgione, Tintoretto and Tiepolo: we can thus see that the fullers' corporative hall in Pompeii is no exception in an Italy so prodigal of her wonders.

On the same side of the Forum as the Building of Eumachia, and almost in the south-west corner, is situated the Comitium, built by the Samnites and restored by the Romans, whose use of it has given rise to much controversy: it has been explained as a school, with the recesses in the walls for bookshelves, or as a polling-office at the entrance of which barriers could be set up to channel the mass inrush of the electors – or these might have served to check the tumultuous exit of the pupils. On the short south side of the Forum, facing the Temple of Jupiter, there are three rather unassuming buildings which do not make much claim on the visitor's attention; it was here that the aediles, the duumviri and the decurions, who were the principal magistrates of the city, were located.

The aediles, two in number, had as their function the supervision of the city's sanitation arrangements, the upkeep of roads, markets and thermae and, important assignment, the organization of public games, which at Pompeii as in Rome held a major place among the pursuits and preoccupations of the populace. Accordingly as they presented more or less magnificent spectacles, the aediles were popular or the reverse, and as it was customary for them to defray the expenses of these games, their generosity was measured in terms of the number of wild beasts killed in the *venationes*[23], and of the pairs of gladiators cutting each other's throats in the arena.

The duumviri, who sat in the neighbouring building, enjoyed judiciary power and administered the establishment of electoral registers and the census. As for the decurions, they formed the Supreme Council of the city: a hundred persons chosen from among the most influential and distinguished citizens and representing the *vox populi* in the administration of public affairs. It is logical that the Comitium where the electors swarmed to appoint officials should be very near the council places of the city's three leading political jurisdictions. These three buildings comprised what was called the Curia, where the city archives too were kept.

At the south-east corner of the Forum, divided from the Temple of Apollo by the Via Marina, stands the Basilica, which at Pompeii as in all cities of the Roman Empire was at once a law-court and the favourite resort of curiosity-seekers and idlers. They came here to listen to the trials, admire counsels' eloquence and pick up news, and they amused themselves, when there was nothing better to do, by scribbling on the walls anything that came into their heads. It will be remarked, however, that the graffiti of the Basilica regulars differ considerably from those to be read on walls in streets or taverns; among the former are often found verse quotations, arguing a certain culture on the part of those who scrawled them, and poetic attempts too by amateurs who had probably not found publishers and had hit upon this inexpensive means of bringing their works to the notice of their fellow-citizens.

This is the most important and impressive of the public buildings in the Forum (with the exception of course of the temples already described), and the vastest and most characteristic of that basilical design which was to endure into Christian religious architecture. The recent

108

discovery of some tiles, of Oscan manufacture, which covered the roof, enables the construction of the Basilica to be traced back to the pre-Roman period, to around 130 B.C. We know to an exact date that it existed in 78 B.C., because on the 3rd of October, the 5th day before the Ides of October, in that year, one Pumidius Dipilus chose to write his name on the wall, together with the date and the names of the consuls in office at that time: Lepidus and Catulus.

From our knowledge of the approximate number of the population of Pompeii, and taking into account that the proportion of slaves was very considerable, it would seem that for the court of a small city the Basilica had vast dimensions and a quite special magnificence; this is owing to the building's serving also as the Exchange, where businessmen or speculators would meet clients, tradesmen or friends at appointed hours.

The Macellum, occupying the exactly opposite corner, the north-west one of the Forum, is a covered market built in the Imperial era. Its design is rather singular, and puzzling today when only traces of it remain; it was a large rectangular space surrounded with porticoes in which were wedged shops, which did not preclude the columns being of magnificent white Carrara marble elegantly wrought.

At the centre, forming a regular dodecagon, was kept a space bounded by twelve rectangular bases, which have aroused the curiosity of archaeologists; it was once imagined that this building was a temple where statues of the twelve major gods figured on these pedestals. We know today that we have here a covered market the roof of which rested on twelve columns, and of a type which was quite common in Rome, in the Italian cities, in Greece and even in Asia. This small round market was called a *tholus*, and there can be no more doubt as to its function since it has been seen to figure, as the representation of a Roman market, on a coin of Nero, and particularly since at the time of the clearing of the pool in this Pompeiian tholus, there were found a quantity of fish scales. This pool was connected by an underground channel with the sewers; and it was here that the fishmongers whose baskets were set out under the tholus roof washed and scraped their merchandise before handing it over to their customers.

There were not only stalls in the Macellum but also small chapels dedicated to the godhead of the emperors, auction rooms, the meeting-place of the corporation of Augustales entrusted with celebrating the cult of the emperors, a money-changer's booth where a great number of various coins have been discovered, and displays of fruit and vegetables. Everywhere were exquisite paintings illustrating the articles of the trade done in this place, the objects depicted naturalistically with that charming sense of realism and gracefulness which is a great value of Pompeiian painting.

And to ensure that all customers would be certain of getting fair weight, the inspectors of weights and measures had established tables containing the standards fixed by the duumviri Clodius Flaccus and Arceus Arellianus according to the decree of Augustus who, to facilitate trading throughout the Empire, had prescribed a uniformity of measurements in keeping with the figures in use at Rome and had abolished the local Oscan and Samnite traditions as sources of perpetual dispute.

There is also another Forum, more ancient and less monumental than that which we have just visited, and highly interesting from the points both of its antiquity and of the buildings with which it is encompassed. It is called the Triangular Forum and is situated by the ramparts in the vicinity of the Porta di Stabiae on a sort of rocky spur created by great flows of lava in prehistoric times. Possibly on this spot, easy to defend by reason of its steep situation, the first occupants of Pompeii built their original city. The Greeks early chose it for its beauty and strategic advantages, and in the middle of the sixth century B.C. they built here a temple, dedicated to Hercules, which is the oldest in the city.

From this natural bastion, become by dint of the consecration of the temple an 'eminence', an acropolis atop which they had a magnificent view over the surrounding country and the sea, the Pompeiians of the sixth century beheld the extent of the lands which were their property or were to become so. Of the Doric temple itself, not much remains, for it was renovated several times, in the Samnite period and by the Romans, and ended by being integrated into this Triangular Forum surrounded by a portico of a hundred columns in a noble, simple style of architecture worthy of the original temple.

The Triangular Forum held an important place in the life of the city, less important certainly than that of the principal Forum, but nonetheless essential, for it stood near the Temple of Isis, one of the centres, as we have seen, of the Pompeiians' religious life, and it also owed a considerable animation to the fact that the Palaestra and the two Theatres, the Great and the small Covered, communicated with it.

From Roman custom, the Pompeiians had acquired a passion for the theatre. But it does not seem that there existed here, as at Rome, the same enormous idle population, fed at the State's expense, entertained through the generosity of the magistrates or of those who aspired to office, and, needing endlessly to be diverted just because it had nothing to do, becoming turbulent as soon as it was no longer supplied with the games it demanded. At Pompeii, matters were different; this was no capital but a small provincial city devoted to industry and business and most probably not containing such a restless and dangerous plebs as seethed in Rome. The theatres were not the less frequented, for however industrious the merchants and the workers might have been, it was necessary to take account of the considerable number of holidays set aside in the Roman calendar for religious celebrations, or civic holidays naturally given over to games; spectacles were thus extremely frequent and the theatres periodically filled with an attentive and noisy throng clamouring to be entertained. The Theatre at Herculaneum must have held about 2,000 or 2,500 seats, and as the population of the city, much less considerable than that of Pompeii, could scarcely have numbered more than 5,000 inhabitants, it can only be concluded that in order for the Theatre to be full, as it always was since these spectacles cost nothing, one inhabitant out of two, including women, children and slaves, must have attended the performance.

The Great Theatre had been hollowed out in a sort of natural concavity, and from the tiers of the *cavea*, that is, the hemicycle occupied by the spectators, they had an admirable view, beyond the stage wall, over the valley of the Sarno and the Lattari Hills. In its original architecture, it goes back to the second century B.C. or the second half of the third, and its impressive dimensions testify to the Pompeiians' keenness on the spectacles presented here. How many spectators could be seated in the rows of the *cavea*? It is impossible today to tell exactly, for unlike the Herculaneum Theatre which was literally swallowed up in a torrent of mud preserving it intact, that of Pompeii underwent heavy damage in the downpour of volcanic matter, and several rows of tiers are lacking today, which prevents us from reckoning the building's capacity.

It was built according to the principles previously laid down by the

111

Greek architects and adopted from them by the Romans, and provided with all the refinements which delighted the spectators, in particular a device for sprinkling the audience, during the intervals, with scented water, wonderfully pleasant on really hot days; these perfumed showers were called *sparsiones*, and the days on which they were to occur were announced by posters. The inscription *sparsiones vela erunt* (*vela* being awnings) reassured those spectators who might have missed the spectacle for fear of the excessive sun. This *velum* was stretched across the *cavea* and cast a gentle shade over the audience.

Another ingenious mechanism[24] made it possible to convert the stage into a *piscina* in which probably mythological scenes, with tritons and sirens as protagonists, were enacted. The dimensions of this stage, although huge for a provincial city, would not have lent themselves to *naumachiae*, that is, mock naval combats such as were put on in the great Roman circuses, and during which ships battled against one another. Today the elements of the machinery are still in place, to operate the scene-changes and the surprise-effects of which the ancients were so fond, and it would be quite easy, with the slidebars fitted to this purpose, to work the curtain, which was raised vertically from the ground instead of descending from the arch as it does today.

The design of the Great Theatre and its proportions show that it had been built in the era when the Hellenic influence prevailed over Campania, but it was restored by a Roman architect whose name has come down to us through an inscription, Marcus Artorius Primus, who provided all the improvements necessary to fit it to the uses required of it.[25] With the exception of the small Covered Theatre or Odeon, next to the Great Theatre and serving as a 'chamber theatre', a hall for concerts and lectures, and reserved for an exclusive public, and with the exception too of the Amphitheatre, situated in the north-east corner of the city enclosure and used for the circus games, there did not exist any specialized theatres in Pompeii. The plebs and the cultivated people, officials and workers, came to hear the same plays in the same place and doubtless took the same pleasure in what was presented to them.

What then was the repertoire of the Great Theatre? Undoubtedly the same as that of theatres in other cities of the Empire: Greek or imitation-Greek tragedies, comedies, burlesqued mimes and *atellanae*. The *atellanae* were a kind of popular comedy, farces in which can be

112

recognized one of the remote origins of the *commedia dell'arte* which was to flourish in the eighteenth century. This comic genre, a very special one, had been born in a small Campanian town, Atella, from which it took its name. Initially the *atellanae* were meant to ease and relax the audience after the performance of tragedies, but subsequently they were enjoyed for their own sake and played alone without having been preceded by harrowing or pathetic dramas.

The Roman public adored the *atellanae*, at which certain celebrated writers, such as Novius and Pomponius, made their name, because these farces evoked the popular picturesque types which were so familiar and whose burlesque drolleries were so well-loved. Like the Harlequin and the Pulcinella of the *commedia dell'arte*, these types were shown in the most unexpected situations and the ones most productive of marvellous gags. Maccus the glutton turned banker or publican, Pappus the idiot put himself up for office, Bucco the hunchback became a general or gladiator. There were psychological depths in all this, but the public split their sides with laughing. The character of the mimes was no more elevated; they might be compared to music-hall numbers of a rather low level, interspersed with dances, clowning, obscenities, feats of skill and athletic exhibitions, the whole ending with a procession of nude girls.

The status of actor was hardly a respected one, and if it happened that a person of quality appeared on the stage, in so doing he forfeited his title of nobility and toppled down to the lowest level of the social scale. Caesar punished an equestrian knight, Laberius, who had achieved a considerable fame as the author of mimes, by forcing him to appear in one of his own pieces, after which the poor man, having lost his rank and prerogatives, could only retire to his house to brood over his humiliation until the end of his days.

To satisfy the distinguished and cultivated part of the audience, tragedies by Seneca, Ennius, Accius and Livius Andronicus were performed, as well as the comedies of Plautus, Terence, Caecilius and Ambivius, which enjoyed an immense reputation; but there were probably also successful authors whose fame was as ephemeral as it was resounding, and who after having moved or amused generations of Roman citizens fell into oblivion and handed down neither their works nor their names.

More refined entertainment, as we have seen, was to be had in the Odeon, the small Covered Theatre next-door to the vast stage where mountebanks and clowns succeeded tragedians. This little theatre, which did not exist before the Roman conquest, was built at the expense of two duumviri, M. Porcius and C. Quinctius Valgus, who gave this handsome present to their fellow-citizens after the defeat of the allies, that is to say about a century before the eruption of 79. The general plan is the same as that of the Great Theatre, on a much smaller scale, and the machinery is elementary, for performances here were of subtler quality than the spectacular plays which delighted the ordinary public. The fact that it was covered indicates that concerts were frequent here, and that there existed in Pompeii a coterie of music-lovers capable of appreciating instrumentalists and singers in these most favourable listening conditions.

In Pompeii as at Rome, actors were very popular, but much less so, of course, than gladiators and athletes. The actor Sorex, a bust of whom has come down to us, was a notable figure in the city, and it seems that a certain Actius scored a great success during a tour, for inscriptions have been found scrawled in wall graffiti expressing the people's regret to see him go and their hope of his early return. It is from one of these graffiti that we have also learned of the existence and popularity of an actress, Histrionica Rotica.

The scene on a holiday at the Amphitheatre displayed a much greater crowd than that filling the two theatres, for it was there that the performances dearest to the heart of the populace were held: the circus games. The duumviri Valgus and Porcius, the Odeon benefactors, were also substantial donors to this immense arena, built in 80 B.C. and designed to hold 20,000 spectators: that is, probably the whole of the Pompeiian population. So that it might always be full, it was also open to visitors, whom the announcement of an unusually glittering performance always attracted in great numbers. On days when numerous pairs of gladiators appeared in the arena and immense massacres of wild beasts took place, the entire population of the vicinity would flock here. This was highly profitable to publicans and to dealers who had the privilege of setting out their baskets under the outer arcades, and who did well out of the influx of keen sport-

114

fanciers who ate hugely and drank hard and, in the case of the country-folk, also took the opportunity of making some purchases.

But it also might happen that the bloodthirsty circus spectacles would work up emotions to such a pitch that in the tiers fights would often break out between the partisans of one or other of the gladiators, and they would come to blows with as much ardour as their champions. There was that occasion of a veritable pitched battle between the Pompeiians, in their own Amphitheatre, and the contingent from Nuceria, who had turned out in force to attend the performance; the Nucerines, being fewer, had the worst of the tussle. As already mentioned, however, the outcome was that Rome ordained the closing of the Amphitheatre for ten years so as to prevent a repetition and punish the Pompeiians for having broken the laws of hospitality.

The dimensions of this building, as seen from the highest tier, are very impressive indeed; this must have been a splendid scene when filled with a colourful, loud throng, heated by the sun, the trumpet-calls and the sight of blood, standing up in their rows and feasting cruelly on the death of a host of men and animals that killed one another simply to amuse the onlookers and satisfy their perhaps unconscious sadism. This Amphitheatre, which knew the great days of Pompeii, apart from the ten years, from A.D. 59 to 69, when by the order of Nero it remained out of use, measures 142 yards along the length of its ellipse and more than 112 across its width. It was surrounded by trees, and the corner towers of the disused fortifications served only to support the poles atop which the *velum* was extended. The Amphitheatre was quite simple, allowing of no machinery, and without those basements, designed for menageries of wild beasts, which made the Colosseum of Rome so impressive. It would seem that the animals participating in the games were confined in a neighbouring building while waiting their turn to enter the arena, and were brought in cages by the same way as the spectators used to get up into the rows. The site of the barriers, which at that moment would be raised to divide the people from the animals, has been located.

The performances held in the Amphitheatre were probably interspersed with dancing, jokes and more or less obscene acts; but the essential part was the gladiatorial combats and the *venationes. Vena-*

115

tiones was the term for those sham hunts which are seen to figure frequently on the frescoes of Pompeii and Herculaneum, and which ended simply in the killing, either by men or among themselves, of animals maddened with spear-thrusts through grilles separating them from the first rows of the audience. The passion of the Latin people for this kind of entertainment was so great that even a philosopher-emperor like Marcus Aurelius could not stop them and had, even if reluctantly, to be present one day at a coursing of a hundred lions which soldiers, posted in the tiers, assailed with arrows. The interest of these savage contests was heightened with infamous refinements: that, for example, of tying together a bull and a panther who, unable to get loose from their halter and each thinking the other to blame for this confinement, would tear each other to pieces. At great expense, exotic animals were imported from Africa and the Orient, to be made to fight one another or tear apart harmless creatures like deer or gazelles. At the end of the day the corpses of those slaughtered, gladiators and animals, were taken from the arena by the *porta libitinensis*, the 'gate of death', the sight of which can still make the visitor shudder.

If the *venationes* were very popular with the Pompeiians, their preference was above all for the gladiatorial combats, the practice of which, Etruscan in origin, had been introduced on the occasion of funeral ceremonies; subsequently they became simply performances, preceded by a brief religious observance which had the object of disguising their horror by attributing a sacred finality to them. In reality the gladiatorial contests were the source of a highly profitable enterprise: the *lanistae*, owners and trainers of gladiators, rented or sold their charges at a very high price to rich citizens who wished to ingratiate themselves with the people and gain their votes at the election by offering them this choice spectacle, which obviously cost a great deal. The training of a gladiator lasted quite some time; and the appearance of a 'star' who had won numerous combats, and who by virtue of this enjoyed an enormous popularity, in a performance staged by a duumvir would gain the latter kudos proportionate to the amount of gold that he had spent on exhibiting this hero.

Initially the gladiatorial contests were, again, only the accessory of a funeral service designed to assure to the deceased that periodic offering of fresh blood, that is to say of vital energy, which he needed to subsist

116

in the next world. In the Nekia, that book of the Odyssey relating the descent of Odysseus into hell, the traveller begins by pouring blood into a pit around which the shades then throng avidly. All such usages of the peoples of antiquity bear witness to the fact that human blood was the most effective means of obtaining this temporary resurrection.

At the period when these contests remained thus closely linked to a religious function, they took place in the neighbourhood of the tombs, or in the Forum, or in the vast quadrilateral, situated behind the stage of the Great Theatre, which served as lobby to the spectators who waited there for the beginning of the performance; this place was used as practice-ground for the gladiators who, from the reign of Nero, were lodged in rooms above the portico, and there received the visits of their ladies, as is demonstrated by those skeletons of jewel-bedizened women.

The popularity enjoyed by the gladiators considerably exceeded that of the actors and even of the mimes beloved of the masses; by a singular evolution of custom, these poor creatures fated to be victims of funeral sacrifices, and to whom there remained a chance of survival only if they killed all their opponents, had ended by being the object of a veritable cult which can be compared to that today of cinema-stars. But to this cult was added the halo of danger and the sombre fascination of death.

Progressively the funeral rite was transformed into a public show for the performance of which were built those immense amphitheatres where the whole population of the city could be comfortably seated, certain distinguished citizens enjoying the privilege of the *bisellium*, a seat twice as wide as that of the common people. It was probably this temporary glory in which they could bask which sometimes led free men to take up the cruel career of gladiator. Not all, it is true, died in the arena; some, grown old and no longer fit for such martial games, retired and were content to teach the charges of the *lanistae*, if they did not themselves become *lanistae*. Most often these fighters were recruited from among wretched debtors unable to pay their creditors, prisoners whom the endless wars on the Empire frontiers brought in droves to Rome and all Italy, or slaves especially well equipped for this dangerous sport requiring strength, skill, courage and ferocity.

Pompeiian paintings, bas-reliefs of certain tombs, and drawings sketched on walls show the appearances of different categories of

117

gladiators: the *retiarius*, armed with a fisherman's net with which he immobilized his adversary and with a harpoon to finish him off; or the *thrax* (the name derived from his country of origin, Thrace), heavily armed, with a short sword, a bronze, vizored helmet and a shield. In the Naples Museum can be seen complete gladiatorial outfits discovered in the ruins; some are magnificently ornamented, with the helmets decorated with figures in relief, and the finely-chased greaves are true works of art. When the high noonday sun gleamed on the polished head-dresses, when the proudly brandished swords threw off sparks, when the public, on its feet, cheered its favourites and the long trumpets played a military march, the Amphitheatre of Pompeii must have taken on a most wonderful aspect.

The spectacle began with a procession, comparable to the *paseo* of the present-day *corridas*, in which those about to die saluted the people, throwing out their chests and showing off their costly armour, which was often the gift of some beautiful woman taken with their rugged maleness. Next, the director of the games would consecrate the spectacle to the Manes, that is, to the spirits of the dead, so as to keep faith with the tradition and original function of these cruel sports; there existed moreover in the Amphitheatre a kind of well which was reputed to connect the world of the living and that of the dead. Finally the contests began. The men who defeated their opponents returned to their barracks to await the next combat, or again risked their lives. Their best fate, to which they all aspired, was to have their safety assured by some sporting enthusiast or a rich mistress who would buy them into the *lanistae;* but it also might happen that certain retired ones, bored with their leisure, would be overcome with nostalgia for the arena, to which they would return, this time of their own free will.

Of all the graffiti covering the walls of Pompeii, the greatest number refer to gladiators; their admirers recall their numerous victories, their successes with women, the details of their fighting method. Sometimes even, incidents not at all to their credit are related. In the House of Siricus we encounter the mention of a certain Polycarpus who in a shameful fashion fled from his adversary, and in the atrium of the House of the Centenary a more complete inscription apprises us that 'Officiosus fled on November 6th in the consulate of Drusus Caesar and Marcus Junius Norbanus'. It was rare for a gladiator to be so immortalized for having shamefully turned tail on his enemy. Most often those whose names have come down to us are extolled for their victories. The tomb of Umbricius Scaurus, in the Necropolis of the Porta Erco-lano, has preserved several bas-reliefs depicting circus sports, with names of the gladiators, their portraits and the number of their victories. Thus we learn that Nobilior was victorious eleven times, and Bebrix fifteen times. This is nothing, however, beside the fifty victories of Auctus and the fifty-six of Severus. As we have noted, it is not always their triumphs in the arena that are proclaimed in this fashion, but often too their amorous successes. One Celadus is hailed as the *supirium puellarum* and the *decus puellarum*, in other words as the local heart-throb.

The most vivid, picturesque and probably most consummate images of certain gladiators have come down to us in the form of caricatures scrawled upon walls. Mazois reproduces several of these, and some continue to exist on the walls of the passage connecting the Great Theatre and the portico of the gladiators' barracks, and in the House of Obellius Firmus near the Porta di Nola. The unknown artist gave to his virtuosi of the arena the comic demeanour of the braggart in the comedies of Plautus and of the *miles gloriosus* in the *atellanae*. The out-line is full of spirit and dash, emphasizing chiefly the arrogant bombast and pretentious conceit, the swaggering pose of these popular idols; they walk vaingloriously with an assumed dignity, and the plumes float on their helmets as if wafted by the winds of fame.

But a more exact portrait of the gladiator can be found in the statuette serving as sign-board to a tavern in the vicinity of the Porta di Nuceria, not far from the Amphitheatre. This tavern must have done a thriving trade, for it was located on the road which the country folk and people from nearby towns took when they came to attend the sports, especially the Nucerines, before the brawl of A.D. 59 discouraged them, doubtless for some time to come, from sitting in the same stands as such aggressive hosts, even after the punitive delay of ten years had passed.

This statuette is one of the most interesting discoveries quite recently made in an area not yet completely cleared and certainly very richly endowed. It was one of the trophies of this inn, which provided its clients with a triclinium under a rustic arbour, and tables in a peaceful garden where those passing could stop to eat and quench their thirst

119

before going on to take their seats in the Amphitheatre. They were invited in to this place, those of them in particular who adored the gladiatorial contests, by the pleasant look of this smiling figure – perhaps a portrait taken from life – wearing the characteristic accoutrements of the *parmularius*: the vizor-less helmet, the short sword, and more especially the small round shield, the *parmula*, to which he owed his name. The gladiator of the inn of the Porta di Nuceria was leaning with his left hand, that raising the shield, on a statue of Priapus, doubtless his patron god, which hoisted the insignia of a formidable virility. For, and it is readily understandable, Priapus and Venus were of all the inhabitants of Olympus the chosen helpers of these 'demi-gods of the arena', who would address a humble and fervent prayer to them before going in to kill, or be killed.[26]

The Thermae

When the Pompeiians had attended to business, and strolled through the Forum to pick up the news of the city and the Empire, they would then, before going to hear a tragedy by Seneca or a comedy of Terence or to be seated on the tiers of the Amphitheatre in the place appropriate to their position and social standing, assiduously visit the thermae, as did also the Romans. The thermae were not mere bathing establishments, though they did fulfil that function; to reinstitute the Roman thermae today it would be necessary to assemble such divers arrangements as a Turkish bath, a club and the varied grounds of a sporting association. Moreover, the Romans, spending a good portion of their day there, were anxious to have them comfortably, luxuriously and splendidly decorated. The magnificent stuccos of the vault of the *apodyterium* in the thermae called Stabian because they are situated at the corner of the Via della Abbondanza and the Via di Stabiae, comprise one of the most exquisite masterpieces of this art; and the more classic and sober but quite as magnificent decorations of the *tepidarium* in the Forum Thermae show that for this utilitarian establishment, where the water-vapour would probably quite soon damage the delicate reliefs, which were treasures of virtuosity and talent, more was spent than on any temple or private house. It also might happen that – supreme refinement – the ceiling over a *piscina* would be covered in a mosaic representing in brilliant colours an iridescent world of fish,

120

crustaceans and fantastic creatures reflected in the water, the blue depths of which so effectively acted as a mirror that the swimmers had the impression of moving among an extraordinary marine fauna and in an atmosphere comparable to that of the enchanting blue grotto of Capri.

Observing, in this astonishing suite of magnificent rooms which made up the thermae, that the lavatory seats were of marble and that the elbow-rests there were supported by chimaeras or dolphins, we tend to feel that nothing in the modern world can equal such luxury lavished on places where ordinarily a strict cleanliness suffices. We must take into account, however, a characteristic fact of Roman habits: great conversationalists, the frequenters of the thermae liked to open or pursue their discussions even in rooms where normally solitude is preferred: hence, these alignments of marble seats one beside another where they could settle down to chat completely at leisure. This is not the least of the curiosities of the thermae, surprising as they are in their revelations of idiosyncrasies of ancient life. The most informative, because they are in the best state of preservation, are those of Pompeii and Herculaneum, while those of Rome scarcely allow of our divining the particular use of each room and have kept hardly anything of their opulent decoration.

Thermae do not go very far back in the history of Roman civilization, and Pompeii even took precedence over the capital of the Empire in this respect, for she had thermae with palaestrae – that is, open-air sports grounds – long before Rome had built any. Initially, the private house had its own bathroom in which the bath was heated by the kitchen range; bathing establishments were afterwards set up by private enterprise – as we shall see to have been the case at Pompeii. The thermae properly so-called, vast, magnificent and complicated, were launched by Agrippa and soon adopted enthusiastically throughout the dominions during the last years of the Republic.

The Stabian Thermae were the oldest such establishment in Pompeii, since they date from the Samnite period in the second century B.C., but they were enlarged and restored at the beginning of the first century A.D. by courtesy of the duumviri C. Ulius and P. Aninius. They occupy an extremely large square bordered by the House of Siricus on one side, and on the other three by the Via del Lupanare, the Via dei Holconii and the Via di Stabiae. (It must be emphasized once again that these names were assigned in our time when the plan of the city was established, and we are absolutely ignorant of what the ancients called the streets.)

Visiting the Stabian Thermae and going from room to room, following the actual itinerary of a Pompeiian coming to the baths, we shall re-enact in its precise detail the average man's day in this establishment where everything was perfectly organized for health, comfort and pleasure. Let us call him Trebius Valens and accompany him on the stages of his progress through the various parts of this place from the moment of his entry through the main door opening on the Via dei Holconii, to that of his leaving by one of the minor exits, those for instance leading into the Via del Lupanare; which does not necessarily mean that Valens will be making for the brothel (*lupanare*) here, on emerging from the thermae.[27]

After Valens has crossed the vestibule, the walls of which are painted brightly in red and yellow with attractive landscapes, he enters the great courtyard of the palaestra, where bowls, for which a side without columns is reserved, wrestling, boxing, running, hurling of the discus or weights are at his disposal; under the eye of a statue of Mercury, who presides over physical exercise, Pompeiians of all ages give themselves over to their chosen sports. The public palaestrae, located one beside the Triangular Forum, the other – the larger – near the Amphitheatre, are frequented by the lower classes.

When he has worked up a sweat and is tired out, Valens dives into the cold-water piscina, then passes on at once into the room where attendants seize hold of him, scrape away with strigils the sand sticking to his limbs, and rub him down and massage him with oil. While giving himself up to this invigorating and restful treatment, Valens, reclining on a bed, admires the fine stucco ceiling-reliefs picked out with vivid colours, which portray, within a framework of illusory architectural vistas and clever *trompe l'œil*, mythological scenes of which Icarus, Apollo and Hercules are the heroes. Before entering the palaestra, Valens took off his clothing, which he left in the cloakroom called *apodyterium*, as splendidly decorated as the massage rooms and in which each client has his own compartment reserved, looked after by an employee of the establishment.

Now that Valens has devoted to physical culture the time that he feels necessary, has relaxed and rested and has felt his body take on a pleasant suppleness, he enters the actual baths themselves. We would be wrong to imagine that this part of the building, any more than that already described, is prosaically adapted to hygienic requirements: all portions of this place are as magnificently decorated as the rooms already passed through; everything is so ordered in the thermae that visual pleasure heightens the physical satisfaction provided by the bath. Each detail of the rooms' ornamentation is vouchsafed the most exquisite taste, and the harmony of colours and reliefs derives from perfect proportioning, ingeniously applied in each room: so these are more than just garlands of flowers and fruits with cherubs swinging from them, mock-draperies which seem to fall pliantly, statues of gods and heroes in bas-relief, sunken panels of arches giving the illusion of great depth. We can thus understand why the Pompeiians spent so much time in the thermae; here were some of the most finished delights ever invented by decorative art. The cool, milk-white stucco, the polychromatic marbles, the gildings and the highlights of bright colour created an atmosphere of pleasant well-being and of visual delight.

The *tepidarium* offers Valens a lukewarm piscina, in which he bathes as it suits him, unless he prefers to absorb the tepid air filling this room, before giving himself over to the heat of the *caldarium*, where he is greeted by a stifling, scorching steam, which can however be tempered thanks to a round casement opening in the vault to let out the excess vapour. According to whether he is taking the hot-water or the hot-air treatment, Valens dives into the piscina or walks all round it. The hot water is provided by a boiler and the hot air by a hypocaust, an installation of terra-cotta pipes placed inside the walls and under the floor, the heat filtering through the crevices of the bricks. The bather was thus immersed in heated air circulating all around and after a certain time becoming insupportable; he would then return to the lukewarm atmosphere of the *tepidarium* where the masseurs took hold of him once again, rubbing him with oil and perfume, after which it only remained for him to complete the cycle of the bathing procedures as he had begun it: by a good cold bath taken, this time, not in the outdoor piscina of the palaestra but in the hall of the *frigidarium*.

The cold bath in the open air being one of the favourite pleasures of the Campanians, the session in the frigidarium had to give the users of

123

the Pompeiian thermae at least the illusion of the out-of-doors. To this end, the walls and ceiling of this room were painted naturalistically and in effective *trompe l'œil* with all sorts of flowering trees; the scene was one of orchards, of plants climbing on trellises, of birds pecking at fruit: all this depicted with a realism aimed at convincing the beholder that he was looking at an outdoor scene. Paintings of this kind are met with also in that house of the New Excavations unearthed in 1954 and called the House of the Orchard, home of a horticulturist who had had enchanting frescoes executed in it, which are highly interesting too for what they tell us about the chosen fruits grown in first-century Campania.

The Stabian Thermae were divided into two sections, one for men – the larger and more luxurious, since men stayed longer at the baths – the other for women, separate doors leading into these sections. Between these extended the complex system of boiler-rooms, which with their furnaces and boilers supplied the network of underground and intramural pipes.

Up to the Roman conquest the Pompeiians had felt that the Samnite thermae were sufficiently convenient and pleasant, but it was one of the first acts of the city's new masters to construct new thermae in the neighbourhood of the Forum; these are divided from the Temple of Jupiter by the Via degli Augustali. They too occupy an entire block, but have only a somewhat restricted palaestra or rather a garden encircled with benches on which those who liked coolness and shade might rest.

Otherwise, the Forum Thermae are laid out almost in the same way as the Stabian ones, but the decorations are still more beautiful and subtle: the illusory landscapes, conceived with Impressionistic refinement, in the frigidarium, are more poetic than those of the Stabian Thermae, and the marbles richer and rarer. The room whose paintings and sculptures are in the best state of preservation is the men's tepidarium; this room was not, like the corresponding women's one, maintained by a hypocaust with underground pipes, but by a great bronze brazier placed at one end of it. The decorative features sculpted on this boiler, which is of splendid workmanship, bear what might be called heraldically the 'canting arms' of the wealthy Pompeiian who had presented it to the Thermae; because he was called Vaccula, a sobriquet

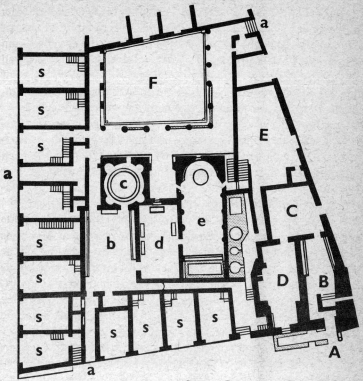

GROUND PLAN OF THE FORUM THERMAE

a entrances to the men's baths
b *apodyterium*
c *frigidarium*
d *tepidarium*
e *caldarium*

A entrance to the women's baths
B *apodyterium* and basin in the *frigidarium*
C *tepidarium*
D *caldarium*
S *tabernae*
E uncovered area
F *palaestra*

meaning 'little cow', cows' heads were designed on the boiler and on the bronze benches likewise donated by him.

It is not to be supposed that this was a joke. The nickname formed part of a man's name, of which it constituted the third part; in the case of this donor, Marcus Nigigius Vaccula, the first part is (as it were) the Christian name, the second the family name, and the third the nickname. The latter could be illustrious (Germanicus, the conqueror of Germany) or could refer to some physical peculiarity (Cicero, the wart) or, as in the case of Vaccula, to a comic likeness.[28]

To facilitate the use of the Forum Thermae by clients who wished to bathe there at night – and night fell early in winter, even at Pompeii – a complete system of lighting, comprising exactly 1,328 lamps, was installed: at least, this is the number which have been found. Juvenal rails against this mania which impelled the Romans to frequent thermae even by night, as if they did not spend enough time there during the day.

The population of Pompeii continued to grow; and as democratization caused the lower classes, as they came into prosperity, to want the same comforts and pleasures as the nobles and the rich, the Stabian and Forum Thermae were deemed insufficient. When the eruption of 79 occurred, new thermae, which are called the Central Thermae, were under construction at the corner of the Via di Nola and the Via di Stabiae.

The building remained unfinished, and what has been unearthed is, as with a number of other monuments, a work yard, where big blocks of stone, ready to hand for the workmen who fled hurriedly at the onset of the eruption, were still to be seen. Only the main work had been completed, which allows us to comprehend the lay-out of the premises, rather different from that encountered in the Forum and Stabian Thermae. New ideas and different tastes governed this construction and, first and foremost, the wish to fill with light the rooms that had formerly remained dim. Seneca, to whom are owed some picturesque descriptions of thermae, thus explains this change: 'The old baths were confined and dark; our ancestors thought themselves warm only where it was not light. Today we describe as "baths where you moulder" those which are not so laid out that from beginning to end of the day they are flooded with sunlight through large windows; we want to be tanned by the sun, at the same time as being washed, and to have a long view, from the bath, over the countryside and the sea.'

To satisfy this wish, the Central Thermae had large glass windows, while in the Forum Thermae there were only narrow round openings, or a thick pane set in a metal framework, resembling the port-hole of a ship's cabin, to be opened at will.[29] Large windows were a feature of the new principles governing the construction of thermae in general, and also the fact that the first floor, which had not been finished by the day of the catastrophe, would have included all the annexes which wealthy Pompeiians thought necessary in a public establishment: games- and lecture-rooms, a library, a restaurant, drawing-rooms for conversation, and rest cubicles.

This change of custom arose from the habit becoming widespread of providing wealthy private houses with their own thermae, thus sparing these privileged people the necessity of going out for their baths to the public thermae. But if they no longer needed these for bathing purposes, they felt that the thermae should maintain and further develop their character of gathering-places which made them so valuable in the social life of the Pompeiians, who like all Southern peoples had little taste for solitude and the retirement of their own houses. The new thermae therefore had to be built in such a way that every possible diversion could be found in them and that, to carry the thing to its extreme, an eccentric could spend his whole life there without any need to go out.

We discover in the Central Thermae yet another extremely new feature which evidently corresponds to a factor recently appearing in Roman habits: a room which existed neither in Forum Thermae nor in the Stabian ones, and which is called the *laconicum*. This laconicum was a square room lit by five oval windows in the corner and by a round skylight at the top of the vaulting, these five mobile openings being fitted with panes; and it would seem that in conjunction with the tepidarium this was where bad digestions, resulting from that excess of feeding to which the Romans in the last years of the Republic and at the onset of the Empire were regrettably addicted, were treated. The description of interminable banquets, spiced with divers attractions, at which innumerable and extravagantly choice dishes succeeded one another, interrupted by the guests' going off to vomit, after which they would return to eat some more, proves that the employment of the

127

laconicum was not superfluous, and that gluttons must often have come there to expunge the unhappy consequences of excessive banqueting.[30]

There existed yet a fourth thermal establishment, of which unluckily there is nothing to be seen, as it was reburied after its discovery; it was situated in the neighbourhood of the Amphitheatre. On the other hand, we know through inscriptions of the existence of privately owned thermae – the public ones were a municipal foundation – whose proprietors publicized them on walls of the city. These are the thermae of Marcus Crassus Frugi, which were managed by his freedman Januarius, and which utilized warm-water springs gushing from the sea. 'Sea water and bathing in soft water' read the publicity inscription placed on the Via dei Sepolcri and giving directions to this establishment. Its profit to Frugi proved not to his ultimate advantage, for he increased his fortune and thereby also the cupidity of Nero, who in A.D. 64 had him executed so as to seize his estate.

9. Suburban Thermae at Herculaneum, showing the stucco decoration of the walls, and also the wooden door still *in situ*.

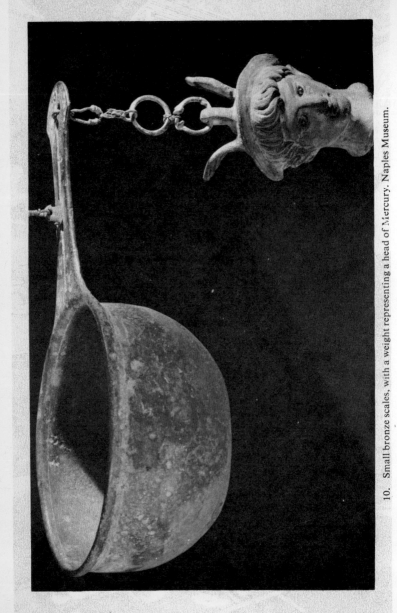

10. Small bronze scales, with a weight representing a head of Mercury. Naples Museum.

11. Terra-cotta vessel depicting Isis. Naples Museum — found at Pompeii.

12. Wooden bed in the House of the Partition, Herculaneum.

13. Enamelled terra-cotta lamp decorated with figures, and with two burners. Naples Museum.

14. Silver strainer. Naples Museum.

15. House of the Vettii at Pompeii. Detail of the fresco of cherubs, in the great triclinium.

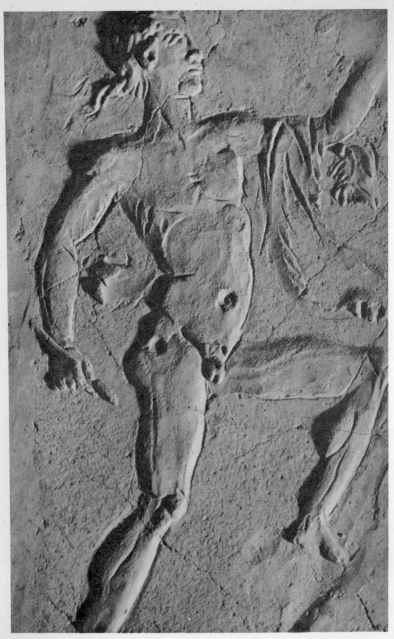

16.   Stucco bas-relief. Naples Museum.

THE LIFE OF THE PEOPLE

'*Salve Lucrum*'

ENTERING the vestibule of the House of Vedius Siricus, who with his partner Nummianus directed an important commercial enterprise, we are arrested by an inscription in the paving, meant to stop the visitor short and fix his attention: '*Salve Lucrum*'.

Hail, Profit! This is a whole way of life: Siricus did not say 'Hail, money', or 'Hail, fortune', for fortune or money could be hereditary. His salute was addressed directly and exclusively to profit, to the money made in commerce, industry and business: that is, not only to all that money can buy, but also and perhaps especially to the pleasure of amassing it.

Welcome to money. This phrase so eloquent in its brevity can be taken in two ways. It welcomes Siricus's friends to his home, people of his own class who love making money and who do make it; but it could also be an invitation to money itself, an appeal to money: let it come, it knows that it will be well received in the Siricus establishment.

Let us place another allusion beside this one. Let us enter the shop-cum-house of Verecundus, an important cloth merchant, very rich and very religious too, who solicits the gods' protection for the success of his business. It was often thought in antiquity that wealth, like health or happiness, was bestowed by the supernatural powers on the men whom they thus favoured. From this arose all the precautions taken to assure the gods' protection and benevolence; their images were painted or sculpted in homes and shops; today, in very many Italian cities, a representation of the Virgin with the Infant Jesus, before which a lamp is kept perpetually burning, has replaced Venus, Mercury, Hercules, or Priapus, who were worshipped as powerful auxiliaries.

Charms and spells were also made use of to ward off from people themselves and from their property the evil spirits that could be harmful to business. It sometimes happened that these malignant spirits were

129

sent by a competitor and rival; thus people carried on their persons and hung up in their rooms and shops magical objects capable of arresting and exorcizing evil powers. Similarly today's Neapolitan frequently keeps a coral 'horn' with which he neutralizes the fatal effects of meeting a *jettatore*, someone possessing the evil eye.[31]

The use of protective talismans is an elementary method of defence against enemies known or unknown who might secretly attack one's life, health or produce; to invoke and flatter the gods is on the other hand to acquire a powerful ally for good and against evil. The proliferation of divine effigies in the business districts of Pompeii is an evidence not so much of the citizens' piety as of their confidence in the possibility of these gods' intervening in individual destinies, for good or for harm according to whether they were favourable or hostile.

Verecundus would be careful not to neglect such protectors; moreover the shops which comprise the ground-floor of his house and which open on to the street, contain prophylactic paintings, whose magical function is highly important for the light that they throw on Pompeiian customs. On one of the pillars is depicted the Pompeiian Venus; this will be described below in the chapter devoted to art, for it is one of the most remarkable and characteristic frescoes of Campanian painting. Below this Venus, who is mounted upon a chariot drawn by elephants, are simple scenes of work in Verecundus's shop and sale-room.

The other pillar is consecrated to Mercury and to another episode in the workaday activity of the cloth merchant, but it is the figure of the god that holds our attention by virtue of its correspondence with Siricus's *Salve lucrum*. It would not seem that the same artist painted the two pictures, although they adorn the same house. The triumphal Venus in fact shows a skilled and subtle art in its composition and execution, and the painter's solution of the difficult problem of representing four elephants full-face is highly curious and remarkable.

The Mercury, on the contrary, betrays a rather clumsy, almost naïve technique, and is destitute of that character of sacred grandeur and majestic solemnity found in the Venus. The painter depicted a temple, seen three-quarters-on and in clumsy, vague perspective, from which the god himself is emerging. Mercury is wearing his wingèd greaves, his headgear similarly wingèd, and he holds in his right hand a sack of money and in his left a caduceus. This is no statue but a living per-

130

sonage, whose cloak is swelled out by the wind and who seems himself on the point of taking wing; for this reason, no doubt, his hat is fastened under his chin, to prevent its being carried away by the rush of his flight.

The facial expression is almost a caricature: the eyes are protuberant, a short beard covers his chin, his meagre, weak profile is that of a miser rather than a god. Mercury is clearly about to leave his temple and soar into the air. Where is he off to? Naturally to carry his bag of money to his faithful worshipper, to him who piously had the god painted without suspecting that this image might be sacrilegious and blasphemous. To whom would the money-bag be carried, if not to the good and faithful Verecundus, well-known to the god and esteemed by him for that money-earning talent. Money attracts money. Let Mercury give to the rich: Verecundus is more than ready to receive the gift, and he too, with his colleague Siricus, murmurs like a prayer: Welcome to money.

The fact that numerous shops and work-rooms adjoined patrician houses and in some cases were even part of them, demonstrates that Pompeii's upper society did not disdain the profit accruing from letting out rooms on their ground-floor for business purposes, and that probably they themselves, these more or less impoverished gentlemen, sold the produce of their lands or workshops through the medium of their slaves. We have already noted the course of democratization, which entailed the rise of the working-classes to municipal office, since anyone could accede to this; the beggars themselves, assembled into guilds, presented their candidates for election, with a view to the advantage which they and their profession could derive from the promotion of one of their number to an official post.

A kind of jumble – if not a confusion – of classes at the beginning of this era made it difficult any longer precisely to distinguish a man of the old merchant class or of genuine aristocracy from a parvenu – *salve lucrum!* – for their habits and way of life were very much alike; only the degree of fortune differentiated them. As for luxuries, those of the new-rich frequently equalled those of long-established fortune.[32] Women too were observed to take a hand in business; a lady as rich and distinguished as Julia Felix, whose villa, splendidly restored during the recent excavations since 1950, occupied a considerable space at the eastern end of the Via dell'Abbondanza, quite near the Amphitheatre, had notices of the premises which she let posted in the city. Such announcements would read thus: 'To let, in the property of Julia Felix, shops with rooms above, baths of Venus, a first floor.'

At Pompeii, as in Florence of the Middle Ages and the Renaissance, the woollen craft enjoyed great prestige and indubitable prosperity. Landowners reared immense flocks of sheep, and it is likely that the peasants brought the product of their shearing to market in Pompeii. In houses of the city, work-rooms made over to the various operations of woollen-manufacture have been discovered; weavers, dyers, felt-makers and dealers in manufactured cloth were numerous, and their influence made itself felt in the political life of the city. Fullers are known to have held high office: for example, Marcus Vesonius Primus, who was duumvir in A.D. 34, had his vats and wheels in his elegant house, his ovens under his peristyle, and his shelves on which the fuller's earth was stored in receptacles similar to present-day washing-machines – all somewhat marring this fine mansion.

Another of his class, Lucius Veranius Hypsaeus, had his fabrics dried on brick pillars[33] between the grand Corinthian columns of his atrium, and he let the latter be daubed with clumsy and naïve paintings illustrating the various stages of this industry. The fulleries that have proved most informative to us are those which, like the Fullonica Stephani, have preserved their equipment almost intact; today, in nearly as good condition as if ready for use, the great screw for pressing the cloth can be seen there beside the entrance door, as well as the communicating basins for washing, immersion and drying, in which the fullers kneaded with their feet like the figures in the paintings of the House of Hypsaeus, the wool being immersed in a liquid which took out the animal grease. For greater convenience, the owner converted the impluvium of the atrium into a kind of piscina in which the wool was soaked in the soapy liquid which removed its impurities.

After the production stage which it reached with the fullers, the cloth was passed on to the dyers; here too we have numerous and valuable evidences of the operations it underwent. In the recent excavations which brought to light the enchanting House of the Ephebus, the installation of a quite complete dye-works was discovered under a portico of Ionic columns. The basins into which the cloth was plunged for its colouring bath and the cauldrons in which the material was boiled have been very well preserved, and the lead pipes for water supply are

132

still to be seen, as well as, in the courtyard, heaps of ashes from the furnace, and amphorae which had contained the colouring matter. In the House of Urbanus in the Via di Stabiae, in the neighbourhood of the Central Thermae, nine stoves occupy the site of a garden where the roar of the fire replaced the singing of fountains, and they dishonour an elegant house with their blackened brick basins.

If works and shops devoted to the woollen industry and trade are numerous, bakeries, distributed through all the districts, are equally so, and in some of these the bread was still in the oven when the eruption scattered the inhabitants. The one believed to have belonged to the baker Modestus, in Region IX, and that in the Vico Storto, both typify the establishment of one of these artisans who from the receipt of the grain to the sale over the counter performed for themselves, with the help of their children, associates and slaves, all the operations in the making of bread.[34] In the courtyard was the mill, composed of two cones of hard stone fitted one into the other, between which the wheat was crushed; the flour fell on to a stone table where it was kneaded; and it was only a few steps across to put the loaves in the oven. In Modestus's establishment, there was also a sort of barn where the sacks of grain were stored, and a little stable housing the asses who turned the mill; at Herculaneum has been discovered one of these mills, beside which – a rather touching detail – the bones of the ass, who fell victim to the eruption, are mingled with the grain, in that kind of furrow or rut in the ground which surrounded the *pistrinum*.

In front of the oven there was a long stone table on which the baker made his bread. A metal plate closed the mouth of the oven. Among the loaves found there, charred since the man was unable to take them out in time, several still bear a mark which was probably the maker's signature, the trademark, which a rival would counterfeit at his peril. These loaves are usually round, shaped like tarts and divided on top by lines raying-out, to facilitate the cutting. Bakeries also made pastry and sold flour retail, some having been found on occasion in those large vessels called *dolia* kept under the counter on which the bread was displayed.

In accordance with the southern custom, the greater part of commercial transactions took place in the street, the shops were largely opened on to the pavement, and the artisans worked on the threshold, where pedestrians would frequently stop to chat with them. Bustling and noisy, the great arteries and the alleys of Pompeii were well suited, by the lay-out of the shops, to long hagglings and discussion over purchases. All produce was within easy reach of the customer and his scrutiny; and because handiwork was still the rule, everyone knew everybody else in this small provincial city, and appreciated his neighbour's ingenuity or talents.

For us too, these good workmen and dealers become as familiar acquaintances when, although they have vanished, we discover their bench or counter ready to receive them once more on their return from the tavern where they have gone to drink a bottle of Falernan wine. We know the particulars of their lives; we know, for example, that the retired centurion Caesius Blandus made over premises in his house at the corner of the Via degli Augustali to one of his old soldiers, cobbler by profession, who left us his tools on the marble table where he worked. We know also that – next to the House of Blandus, an officer of the Ninth Praetorian Cohort who had adopted as his Arms a ship's tiller and had it delineated in mosaic on the threshold of his door – the inn called the Hospitium Sittii, a simple one as it contained only one triclinium, had been established by Sittius Nucerinus, a veteran of the African armies who had served under Caesar and brought back from his exotic campaigns the figure of an elephant which served him as sign-board.

We are familiar too – but her reputation is less pure – with the notorious Asellina who kept a *thermopolium*, a tavern where hot drinks were served,[35] in the Via dell'Abbondanza. The stoves in which the wine was heated, the amphorae of Campanian wine, the goblets and mugs are ready to the visitor's hand, but the charming presences which enlivened this rather dubious establishment are gone. Bronze coins are still in the cash-drawer, bronze and earthen vessels still adorn the shelves, but where are the pretty girls whose names we read on the walls? – Smyrna, Maria Aegle and Asellina herself who probably managed this accommodating troupe, who in the first-floor rooms would meet those clients whose interests here were other than mere liquid refreshment.

As well as legitimate trades, there were at Pompeii as in all cities establishments which served at once as taverns, gaming-houses and houses of assignation or, to put it more bluntly, discreet brothels. The Taverna Lusoria, situated near the House of the Golden Cupids, displays as its sign a vessel flanked by two phalluses: this alone would suffice to indicate to clients the kind of pleasure available in this attractive building, whose proprietor freely offered credit, as is shown by the sums chalked up on the walls, representing unsettled accounts allowed to run until the day when the eruption cancelled all debts and wiped out all claims. The ground floor was for gaming and drinking, while amorous couples found discreet corners on the first floor.

Less discreet than the Taverna Lusoria, the Lupanare paraded its immoral promises beside Sittius's inn. It consisted of a ground floor where a passage decorated with obscene frescoes, perhaps intended to rouse the clients' fancies or enable them to indicate their preferred sport, divided two rows of cubicles where there was just room for a bed, and which only a curtain separated from the corridor. For connoisseurs who wanted more intimacy and quiet, and who eschewed the promiscuity of the ground floor, a first floor, extending over the street in a large balcony, provided discreet little rooms.

It would seem likely that, their fling over, those clients of the brothel who were visitors to Pompeii would return to their lodgings in the inn hard by, which, again, was not very grand since it had only two private rooms and three dormitory ones where several persons could pass the night together. Giving in to the habit which certain men have of scribbling on walls whatever comes into their heads, several clients of this hotel have thus perpetuated themselves; one Vibius Restitutus bewails the absence of his dear wife Urbana; some touring mimes, doing a stand at Pompeii, announce that they belong to the company of Actius Anicetus, that actor adored by the public, whose departure is regretted, we have seen, in many inscriptions; and someone from Pozzuoli, Julius Speratus, disappointed in Pompeii whether it is on business or for amusement that he has come here, affirms that there is nothing in the world so beautiful as Pozzuoli.

As we thus proceed, from shop to shop, surveying the luxurious stores of the Via dell'Abbondanza and the humble back-street stalls, at each step we encounter these disturbing evidences of the life of the people surprised by the cataclysm. Here, behind Eumachia's monument, is a large tannery in which the great table for scraping the hides and the vats where they were cured in a bath of tan would be usable at any time, and on the floor are the necessary cutters and scrapers. Here, close to the Necropolis of the Porta Ercolano, we have these potters' kilns in which funeral lamps were baked, as well as vials for perfume and vessels in which the offerings meant for the dead were deposited. Here we have the House of the Surgeon, whose instruments, previously discovered in the old excavations, are today at the Naples Museum, where likewise may be seen, in the room reserved for scientific objects, the *groma* of Verus the blacksmith, maker of bronze implements, who lived near the House of the Cryptoporticus; the *groma* was a rather complicated and highly ingenious apparatus serving to measure the area of fields.

Now we come to the salt warehouses (*Statio Salinensium*) which were also used for guild-meetings of the salt-pit workers, and another guild-hall, that of the armourers, called the *Schola Armaturarum*, unless it could have belonged to a young men's club for military sports. The paintings on the walls and pillars depict martial trophies or eagles, and on the walls of this long rectangular room which has the genuine look of an armoury are also ranged shelves and cases containing fine plumed helmets, shining armour, chased greaves and the handsome swords which must have been the pride of this guild's members.

In the same district may be observed a curious detail which is important to our picture of popular life. Lavatories were placed at the people's disposal in all public places: the Forum, the thermae, the theatres. It chanced, however, that certain resourceful spirits regarded it as a pity that these arrangements, which could be highly profitable, put money into nobody's pocket. Thus it came about that clever tycoons – if it is permitted so to call them – set up urinals at certain street-corners. One has been discovered just at the corner of the lane which runs beside the House of Julius Polybius; this contrivance consists of the lower half of an amphora hung on the wall, and the product was sold to the guild of fullers, who used this liquid, together with potash and other de-greasing substances, supplies of which have been found in fulleries, to cleanse the wool and cloth.

Walls That Talk

As the walls of houses fronting on the street were cleared of the thick crust of ashes, mud and lapilli clinging to all the buildings, it was seen that they were often daubed from top to bottom, in large black or red letters, with placards – there is no exacter word for these – extolling the merits of candidates for public office, announcing auction sales, promising magnificent spectacles in the arena of the Great Theatre. There were also the famous *albi* in the Forum: boards of official postings, giving notice of lost property, slave auctions, police regulations and sentences of the Court. When these announcements became out of date and inapplicable, painters came with ladders and white-washed the entire wall in readiness for new publicity.

But as well as official notices, there were all those by private individuals who wished to acquaint their fellow-citizens with what they had for sale or to let, or who were seeking lost property. Everywhere were thus displayed phrases such as: 'So-and-so's boiler has disappeared from his shop: whoever returns it to him will be given a reward of 15 sesterces, 10 for anyone informing against the thief.' It would seem that certain walls were especially appropriated for placardings, since the façade of Trebius Valens's house is covered with various notices in enormous letters, among which there was naturally the announcement of gladiatorial contests in the Amphitheatre, with *velum et sparsiones* (we may note here that certain scholars interpret '*sparsiones*' in this context as meaning largesses bestowed on the people, rather than sprinklings of scented water) giving the names of the combatants and of the generous organizer of the sports; also, exhortations by Trebius Valens himself urging the citizens to vote for the candidate of his choosing.

In the inscriptions of a political nature, we find the characteristic elements of civic life in the Campanian towns. Firstly, a very strong patriotic feeling for Rome, and a devotion to the emperors who favoured Pompeii's commercial upsurge. The epoch of pro-Samnite patriotism being affirmed in the Social War was now long forgotten; today the point of the stylus imprinted effusions like this: 'Romulus is in heaven' or 'Long live Augustus' or 'Up the two Fabii'. Submission to the Empire and allegiance to Rome, whose inhabitants came in such great numbers to live at the seaside, caused the Campanian cities to become more and more closely integrated in the State against which they had once fought.

All political fervour was concentrated in the elections for municipal posts, which were contested by the ambition and vanity of all classes of citizens. The beggars, we have seen, themselves put up candidates and actively intrigued to get them in; and certain societies were formed to support such or such candidacy. Some had a religious basis: they united the followers of Isis, the *Isiaci*, or those of Venus, the *Venerii*, and certain placards probably originating from these latter are signed by Venus herself: *Scripsit Venus Pompeiana*.

Other societies united the inhabitants of a given neighbourhood, the *Forenses*, for example, who lived round about the Forum, or else provincials settled in Pompeii who were drawn together by a common attachment to their home-town. Some placards originated from the candidate himself, others, more numerous, from his supporters, who spoke for him and canvassed passers-by to give him their votes. Sometimes an elector would even be addressed by name, to arouse his personal interest: 'Rufinus, support Popidius Secundus's candidacy, and in return he'll make you aedile,' or 'Proculus, support Sabinus, and in exchange he'll support you.'

The owner of the house on which the poster was painted was likewise indicated by name, and it seems that the inscription could not be made without his approval, free or bought. Certain householders refused to have their walls bedaubed and said so in terms which must have been similar to those of this 'placard against placarding' found in Rome: 'Painter I beg of you not to write anything here; if you inscribe a candidate's name, may he fail in the elections and be excluded from all office.'

When Cicero said, jestingly, that it was easier to be a senator at Rome than decurion in Pompeii, he was alluding to the frenzy and even violence of these electoral campaigns, where there was no question of parties or opinions, but only of private or corporative interests. The porters, carders, muleteers, bath-stokers, waterers were as exacting and clamorous as the members of powerful guilds, fullers, physicians, bakers, goldsmiths or innkeepers.

Among these electoral societies are encountered certain ones springing from the fertile imagination of some ironic and whimsical *scriptor*: those, for example, of the *pilicrepi* or ball-players, of the *seribibi* or late-night tipplers, of the *larunculi* or petty thieves, the *dormienti omnes* or snoozers. Humour, evidently, never lost its prerogatives, even in circumstances as serious and as turbulently emotional as the Pompeiian elections. Indeed the inscriptions at times assume a rallying tone; they label as an ass or an ox anyone who will not vote for a certain candidate, and it even happens that certain *scriptores* put forward quixotic or subversive views in the style of: 'The city is too rich; I propose a sharing-out of the public treasure among the inhabitants.'

Ordinarily, the people recommending a candidate extol his virtues, merits, disinterestedness and devotion to the public weal.

The egregious baker Paquius Proculus, whose portrait is one of the masterpieces of Campanian art, was unanimously elected aedile; placards thus salute his victory: 'All the Pompeiians have created Paquius Proculus, deserving of the Republic, aedile'; and 'The entire mass have approved the candidacy of Proculus for the office of aedile; it is what his honest virtue and piety merit.' Women are as fervid as men in praising their favourite's abilities, and take pride in associating their names with that of their candidate: for instance, the women Statia and Petronia who recommend Marcus Casellius and Lucius Albucius, declaring: 'May the colony always have such councillors.'

As for the candidate, he never appeared to speak in his own behalf; he had no political platform as it were, only qualities which spoke for him, and it was his friends and neighbours, his clients and tradesmen who vaunted his merits; sometimes a diminutive friend, a child, *animula*, the 'wee soul' who in bold red characters had the name of her chosen candidate written up.

In such personal cases, it might well be supposed that electoral graffiti and the amorous ones could coincide. From what the Pompeiians wrote on walls, their main preoccupations would seem to have been politics and love. We have seen what the walls disclose of electoral customs; now let us hear what they have to tell us of intrigues and passions.

We have already read what the visiting functionary, bemoaning the fate which had separated him from his doting wife Urbana, wrote on the wall of his hotel room, where, more than any other place, he regretted his solitude. In houses, under the Forum portico, on the plaster of alley-ways, in front of the *thermopolium* while drinking a glass of mulled wine, or while waiting for the farrier to shoe his horse, the lover, thinking of his girl, would give vent to his plaints and desires, or his bitterness and mockery. A multitude of touching or erotic stories are thus inscribed in brief sentences which indicate the sufferings, the pleasures shared, the joys of hoping or the boredom of satiety.

These inscriptions are very numerous and varied. Some are the work of a lover who fancied himself as a poet. 'Today anger is still close to me, keep well away; believe me, if she wept, love would return.' Or: 'When I write, it is love that dictates and Cupid himself guides my hand: I could die, though I were a god, if bereft of you.' Here are some pleasant lines: 'You have never seen Venus? No need: look on my fair one, she is as exquisite.' An experienced lover composed this unlooked-for paraphrase of the *Pervigilium Veneris* (which had not yet been written perhaps, but was to express some eternal truths): 'Prosperity to him who loves; woe betide him who knows not how to love; doubly woe upon him who stands in the way of love.' And a philosopher affirms: 'To try to sunder lovers is to seek to contain the wind in a goatskin or stop the cool chatter of running water.'

Other inscriptions tell an anecdote. In front of a tavern, the driver has stopped to quench his thirst, while in the vehicle a young man fumes at the delay, for the driver has met friends and is gossiping, deaf to all appeals. What to do? In turn, the impatient young man descends from the vehicle, takes a style out of his writing-case and like someone today scrawling on a pad while waiting for a telephone connexion he writes on the tavern wall this pleasing verse: 'Ah! If you knew how love is consuming me, you would hasten to convey me to my beloved. Quickly, hurry, empty your cup, climb into your seat and take up the reins. Whip your mules, my good fellow, and gallop to the house of my fair one.' Not all lovers, unluckily for them and their beloved, are poets; one could find nothing to write except: 'Hail, Victoria. May you, where'er you go, sneeze merrily.' Elsewhere two sentences on two different walls describe the start and finish of a love-story: 'Here Romula and Staphylus met.' 'Here Staphylus met Quieta.' Fickle Staphylus.

Not all the graffiti were as amiable. Scorned or discarded lovers take revenge in writing. One lays the blame on the goddess herself who inspires love. and he blasphemes: 'I could caress Venus's ribs with a stick, and whip her buttocks with a switch: she pierced my heart, and I would gladly break her head with a cudgel.' Elsewhere it is the husband of a frigid woman who is complaining: 'What use to have a Venus if she is made of marble'; and a dismissed suitor who slanders the in-different girl: 'Lucilia sells her body.' The walls speak with all the voices of love. That of jealousy: 'Let him who takes my sweetheart from me be devoured by the mountain bear.' Suspicion: 'No more question of it – Romula, my mistress, has slept here with her lover.' Philosophic resignation: 'Love comes and goes, so what does it matter?' Flattery: 'Castilia, queen of Pompeiians, sweetest heart, hail.'

Women also made use of the walls to reply to their suitors, but not always with tenderness and kindness. We can admire the short shrift that one beauty gave her lover: 'Serena has had enough of Isidore.' And this salutation of Vergula's to Tertius: 'You are too ugly.' And this scornful goodbye from Livia to Alexander: 'What do I care if your health is good or bad? Do you think I would mind if you dropped dead tomorrow?'

After the amorous inscriptions, we have the prating of drinkers who decorate the *caponae*, the *biscae* or gambling-houses, or the *tabernae*. Some became expansive in their cups, like the fuller Cresces who besmeared an entire wall of a tavern in the Via di Nola with pouring out his friendliness towards the whole universe: 'Long live the Cam-panians. Long live the Nucerines! Up the Pompeiians! Up the fullers!' and who finally signs: 'Up the fuller Cresces.' Others eructate like a hiccup the blissfulness of excess: 'Blessed be the gods: here are we swollen up like goatskins.' A malcontent blames his state on the bad wine served him: 'May you, landlord of the devil, die drowned in your piss-wine. You sell the inferior stuff but you keep for yourself, you swine, the good bottles.'

The parasites and spongers whom we know to have been so numerous in that period and country, from the satires of Juvenal, the epigrams of Martial and the *Satyricon* of Petronius, commit to the walls their appetites and designs: 'Good health to him who invites me to dinner.' But the reprobate has not yet been heard, he is still fasting: 'He at whose house I am not dining is a barbarian.'

It also happens, however, that sober folk take up their styles and imprint moral advice, though it be only to remind their guests of the elementary requirements of decorum. In the house called, for this reason, that of the Moralist, the walls of the triclinium bear, instead of pictures, counsels which would seem superfluous in the home of so distinguished a man, who would receive only his peers. Let us read them. 'Let the servant wash and dry the guest's feet. A towel protects the bed pillows; be careful of our linen.' (Juvenal and Martial often allude to the disgraceful habit unscrupulous guests had of carrying off their hosts' napkins; it was for this reason, doubtless, that at most dinners napkins were not laid out for the guests: each one brought his own.) The other injunctions of the Moralist are of a more elevated kind: 'Ignore impure glances and do not give the glad-eye to someone else's wife; be chaste in your speech; abstain from anger and back-biting, if possible; if not, be off with you and return to your own home.'

Some inscriptions requested passers-by not to damage the houses. The gods' anger was invoked on those infringing this prohibition: 'Let the wrath of Pompeiian Venus fall on whoever does any damage here.' Especially unwelcome were passers-by who took advantage of the loneliness of an alley or the darkness of the night to save themselves the trouble of going to the lavatories. The *cacator* is requested to move on – to the next house, probably; or he is more severely threatened by setting up a picture of two serpents in front of a man squatting: '*Cacator*, beware the punishment.' A poet improvised a verse invective against the *stercorarius* who 'forgot himself' at the foot of the former's wall.

Sometimes a euphemism is used for these trying characters. Thus, in the Via del Lupanare are seen the two traditional serpents which probably symbolize the divine vengeance protecting the house, accompanied by this phrase: 'There is no room here for loafers, move on without stopping.' An image of Venus, Minerva or Fortune serves as reminder that these goddesses are ready to punish the offender: which appears to us much ado about a minor offence.

Among the aptest of the inscriptions is that printed by someone unknown who, after having spent some time in reading the electoral and advertising placards, the amorous epistles and nonsenses like 'On September 27th a woman from Pozzuoli was delivered of three sons and two daughters,' 'On the eve of the Kalends of May I put the eggs under the hen' or 'Faustilla owes me 15 denarii plus 9 as interest,' plus the obscenities which in all ages and countries have amused graffiti addicts, ended by writing in his turn: 'I wonder, O wall, that you have not yet collapsed under the weight of all the idiocies with which these imbeciles cover you.'[36]

142

More or less humorous drawings, among them indecent pictures of Priapus and phalluses, which were a good-luck sign, often accompany the inscriptions. Amateur caricaturists would sketch on the wall of a house their grotesque portrait of the owner; a certain Rufus lent himself to these distortions by the extraordinary and ridiculous dimensions of his nose, which the malice of the draughtsmen readily transformed into a phallus. It was also found diverting to represent the heroes of Homer and Virgil in a burlesque fashion. The gladiators, those popular idols, did not escape this satire, any more than did actors, dancers and mountebanks.

To carry out these comical parodies, what was required? A stylus to write with; often even a nail or a bit of wood which was conveniently to hand; or the parasite who had dined badly at a rich man's table might pay him out by exposing him to ridicule, on leaving the triclinium, with the point of a tooth-pick.

THE POMPEIIANS AT HOME

Restoration and Presentation of Private Houses
THE remarkable state of preservation of the Pompeiian private houses allows of a method of restoration and presentation which it would have been very difficult, in general even impossible, to apply to public buildings. As a result, however well restored may be the theatres, temples, structures of the Forum, Amphitheatre, even the thermae, all these latter do not by any means present the highly authentic, fascinating character which arrests the visitor as soon as he sets foot in a private house.

The ambition of re-establishing the Forum in its exact state of 79 was absurd, though this aim is legitimate in regard to buildings which by their lay-out and actual dimensions lend themselves more to an entire restoring. Such restoration has today attained a degree of excellence and completeness which reconciles strict scientific accuracy, inimical to all extravagances, with the desire to capture visitors' imagination and sensibility and to arouse in them that impression, which cannot be had in any other ruins in the world than those of Pompeii and Herculaneum, of an utter familiarity between the person of today and these things of the past.

From the first years of the twentieth century – let us say 1910 – can be dated the care which the directors of works at Pompeii and Herculaneum have devoted, in clearing the houses, to recovering the upper portions as much as possible. Till then the chief preoccupation had been the *plan*; now it was endeavoured to preserve and repair the *elevation*. To nineteenth-century visitors these cities would have looked as if consisting only of ground-levels; in reality these houses had storeys, and it was of extreme interest to restore the ceilings, the walls upstairs, the staircases, and the roofs with their tiles. The restoration from 1910 of the Via dell'Abbondanza, nearly two-thirds of a mile in length and lined with shops and dwellings, showed the immense possibilities of this principle of actualization of the past, the influence of which is being still further and further developed.

Private houses having recovered their storeys, ceilings, partitions, roofs and doors, there was now lacking only furniture to give the visitor the impression that he could straight-away settle in and live here. The idea of familiarity thus replaced that of singularity. It is no longer the strangeness, indicative of the remoteness in time, which is the essential of the Pompeiian and Herculanean house, but on the contrary its 'actuality', since it is perfectly habitable and in fact so well ordered that most of the visitors who come out of mere curiosity are won over by the felicitous proportions and subtle harmonies of their surroundings, and would wish to live in such a home.

The furniture unluckily was in almost all cases destroyed by the catastrophe, except of course for those objects which could stand up to the weight and heat of the burning ash and fiery mud: marble tables, for instance. And as the scruple of perfect accuracy precludes introducing into these houses an article which was not unearthed in them by the digger's spade, the aim of representing these apartments as they were before 79 has been given up; furnishings are thus very rare, but always those which were really here, and which have been kept in exactly the same place.

There is however one part of the house which is easier to 'revive' completely: the garden. In the gardens, in fact, have been discovered piscinae, basins, pipelines, fountains and often even the line of flower-beds and walks, and the remains of trees calcinated in the holes into which they had sunk. With complete adherence to the original plan, it has proved possible to restore these gardens to their original state, with scrupulous care too as to the species of trees and shrubs which grew in them; these are known through analysis of the rubble and from frescoes in which landscape and orchards are depicted. This vegetation has been scientifically studied, by Comes in particular, who compiled the extremely thorough and extensive list of flowers, vegetables, fruit trees and ornamental or shade trees. In the frescoes of the House of the Orchard, discovered in the present excavations, a type of lime, introduced into Campania only in the first century according to botanists and constituting at that time a rarity and oddity, has been recognized.

It is therefore the gardens, such as they are today presented, which cause the visitor most to marvel, since they are alive with all the gorgeous profusion, dazzling and scented, of this Mediterranean vegetation, to which are added the African palms that do so well in southern Italy.

Among the masterpieces of restoration and presentation must especially be cited the portico of the House of the Tragic Poet, the two *cubiculi* of the House of the Orchard, the terraces of the Villa of the Mysteries, the triclinium of the House of the Moralist, the peristyle of the House of the Silver Wedding, the atrium of the House of Caeius Secundus, the nymphaeum of the House of Loreius Tiburtinus, the peristyle of the House of the Vettii, the garden of the House of Marcus Lucretius, and the peristyle of the House of the Golden Cupids, where the *oscilla*, those large medallions depicting figures of gods or genii, hung there by the owner, still sway in the breeze.

Plan and Interior Lay-out of Pompeiian House
Before surveying individually the most beautiful and significant houses – for it is not possible to describe them all, and that description itself, with its inevitable repetitions, would run the risk of becoming wearisome – the visitor and the reader need to be made familiar with the general aspect and the various elements comprising the standard house at Pompeii and Herculaneum – as indeed in almost the whole of the cities of Roman antiquity.[37]

The earthquake of 62 and its numerous ravages, which had not yet been completely repaired, as we have seen, when the eruption occurred seventeen years later, are the reason for there remaining, on the day of that final catastrophe, but few houses in the ancient style. Pompeii had besides undergone – much more than Herculaneum, we shall see – the general fate of cities where an enormous increase of population is brought about and where the money, changing hands, shifts the hierarchy of social classes. The need to rebuild houses knocked down by the earthquake, and the desire of the new-rich to transform the properties bought by them, gave a rather new aspect to the private houses, which kept pace with the evolution of manners, customs, tastes and habits.

Among the rare houses that kept their old type, the one to be visited first as the most characteristic is that one called the House of the Surgeon because a whole set of surgical instruments indicating the profession

146

of the owner has been found here. This collection of forceps, extractors and specula is in the Pompeii Museum, the Antiquarium, displayed beside the entrance. (Also on view there are a sworn weigher's precision scales and fine needles belonging to an engraver of precious stones, in whose house was discovered a collection of beautiful gems, completed or in process of being worked; this artist, whose house was cleared during the New Excavations, was called Pinarius Ceriales and he lived in the Via dell'Abbondanza.) Studying the House of the Surgeon from the outside, we notice that it has kept the special traits of the Italic house prior to Greek influences: thick walls of Sarno stone cemented with potter's clay and almost without windows, these latter being more like loopholes and reminiscent of the style in which the original city enclosure was built.

Entering the house, we first encounter a *vestibulum*, on the paving of which sentiments of welcome were inscribed in mosaic: *Salve lucrum*, *lucrum gaudium* (profit is joy), *havetis intro* (greetings to the arrivals) or *cave canem* (beware of the dog) accompanied by a more or less minatory picture of that faithful guardian. Then comes a passage (*fauces*) opening into the *atrium*, relic of the primitive house; and tradition still retains the hearth, considered as sacred, and the altar to the Lares, in the atrium. The roof of the atrium is pierced with a large opening, the *compluvium*, designed to let in the light, and from which a system of channels and gutters diverts the rain-water into a great central pool, the *impluvium*, adorned with statues and water-jets. At the end of the atrium, in the corridor extension, is the *tablinum*, which is as sanctified as the atrium and contains the nuptial bed and the dining-table, both encompassed with a kind of holy respect.

Before leaving the atrium, we may observe that various terminologies applied here, accordingly as the roof of the compluvium rested on beams (Tuscan atrium), on four columns (tetrastyle atrium) or on six columns (Corinthian atrium). Curtains could veil the compluvium opening, to obviate the heat of the sun and also protect the occupants from the curiosity of the neighbours who, according to Plautus, never failed to be staring curiously out of their windows at what was going on next-door. Off the sides of the atrium were small rooms called *cubicula*.[38] Between the atrium and the tablinum stood a kind of sideboard, more or less vast and luxurious, called *cartibulum*.

147

Beyond these essential, basic parts of the family house are the kitchen, garden, wine-room and columned peristyle with its plants and pools of water. The whole is contained within solid, high walls almost devoid of openings, as if to protect the family against intruders.

If the House of the Surgeon represents the original Italic house, the House of the Vettii is the perfect type of the house of the hellenized Samnite period. The changes due to Greek influence alter in no particular the traditional scheme and the ritual position of those elements held up to veneration through that feeling of sanctity which, much more than is usually realized, impregnates all that has to do with the family and its dwelling; the hearth and the altar to the Lares adjoining it form the centre and pivot of the Romans' devotion and piety. The House of the Faun, too, is, in its design and the arrangement of its component parts, the home of a Samnite patrician who has borrowed from the Greeks his culture and way of living.

For the bygone Italic simplicity was substituted a spirit of luxury, splendour, possibly even of ostentation, which did not previously exist here. The austere Sarno stone mixed with clay was replaced by blocks of volcanic tufa, coming mainly from Nuceria and quarries round about Pompeii; this was easily hewn and had a rich and varied colouring.

If we study the plan of the House of the Faun (see page 81), we note important differences from that of the House of the Surgeon. Shops occupy the entrance façade; there are two atria, one Tuscan, the other tetrastyle, placed side by side, separated only by cubicula; there are two triclinia, one a summer dining-room open to the peristyle, and a winter one in the usual place; two peristyles, one of average dimensions and between the rooms, the other immense, occupying nearly half the total house area, all that part facing on the street behind, and containing a small door in this back wall to enable the occupants to slip out quietly and avoid any tiresome characters lying in wait for them in front of the great doorway, the *posticum*.

The same plan is found, apart from a few modifications, in all the houses that we shall visit; to study and define their particularities will be easier once we are familiar with the general arrangement of the rooms and with their functions. We shall begin by going through several houses brought to light in the present excavations, those subsequent to 1952 and for that reason least known; we shall then proceed from the least to the better known, in surveying houses of the New Excavations (1910–52); and finally, to the ones that are most famous, since generations of travellers have already admired them: those of the Old Excavations (pre-1910).

The Present Excavations

The most curious of the houses in the present excavations is the Villa of Julia Felix. This title of 'villa' would seem to indicate that the house is situated outside the walls and in the country, like the Villa of Diomedes, the Villa of Cicero and the Villa of the Mysteries; in fact, it is within the enclosure, at the eastern end of the second region and almost adjacent to the wall in which opens the Porta di Sarno, in that corner where the Amphitheatre and the Palaestra also are. It is called 'villa' because it has a group of out-buildings such as pertain rather to a country house than to a town residence.

The Villa of Julia Felix was one of the first dwellings discovered in the eighteenth century; it had been unearthed in 1755 but, through the discoverers' spleen at not having found in it the hoped-for valuables or enough of them, it was re-buried under its own rubble and was only cleared, completely this time, in 1953. It appears in the shape of a vast residential house, the largest heretofore discovered, to which were adjoined commercial premises which Julia Felix let and which included shops, taverns, flats and the important establishment of private baths, for which we have already seen the to-let notice. Julia Felix also had here a very large garden, for fruit and vegetable growing as well as enjoyment, thus allowing of a comparison of this city building with a suburban villa.

The Villa of Julia Felix is one of those which provide us today with the exactest idea of the character of the person who lived in it and of the social conditions which obliged her to modify her way of life. The frescoes of still-lifes, removed in the eighteenth century, and the Nine Muses of the Louvre indicate a woman of refined tastes and sensitivity to beauty. She was rich, or rather had been. The letting notice of a 'bath of Venus' and a first-floor proves that this patrician woman needed money, since she found herself obliged to make over to the public the thermae which she had had built for her private use.

What then is signified by 'baths of Venus' (*balneum venereum*)? Some

149

commentators have thought that this might be a questionable establishment where the pleasures of love, besides those of the bath, could be enjoyed. That appears highly improbable. The complete comfort of Julia Felix's thermae induces us to translate *balneum venereum* as 'baths worthy of Venus', which is more seemly and more in keeping with the truth, for it is hardly possible to see this dignified matron in the rôle of *meretrix*, or even consenting to make over a part of her private residence to an immoral enterprise. On the other hand, to let her thermae to a baths proprietor, and to let shops on the ground-floor and rooms on the first, was not in the least shaming, and numerous were the highly-respected Pompeiians who did as much.

Leaving her house by the door to the Via dell'Abbondanza, we find on the right the Foro Boario, recently cleared after having been re-buried in the eighteenth century. This designation of 'bovine forum', which dates from the first discovery, arises from the supposition of the archaeologists of 1760, who found the bones of horses and oxen here, that it was a cattle market. Besides, the nearness of the Amphitheatre gives a certain consistence to the theory that animals intended for the venationes and the circus sports were kept in this place. It is thought today, now that vines and installations of presses have been found, that there was a vineyard here, as well as the paraphernalia of wine-making, and a tavern where drinkers came to enjoy the produce on the spot.

In the House of Venus, to the left of Julia Felix's house in the Via dell'Abbondanza, a fresco of Venus bathing has lately been found, and this is one of the happiest of recent discoveries for the boldness of execution, the vividness of colour and the robust, slightly plebeian freshness of the goddess's body reclining in a shell drawn by dolphins. The effect is of the wall ceasing to exist, the blue of sky and water blend so well with that of the atmosphere, and all the more since an illusionist composition of flowering plants transforms the lower part into a verit-able garden.

Another house of the recent excavations, that of Successus, poses a lively problem as to Successus's identity. This name designates the portrait, painted in a cubiculum, of a nude infant depicted as pursued by a goose: the child greatly resembles the statue of another infant, also nude, holding a dove this time, which serves as a leg of a marble table.

Was this little boy twice portrayed, and indicated by name in the fresco, the owner's son, or a favourite slave?

Walk Among the New Excavations (1910–1952)

Since the priestly class had the right of priority in the Amphitheatre and at public ceremonies, we may mention first the House of the Priest Amandus. It is, in fact, a house of modest dimensions, very different in this from Paquius Proculus's vast place next-door. A touching detail makes this religious functionary sympathetic to us; having not enough room to plant a garden large enough to satisfy his love of nature, he indulged himself in a great tree overshadowing his little courtyard. It is most affecting also to perceive drawings, on the white plaster of the peristyle, of children, palm branches, naïvely scrawled figures and, in clumsy lettering, the name of the scribbler's father, since the remains of a little girl were found here among the corpses of men and women suffocated under the lapilli before they could open the door against which they were rushing. Another detail, of interest now to historians since it relates to the slave uprising, is the name of Spartacus – whether or not the famous Spartacus, is not certain – inscribed in Oscan characters under a primitive picture representing a gladiatorial combat.

Moving on from the priest's small house, we look at two vast, luxurious residences which belonged to parvenu merchants. The first is that of Loreius Tiburtinus, whose origins are indicated by his cognomen: he was not a native Pompeiian but came from Tivoli (Tibur). Attracted by the beauty of Campania, or expelled by the political quarrels which periodically exiled numbers of citizens from Rome, he had settled in Pompeii and opened shops which did a thriving business since they fronted on the Via dell'Abbondanza near the Amphitheatre. Loreius Tiburtinus owned here not only one of the loveliest houses in the city, but also a splendid garden of pear, fig, chestnut and pomegranate trees, complete with pergolas containing rivulets and fountains. Roots found in the soil reveal the precise kind of trees selected by Tiburtinus, who also took pleasure in the flowing waters of a long *eurypus* traversing the garden's entire length and supplying the fountains and the mystic springs of the nymphaeum.

The other house belonging to a rich merchant is that of Publius Cornelius Tegetus, which is also called the House of the Ephebus in token of the bronze effigy of a youth, an excellent copy of a celebrated Greek original, which served as the base of a candelabrum; while four figures of pedlars, comic and obscene, support the salt-cellars on the table upon which meals were taken, lit by the bronze ephebus, in the open air. This incongruous juxtaposition of works of grave beauty and repulsive caricatures, together with the sumptuousness of the triclinium couches, now restored to their original state, evince a fondness for somewhat ostentatious luxury. But one fact attests that Tegetus prized his works of art: at the onset of the eruption, instead of taking to his heels he dismounted the candelabrum, detaching the ephebus statue, which he wrapped in a cloth, and only then thought to leave the house; but the ceiling caved in on him, noxious fumes stifled him, and he died clasping to his breast that cherished figure which had cost him his life.

The owner of the so-called House of the Golden Cupids also belonged to that class of wealthy merchants, possibly come from Rome, who brought to the Campanian cities in the Imperial era an ostentation which was not always in good taste. The presence of the Golden Cupids designed on glass, which give their name to the house – the one with oscilla, alternating with theatrical masks, hung under the portico – indicates the wealth of the owner, Cnaeius Poppaeius Habitus, as well as his penchant for the theatrical setting introduced into daily life. Poppaeius, who was possibly a connexion of Nero's through the latter's wife Poppaeia, loved Greek marbles and mythological paintings, and he filled his house with everything that could delight the eye; but it all lacks the tranquil ordering and simple harmony of the House of the Moralist.

Which of the two owners of this last house was the 'moralist': Epidius Hymenaeus or Arrius Polites? The former, it would seem, but they both must have had the same tastes and predilection for a quiet existence, including siestas in the garden and hours of lazing in the broad loggia of the upper storey.

We find another relative of the Empress Poppaeia in Quintus Poppaeius, owner of the House of Menander; he is not to be confounded with the steward, Quintus Poppaeius Eros, who lived in the out-buildings with the slaves and superintended the stables. Slaves and freedmen often bore their master's name, a custom continued sometimes even into eighteenth-century Italy. Quintus Poppaeius, like

Habitus, must have been smitten with the theatre, for certainly the paintings in his house reproduced scenes out of tragedies. He was also a connoisseur of handsome silver plate, and in a vault where his hoard had been deposited during reconstructions on the house, which had been damaged in 62, there were discovered an enormous number of vessels, plates, goblets and more than a hundred pieces of splendid workmanship, which on reception days must have gleamed with wonderful brilliance on the tables, sideboards and side-tables.

Why has the name of Menander been substituted, in the usual designation of this house, for that of the owner? Because in one of the rooms, which is adorned with theatrical masks and effigies of poets, there is the portrait of a man who is unrolling a work and reading it: the title of the play is that of a comedy by the celebrated Greek writer, and so as to rule out any ambiguity, the name was inscribed by the painter on the skirt of the man's cloak.

Yet another theatre-lover, perhaps even an actor or author, is encountered in the House of the Tragic Poet (see p. 67), which of course does not belong to the New Excavations since it was prior to them the scene of Bulwer Lytton's novel *The Last Days of Pompeii*. The house owes its renown not so much to this book as to the fact of its representing, in its arrangement and decorations, the best example of a well-to-do house where neither economy nor extravagance prevailed, but simply a comfortable well-being and rather elegant luxury, at the time of the catastrophe. The owner had not needed to retrench and make over portions of his building to merchants – with the exception of two shops flanking the entry where on the threshold mosaic barks a chained dog whose fearsome aspect justifies the warning 'cave canem'.

The paintings of the triclinium and the cubiculi all refer to episodes from Greek or Latin tragedies, but the mosaic of the tablinum is still more interesting, for it introduces us into the wings; we have left the stage and are now in the province of the director or stage-manager who is in process of showing his players how to act, and who demonstrates what he teaches. This curious mosaic is a document of extreme interest for the light which it throws on the life of actors in antiquity. It is highly regrettable that the house was stripped of its works of art at a period when the sole preoccupation was still to enrich the museums, so that we have to go to the Naples Museum to admire these frescoes and mosaics, of which there remain *in situ* only a few examples, delightful certainly, but insufficient to render the original beauty of the house.

It is also deplorable that all the works of art of the House of the Citharist were removed: the statue of the musician from which its name was derived, the bronze group of animals and the frescoes; but the arrangement of the rooms themselves, and in particular that of the three peristyles, shows what a skilful and artistic effort was made to blend two houses which had been made communicating – something which was very difficult, given the traditional plan, which naturally suffered in such combination.

In the House of the Lararium an even more unusual phenomenon can be observed. Like so many Pompeiian houses, this one had been severely damaged by the earthquake of 62, or else had changed hands on the eve of the eruption. At any rate, the latter caught the painters just in the middle of their work; they left the site at once, never of course to return, and so providing us with an excellent chance of observing their various techniques, for the rooms of the house are not all in the same state of completion. The lararium is finished, as is the triclinium, where the owner had had still-lifes painted, but the atrium still exhibits its walls in the rough state, and the peristyle is blocked with masses of plaster which the stuccoers were going to use in their decorations.

It is not a question of artistic technique but one of historical reference which arises when we enter the House of Casca Longus. This name of Casca puts us in mind of the conspiracy of Brutus and Cassius to assassinate Caesar, and of the rôle which Casca played in that murder. But was he really the owner of this house bearing his name? So it is supposed because the legs of a splendid marble table here are inscribed with that name; but it is also possible that after the defeat of the 'liberals' and the revenge taken by Antony on them, their possessions were sold at auction and that a wealthy Pompeiian or a Roman who established a country-seat at Pompeii might have bought this piece to adorn his residence.

Be that as it may, the occupant of the House of Casca was a theatre-lover. In fact, the most beautiful work of art that he possessed, apart from the enchanting floral decorations on the ceiling of a cubiculum, is a great fresco depicting a stage on which an absurd figure holding a mask to his enormous and immoderately opened mouth is haranguing two women who listen, stricken. I presume that the pale, delicate, interesting figure of the young woman in a purple robe and yellow mantle is an authentic portrait, perhaps that of the actress who played this rôle in a comedy of Plautus or an *atellana*, and for whom the owner of this house, the putative Casca, had a keen admiration – or more than admiration.

There is a mystery also in the House of the Lovers, but here the riddle is not attached to any definite object. Nor does any name allow of our identifying the occupants. The house is not richly decorated, but its proportions are exquisite; the modest dimensions suggest a warm, touching intimacy. Whoever enters here is struck with a singular aspect of harmony and inner well-being. The paintings are quite fresh, as if just completed. This asylum of peaceful retirement may well have been so arranged for two young lovers and for that 'life of honey' to which a verse written on the portico wall alludes – written, if not by one of the lovers, perhaps by a visitor of theirs – and which interprets so well the atmosphere of these rooms: 'lovers like bees need a life of honey'.

The verse in the House of the Lovers celebrates the delights of love; but in another dwelling, that of Julius Polybius, which is decorated with beautiful frescoes drawn after the *Aeneid*, we read a quatrain which strongly reveals that mixture of hedonism and disquiet, of living for pleasure and nostalgia for another way of life, of spiritual anguish standing out in relief against the joys of the senses because they were precarious and of brief duration: that spiritual state which brought about the success of the religions of mysteries, then of Christianity. The verses are: '*Nihil durare potest tempore perpetuo, – cum bene sol nituit, redditur oceano*; – *decrescit Phoebe quae modo plena fuit*. – *Sic venerum feritas saepe fit aura levis*.' ('Nothing can endure forever; when the sun has well shone, it is restored to the ocean; and the moon, however full it was, wanes. Thus often is the wildness of Venus transformed into thin air.')

The house of the two Verus brothers is called the House of the Centenary, since it was discovered in 1879, eighteen-hundredth anniversary of the eruption. For their own amusement and that of their friends, the brothers Verus had a small dining-room decorated with obscene frescoes, which are nearly up to the level of those in the Lupanare and therefore are not generally shown to visitors. We can, however, console

155

ourselves in admiring the delightful nymphaeum and the mythological frescoes, and by observing the changes (or what can still be detected of them today) which altered the lay-out of the premises and the decorations in keeping with the various fashions succeeding one another from Samnite austerity to the classic beauty of the Augustan era and finally the more gaudy luxury of the reconstruction period between 62 and 79, all marking profound evolutions in social life and in taste.

If it is not possible to establish an exact chronology of the houses of Pompeii, by very reason of these frequent renovations, some reveal the approximate date of their decoration, according to the preferences of the taste then prevalent, though also according to those of the owner. It is understandable that Marcus Lucretius, priest of Mars, had military trophies and Victories painted; for his friends, however, he had a nymphaeum laid out which is perhaps the most exquisite in Pompeii. For us, it is interesting also to see here one of the very rare examples of the closed ceiling in what is called the *atrium testudinatum*, from the absence of an impluvium: the rain water, instead of being diverted into an interior pool, was carried to the outside by gutters.

In the House of the Labyrinth is to be seen an extraordinary mosaic paving representing the struggle between Theseus and the Minotaur in the subterranean prison of Minos's palace. The labyrinth, as we know, is a symbolic image of very considerable import: an allegory of human life and of the difficult journeys which the soul must make in this world and in the next before attaining the blessèd condition of immortality. It is not feasible here to indicate all the implications of which this complex and engrossing subject is capable; we must content ourselves with surveying with pleasure, in the garden, a fine box-wood labyrinth, not to the height of a man as in the eighteenth-century mazes, but almost level with the ground, as in those which Adrian de Vries constructed in the sixteenth century.

Certain houses almost seem to have a providence of their own, perhaps linked to the fortune of the men inhabiting them. That of Caecilius Jucundus was providentially spared during the absurd air-raid of 1943 which wrought such havoc – just as its owner had emerged unscathed, as has already been related, from the earthquake of 62. This banker deserves notice for yet other reasons than those bas-reliefs of his in the lararium: firstly, contrary to the case with so many Pompeiians, whose names only are known to us, we are acquainted with his features, because he knew how to be popular with his servants and employees, so that his freedman had that wonderfully animated bust done which greets us today in the atrium and which is a truly speaking likeness, its expression is so vigorous, natural and strongly individualized. We know, moreover, his methods of business procedure, for on the first floor of his house a chest containing a large quantity of wax tablets perfectly intact was found, and the seals of these have had only to be broken to reveal the transactions, highly honest and even generous as they were, of this banker who lent money at a moderate interest and did not harass impecunious debtors.[39] Jucundus's face and his archives present to us a most sympathetic person, and we can understand why his fellow-citizens made him one of their most highly respected magistrates.

At the period when spectacular finds were kept for the visits of distinguished travellers, a house cleared on such an occasion was naturally given the name of the august visitor to whom this was a manner of homage. Thus there are the House of Queen Margherita and the House of the Prince of Naples, as well as the House of the Silver Wedding, thus designated because it was unearthed in 1893 on the occasion of that anniversary in the royal family of Italy. On the other hand, the House of Adonis, that of Castor and Pollux, that of the Hunt, that of Meleager and that of Orpheus are called in token of the most beautiful works of art found in them. Of venerable renown and known throughout the world, so greatly has it been popularized by photography, the House of the Faun owes its name to the admirable statue of the dancing Faun which decorates the peristyle pool, but the house could as well be called that of the Battle of Alexander, for it was here that this extraordinary mosaic which will be described farther on was found. Or the house could even be named that of the Egyptian Landscape, for another mosaic treats this subject, dear to the Romans, of Nilotic landscape represented with more fancifulness than exactitude – or that of Sulla, for it is probably here that the dictator's nephew lived when he was entrusted with the administration of the colony installed in Pompeii to punish it for its part in the Social War.

Sulla had had the moderation not to sack the city, but the intrusion of the legionary veterans now turned farmers on the Campanian lands raised grave problems, and the young Sulla needed much diplomacy to resolve these and to achieve the assimilation of the two antagonistic elements. The House of the Faun made him an admirable residence of vast dimensions, occupying an entire insula of more than 3,250 square yards; like the House of the Silver Wedding which is almost its equal in extent and luxury, it allows of our distinguishing the additions and alterations which changed its original aspect, from the Samnite period to that between 62 and 79 when the city put on a new face.

No less celebrated than the House of the Faun, and likewise a target for all the tourist parties that flock to admire it and sometimes admire nothing apart from these distinguished mansions, the House of the Vettii has been analysed and described so often and at such great length that it seems superfluous to do this once more. It must however be observed that the two rich merchants who had it built, Aulus Vettius Restitutus and Aulus Vettius Conviva (since they bore the same nomen and praenomen, we see the need for the cognomen to differentiate between them), excluded from their home everything that could recall their profession, and they did not follow the practice of so many proprietors, even the wealthy Julia Felix, of letting one or more parts of their buildings. (For plan, see page 94).

In the Vettii establishment, neither the noise of handicrafts nor the hagglings at counters nor the importunate clamour of a tavern were to be heard. Instead of being converted into shops, the ground-floor rooms fronting on the main street have no street-entry and serve as lumber-rooms, wine-rooms or else living-rooms. The brothers Vettii also had pipelines and stones, to keep off the damp from their walls, set up on the pavements, which were thus obstructed.

A look at their house itself shows that the largest amount of space, more than half the total area, is made over to the immense peristyle and the great triclinium adjoining it: much the biggest in all Pompeii. The atrium itself is huge, and here, still to be seen, are the two cupboards or strong boxes filled with valuables; the latter were committed to the protection of a statue of Priapus, of which the pudenda are hidden from view. Adjoining the great triclinium were a dining-room, extensively open on to the whole stretch of garden, and the *gynaeceum* or women's apartments.

The decorative themes of the triclinium are those which would most

158

please refined and wealthy sybarites like the Vettii: cherubs everywhere, the *putti* so adored in the Italian Renaissance, engaged in all imaginable occupations: as grape-harvesters, drivers of chariots, fullers, gardeners, goldsmiths and oil-manufacturers; and whole collections of frescoes on mythological subjects: Pentheus torn apart by the Bacchants, Bacchus and Ariadne, the infant Hercules strangling the serpents.

But it is the garden, especially, which constitutes the masterpiece of the Vettii; the garden which modern restorers have had only to put back in its pristine state, replanting trees of the same kinds in the same places as those burnt down during the eruption, remaking the lovely flower-beds, with their water-jets, fountains and statues. A profusion of flowers once more overruns the space between the colonnades of the peristyle; and they are the same flowers as Vettius Restitutus and Vettius Conviva were fond of, roses in abundance and violets and hyacinths, the scruples of the horticulturists extending as far as ruling out those varieties which it is not quite certain that the Pompeians knew, appreciated and placed in their gardens.

The Suburban Villas

Love of nature, the desire to escape as much as possible from the crowding and hubbub of a small, over-populated city stifling in its enclosure of walls, accelerated during the first centuries B.C. and A.D. this exodus into the country, which was especially manifested in the building of more numerous villas in the vicinity of Pompeii and Herculaneum, along the entire coast-line of the Bay of Naples. The villa was composed of a large-scale agricultural establishment attached to an extremely luxurious squire's seat, which, to the splendour and comfort that could be had in the city, added the advantage of being screened from inquisitive neighbours. Thus it would seem that it was with the intention of avoiding intruders and practising in complete peace a cult forbidden by law, that the owners of the Villa of the Mysteries retired into rustic solitude at a safe distance from Pompeii.[40]

Up to the present, only a few villas have been explored. The so-called one of Cicero had been excavated in 1763, then filled up again after the removal of the pictures and mosaics that could readily be taken out. From the Villa of the Mosaic Columns, opposite that of Cicero, on the other side of the Via dei Sepolcri, came those curious columns to which the house owes its name and which constitute, with their facing of polychromatic mosaic, a very rare decorative effect which is most unusually striking. Also to be seen here is an admirable fountain of glass and shell-work mosaic, which virtually forecasts the style of the Renaissance and eighteenth-century grottos.

Between the city and the Villa of the Mysteries, which is in a more secluded position, we visit the Villa of Diomedes, which provides a first-rate model of the urban house adapted to country life. Had this villa been excavated according to present-day methods, it would certainly be as complete as the Villa of the Mysteries, investigated between 1929 and 1930. It was unhappily prospected between 1771 and 1774, hastily unearthed and stripped of its paintings. There was much horrified exclaiming at the discovery of numerous skeletons of victims of the eruption, who had thought to take shelter in the cellar and were asphyxiated there. Eighteen bodies were crowded together in this room, men and women entangled, and children clasping their parents. The father of the family had almost reached the door, and key in hand, was getting ready to open it when he collapsed, suffocated.

This macabre spectacle of bodies heaped in the basement cast a gloomy shade over the Villa of Diomedes, which itself resembled a corpse, it was so effectively stripped of its works of art. But the house is very interesting for what it tells us about the layout of rooms in these residences at once luxurious and rustic. The cool, airy rooms designed for siesta, the comfortable and luxurious baths, the large promenade terraces encircling the portico, the enormous garden with its piscina and, amidst trees and plants, the summer dining-room, would make it an ideal place for a holiday; from every part of it, the great curve of the Gulf of Naples, the vineyards and olive-oil mills, the well-grown fields and woods abounding in game, covering the slopes of Vesuvius, must have been visible. For a still more extensive view, we climb up to the small terraces of the belvederes rising above the walls on the elevation facing the sea. Everything here was arranged so that the occupants might enjoy the maximum of quiet and peacefulness, reflection and isolation, as well as contemplation of one of the loveliest landscapes in the world.

The Villa of Porta Marina is less secluded than those just described; like the Villa of Julia Felix it is joined to the city, since it was built, at least in part, on the enclosure walls, at that period in the reign of Augustus when the Pax Romana made fortifications unnecessary. Its owners seem to have declined to restore it after the earthquake of 62, and it is thus that it was discovered at the time of the excavations, neglected by its occupants but still possessing fine paintings.

To enjoy the sun, the sea air, the view over the sea and fields, to walk among finely decorated columns with each space between them the frame of a different picture: all this comprised the refined pleasure of these Pompeiians who in this still half-citified dwelling enjoyed vast airy and sunlit spaces, which the crowding together of living-accommodations within the city made more and more rare. We are struck with the spaciousness of the rooms – exceptional in a house of Roman type, in which through inclination or necessity the rooms tend to be very small – with bays extending outwards and allowing of free communication between the interior and exterior.

The occupants of this exquisite and grandiose mansion also were victims of the eruption; like the people in the Villa of Diomedes, they thought to take shelter under the vaulting of an apparently solid room, bringing with them whatever they wished to salvage: money, valuables or just workaday tools; they were hoping that the rain of ashes would be of brief duration. How distressing it must have been for them to say goodbye to all these magnificent frescoes, which could not be taken down as easily as vases or statuettes, we can well imagine when we admire the splendid paintings in the triclinium, which also contained, in keeping with the contemporary mode, little pictures painted on marble, similar to those found at Herculaneum. These pictures, called *pinakes*, were sometimes Greek originals which were extremely costly and were hung in the way a modern collector proudly displays the canvases he has bought. The *pinakes* of the Villa of Porta Marina seem rather to be Italian copies.

Although farther from Pompeii than the above-mentioned houses, the Villa of Boscoreale must also be numbered among the suburban villas; a visit to it reveals other aspects of the way of living in those times. An interesting rough-cast taken from it may also be seen in the Pompeii Antiquarium.[41]

This villa, set amidst vineyards, displays all the features of an extensive wine-producing cultivation in full flow, with its presses, vats and storing sheds. The people who lived here were not rustics: far from it; they certainly possessed the finest silver plate that ever was owned by Campanian gentlemen. And he was certainly a gentleman-farmer, the Roman who was enabled by the sale of his wine to pay for such magnificent works of art. Only the treasure discovered in the House of Menander can rival, in the number of pieces (more than a hundred) and in artistic beauty of workmanship, the famous 'treasure of the Boscoreale', which is among the most prized possessions of several museums, chiefly the Louvre.

The owners of the house, caught in the eruption, tried to hide this treasure in a place where no one would think to search if he was not in the secret of the hiding-place; hoping to recover the treasure once the danger was past, they deposited the sack with the plate in the well of the room containing the oil-press. (The masters of Boscoreale in fact drew on their lands for all necessities of family consumption: corn, wine, olive oil and wool.) Unhappily the mephitic vapour overcame them, and they fell into the well, and their skeletons were discovered at the same time as those precious goblets ornamented with skeletons which passed from hand to hand at the conclusion of a meal, to remind the guests to think of living well, if not of dying well, since, as Lorenzo de Medici was to say: *'di doman non c'è certezza.'*

The history of the Boscoreale diggings is extremely colourful: it has been told in full by Count Corti in his excellent work, *The Destruction and Resurrection of Pompeii and Herculaneum.* It was Fiorelli who took the initiative here after peasants had informed him of the discovery of a large quantity of amphorae and jars in the ruins of an ancient house; but the excavation work was stopped in 1876, as a result of differences with the owners of the plots. It was only resumed twenty years later, with enormous success. Nothing had been moved since the eruption; horses' bones were still in the stable, those of the watchdog near the threshold, and if the amphorae did not bear the name of the maker and the date, as in the House of the Vettii, they testified to the wealth of the vineyards belonging to the master here.

Such are the fortunes of discovery – disappointments and marvellous good luck. Of the latter kind, and one exceptionally important to a better understanding of ancient religions, was the discovery of the initiation chamber of Dionysiac mysteries in the Villa of the Mysteries.

When in 1910 only part of the immense area of the buildings was cleared, it was still not known that the house contained this marvel. In 1929 archaeologists returned to the spot where the soundings and the first clearings had indicated a site of uncommon extent; and it was in 1930 that the initiatory paintings were brought to light. Since that time the labours of restoration and presentation of the villa in its entirety have been completed, and nothing could be more instructive for us, setting aside the artistic and historic interest of the frescoes, which have become famous and have been exhaustively analysed, than the arrangement itself of the various parts of the building.

Before we go through the house, a glance at the plan shows the manner in which the premises were disposed; it will be seen that the whole part facing south, east and west is replete with broad, splendid terraces converted into veritable hanging gardens, today as of old. At the rear are the slaves' quarters, kitchens, baths, store-rooms and repositories for agricultural implements, and the wine and oil press-houses and wheat barns: all this distributed around the great peristyle which though traditionally the centre of the house is here that of the utility rooms.

It will firstly be observed that unlike the town house which is concentrated, within its almost window-less walls bounded by streets, around the atrium and the peristyle, the country house all but does away with walls. To be more precise, let us say that life in the latter is centrifugal, that it moves from the centre of the house, to ray outwards. The town house is forever evading inquisitive gazes and the neighbours' noise: however vast it may be, it is still a very much enclosed shell turned in on itself, and usually open to the sky only in the compluvium and peristyles; painted landscapes replace the view of real ones. The villa, on the other hand, is at one with the landscape; it is laid out in such a way that without going out of it the inhabitants could enjoy at any time of the day an infinitely varying spectacle of light and shade upon the natural surroundings of the house, and upon the sea as far as the horizon.

Fully to grasp this response of the architects to the wish of lovers of untrammelled nature, whether Pompeiian or Roman, temporarily or permanently established at Pompeii, we must approach the Villa of the Mysteries from the side facing west; in the centre of this façade is a large, semi-circular verandah, which affords the finest view in the whole house. This exedra extends to right and left in terraced gardens, laid out upon high stonework walls; the most beautiful rooms are thus as if hemmed in among these hanging gardens which stretch away to the west, south and east, where they are continued by a very long portico which on that side conceals the entire façade of the house, including the utilitarian sections.

The Villa of the Mysteries underwent considerable renovations subsequent to the time of its construction in the second century B.C., and it was in the period of the emperors that it acquired its majestic and final beauty. The presence of a statue of Livia, today in the Antiquarium, proves that its owners had dedicated a cult to Augustus's wife. Seriously damaged by the earthquake of 62, the villa was undergoing repairs. In the cellar have been found skeletons of labourers who were in the course of repairing the walls, and in his cell near the gate, the body of the porter, who had been unwilling to leave his post despite the danger. Two other corpses were found as well: those of the mistresses of the house, judging by the jewellery: a woman and a young girl, whom the collapse of walls had hurled down from a first-floor room to the ground floor where they were crushed under beams of the ceiling.

When the 'initiation chamber' was discovered in 1930, the Villa of the Mysteries became an enigma for archaeologists and religious historians. Although of fairly small dimensions and situated apart from the principal rooms, this chamber constitutes the spiritual centre of the whole house. An atmosphere of intense and occult religiosity which no visitor can fail to sense here still radiates from it, together with the allure of a secret cult which was enacted a few steps from the lararium, behind the nuptial chamber, which seems to be an appendage of it, or rather the sanctuary to which the initiation-room leads like an ante-chamber. The latter is in fact scarcely recondite, since it communicates also with two porticoes which themselves give issue to the hanging gardens outside.

The 'Mysteries' of the Villa of the Mysteries

It may be asked why, when the official Roman religion tolerated alongside itself the presence of so many alien cults, often bizarre and extravagant ones like that of the Black Stone and the castration rites of the priests of Atys, it opposed with an animosity borne out by several

164

decrees the celebration of the Bacchanals. Was not Bacchus one of the divinities reverenced in the Latin pantheon? Why did the *senatus-consultus* '*De Bacchanalibus*' threaten celebrants of the mysteries of Dionysos with the gravest penalties, when worshippers of Orpheus and Adonis were unmolested and a public cult was given over to the Egyptian Isis?

In this lies a phenomenon which can only be recorded here, since we have not the space to study its profound significance and the contingent political complications. The fact remains: in a room of the Villa of the Mysteries there were probably enacted initiation ceremonies into those Dionysiac mysteries of which the different stages are portrayed on the wall in life-size figures, but depicted in a rather equivocal and discreet way so that only the celebrants could receive their sacred instruction.

For us, this teaching still remains conjectural, as the religions of mysteries are not completely known, for that very reason of the adepts having kept them secret, as well as the fact that allusions to them in ancient authors are not always reliable. We concede that as the initiation chamber was virtually accessible to all comers, these mysteries could not enjoy the security from profane eyes which the mysteries of Delphi and Eleusis guarded by celebrating their clandestine rites in caves or underground chapels. The occupants of the Villa did not hedge themselves round with such precautions, which proves that they did not run the risk of denunciation, perhaps by some ill-disposed slave, for infraction of the *senatus-consultus*. On the other hand, nowhere in the house have those holy objects depicted in the frescoes been found: the mystic fan and the sacred phallus. As regards the phallus, which so often appears in ancient decorations: apart from frankly obscene figures, the ancients, it must be remembered, had not our contemporary notion of indecency. No more than in India, where it was worshipped under the name of *lingam*, was a pornographic significance necessarily attached to the portrayal of this object in Rome and the provinces of the Empire. On the contrary, it was widely venerated and religiously worshipped for its connexion with the principle of fecundity, life and virile energy. Quite different ideas occurred to the mind of an ancient according to whether he encountered this image on the walls of a brothel, where its obscene function was unambiguous, or on a statue of Priapus which, despite the exaggeration of the male attribute, was sacred. Today, both effigies are relegated to the 'secret museum', because our affected modesty is incapable of comprehending the ambivalence of such an image.

It is certain, at all events, that no town house could have maintained as well as did this Villa, which was somewhat remote from the city, the secrecy needed for the celebration of forbidden rites, all the more since these were attended by noisy dancing which at Pompeii, where the houses were closely crowded against one another, would have attracted the neighbours' curiosity and malevolence.

Of what consisted the rites enacted in the Villa of the Mysteries? The magnificent frescoes can be regarded as a narrative relating the manner in which the proceedings developed, under the eye of the severe matron who is watching over them and who, probably having the function of priestess, or mistress of ceremonies, sees to it that everything happens according to the meticulous prescriptions of the ritual. The fact too that with the exception of sacred and mythical personages taking part in this, there are only women, and that the initiation chamber is next to the conjugal one, suggests that these rites probably constituted an initiation into a bride's life as well as a promotion to the honour of mystical wife to Dionysos.

Following the progress of the rite, we first see a veiled woman whom we may call the postulant, who entreats initiation and presents herself at the entrance of the room; there she first encounters a nude little child who reads to her the conditions of initiation, the phrases she must pronounce, and the pledges she is going to take. A seated woman listens with smiling solemnity to this lesson, reading over the child's shoulder and making sure that everything is disclosed and well spoken; with her hand, which is holding a stylus, she points out the words, one after another, to the little reader, lest he should omit any. Beside her, a young girl is moving towards the interior of the room, carrying a plate on which are various objects.

In the following scene, we see three women busy round a table. One of them, seated, has her back turned to us, thus concealing the objects that are on the table and not to be seen by us. In this way, should an uninitiated person ever penetrate into the room, he would not observe what must remain hidden: the actual contents of revelation, which only the initiate is authorized to receive. We next encounter a rather enigmatic personage, a bearded figure of Pan, his eyes luminous; he is playing his lyre. This bizarre apparition suggests a question. Is this Pan a god mystically associated with the ceremony and present as it were only in spirit, or are we to suppose that this is a supernumerary who has assumed the mask of Pan and who *is* Pan, since the mask is the character?

Farther along we shall be faced with a similar puzzle when other spirits come into view; the young Pan and female Panisk, nursing a kid, who next appear, can also be interpreted in this dual fashion, as actual or allusive. We return to solid reality when a terror-stricken woman, her lifted arms putting aside her veils, runs weeping towards us. This is either the postulant, come to the second act of this sacred performance, or an assistant announcing a fearsome event to her. What is this event? The appearance of the divine group of Bacchus and Ariadne, embracing, and attended by other Pans, the customary accessories of the Bacchanals – or that kind of wingèd female demon brandishing a whip?

The mythical personages and the participants in the mysteries are in no way differentiated, except by attributes which could be theatre props; and this encourages us to believe that the loves of Bacchus and Ariadne were mimed in a 'tragic play' performed during the ceremonies. Of the legend of Ariadne only its significance, its symbolic value need be remembered. Ariadne represents the human soul conquered, possessed, by the god, uniting with him and becoming immortal. The mysteries had as their object to make of each woman initiate an Ariadne, mystically espoused by Dionysos. Here is an example of that sacred marriage or hierogamy so frequent in the religions of antiquity. I therefore judge that the divine couple and the satyrs beside them, one of these latter – significant fact – flourishing a theatrical mask, belonged really and materially to the ceremony, in the capacity of actors of that mythological interlude inserted in the religious ritual of which it was an integral part. Inhabiting the same space, these personages are of the same nature. It would be difficult indeed to believe that the wingèd female demon brandishing her whip inhabits a different dimension from that of the woman she is flagellating, whom we shall next see. The former wears a theatrical costume, including that pair of wings so often seen on Greek harpies and the Etruscan female spirits associated with funeral cults.

This survival from Etruria, to which are also owed the gladiatorial contests, is significant in the ritual of a mystery of Eastern origin. Dionysos is the god of generation and of the dead; he rules over the underworld, and he distributes in wine, itself also a mystic symbol, vital energy, knowledge, illumination. In his union with Ariadne he infuses his divinity into the human soul which gives itself up to him, which is elected by him, and it is the initiation that leads to this election. He is also the very life-principle, imaged by the phallus covered over with a veil which a young woman kneeling is preparing to unveil for the act of manifesting, of adoration: the revelation.

It is possible that in the orgiastic frenzy which possessed the Bacchants, this adoration of the phallus involved irregularities the nature of which it is easy to guess, and which might have justified the measures taken by the Senate to prevent such abuses. But most probably no such thing occurred in the home of the chaste and stern matron who watches and directs the ceremony. In this patrician house everything passed with an utter circumspection, which the Bacchic *thyase* would not perhaps have respected if it had been enacted in the fearsomeness of caves or the nocturnal solitude of forests.

The phallus unveiled and the loves of Dionysos and Ariadne mimed before her, the postulant understood the spiritual meaning of the mysteries in which she was participating; she had still to undergo the physical trials which form part of all initiations. She had to go through suffering, perhaps further to identify herself with Ariadne who suffered at being abandoned by Theseus on the island of Naxos where Bacchus came to search for her. Unclothed, she kneels before a seated woman, between whose knees she hides her head, and then it is that on that beautiful trembling nakedness the wingèd demon rains down her whip-lashes. The flagellator lashed in earnest, hard and unsparingly; we can divine this from the agonized and distracted expression of the victim, and the consoling gesture of the woman who softly strokes her hair; the painter has magnificently expressed the quivering of the body that trembles under the strokes, but at the same time that expression of suffering is tempered with a kind of holy intoxication which the whip begins to awaken in the initiate.

And here she is standing again and, completely nude and clashing small cymbals, she dances with a swift, astounding rhythm. The sign is given that the god has taken hold of her, that he possesses her in the madness of this insane whirling to which she abandons herself. A dance of joy, but above all a frenzy at once mystic and sensual, this impromptu exaltation in which the individual rejects all her customary, banal social *self* is, like the flagellation, a phenomenon of purgation. It is both orgy and ecstasy, during which a new being is born, this being created by the initiation and henceforth worthy of the god's espousal. The hierogamy will not be depicted, for this sacred, supernatural act is of its very essence un-representable. The vicissitudes of the Dionysiac cult are completed with the last episode, in which are seen a woman and wingèd cherubs proceeding to the ritual toilette of the bride, the cherubs being here the manifest sign that this union is either carnally or spiritually, or in both ways, a hierogamy.

Such is one interpretation that can be given to the frescoes in the Villa of the Mysteries; others are perhaps equally valid. Since the discovery of these fine and striking paintings, much has been written about them. The theory that the supernatural personages are disguised actors, which I set down here for what it is worth, appears to me to justify entirely this clear inference that the actual figures and the gods have the same corporeal substance and move in the same dimension. What, too, could be more simple than to convert attendants into satyrs, Pans and Silenuses? – the mask which is shown us rather indicates as much. As for the flagellation, these, one feels very definitely, are not imaginary blows that make the flesh of the new Bacchant contract and shudder; and the whip is a real one, even if the wings of the Etruscan demon are false.[42]

THE NECROPOLES

At Pompeii as in all the cities of Roman antiquity the world of the dead is clearly distinct from that of the living. The tombs are to be found beyond the city enclosure.[43] But they were not isolated and contained in an enclosed space, as is the practice today; quite the contrary, they were ranged along the routes leading to the city in the neighbourhood of the gates. Instead of being a place set apart for silence, meditation and prayer, the necropoles were crossed by the noisiest and busiest roads. Certain tombs were laid out in such a way that wayfarers could rest in the shade on marble or stone benches, which formed part of the architecture of funereal monuments. The deceased, whose souls were supposed still to be hovering in the places where their remains were laid, thus participated in the happy bustle of peasants coming to sell their fruit and vegetables in the market, and in the conversation of passers-by stopping in the exedrae to discuss business, pleasure, the circus games or political rivalries.

Among these monuments, humble or magnificent, placed without any order on both sides of the road, dealers would set up their stalls in the empty spaces, and this familiarity between the supreme calmness of death and the commercial hurly-burly of the living established a kind of close relationship at once mysterious and benevolent between those gone before and the inhabitants, in whose preoccupations they were thought still capable of taking an interest.

The dimensions and style of the tombs changed at the same time as the city acquired more wealth, power and authority. Initially, it was enough to thrust into the ground urns containing the ashes of bodies burnt on pyres; the place in which these urns were laid was considered as sanctified. Sometimes *stelae* bearing the names of the deceased were erected; it came to pass that the upper end of these stelae was given a rounded shape recalling that of a human head, a custom preserved

170

today in Turkish cemetries, where this appearance of a head is clearly stressed by a turban. At Pompeii the human resemblance was accentuated by representing tresses of hair when it was a case of a woman's tomb. The name of the deceased and a dedication to his spirit were inscribed there.

On the plot where the dead of the same family rested was erected an altar intended for sacrifices and libations, in conformity with the old belief that the deceased continued to survive, in the subterranean world to which he had gone, if he were regularly supplied with the sustenance capable of nourishing him. Wine or milk thus poured on the ground was supposed to reach the shades by a conduit running through the soil, sometimes an amphora the base of which was pierced. A small structure, very simple, enabled relations of the deceased to rest during funeral ceremonies, and this kiosk also served to store the implements of the cult. The fact that these kiosks vaguely resembled sentry-boxes made the first discoverers of Pompeii and some naïve people even today believe that here was the hut of a watchman entrusted with guarding the tombs. This hypothesis was not absolutely absurd, for it is well-known that in antiquity necromancers who called up the shades of the dead were numerous, as were also sorcerers and magicians who made up their philtres or charms out of human remains stolen from the cemeteries.

Men's pride and vanity do not apply only to multiplying in their lifetime the signs of their wealth and power; it was incumbent as well that after their death their last dwelling should continue to perpetuate their distinguished name, titles, functions, splendid feats of arms if they had achieved any, or the gifts they had made to their community. In this way the original funeral kiosk little by little took on monumental dimensions, the nobles and the wealthy vying with one another for the possession of the greatest, most magnificent and gorgeous tombs. A kind of outbidding was thus established in funereal art, multiplying the number of statues, the allegorical paintings, the inscriptions in enormous lettering. The bench reserved originally for the deceased's family became this exedra where whoever wished could come and sit. In the beginning these benches were out in the open, then the custom arose of covering them over with a kind of vaulting, similar to the apses of mediaeval Christian churches, where the tired

171

passer-by or prating idlers could, according to the season, shelter from the sun or the rain.

Archaeologists believe that these structures particularly evolved under the influence of Greece and the East, when Hellenic customs began to hold sway over the Campanian cities. The splendour of the tombs was no longer only a homage rendered to the deceased, who had heretofore been satisfied with an urn or a terra-cotta or tufa coffin containing together with the human remains vases and implements which, so the ancients supposed, the dead person would need in the next world; the vanity of the living too found this advantageous. A funereal monument of splendid dimensions and with superb decoration indicated to all those who passed this way, and stopped in passing to look, the distinguished antiquity of an aristocratic family or the more or less honourably-got fortune of a clever banker or successful merchant. In the case of a personage who had given distinguished service to the city, it sometimes happened that the municipal officials, to honour him, would grant his descendants a plot of ground attached to the *pomerium*, situated beyond the city enclosure, for them to erect a monument commemorating him.

The pomerium was that zone considered as sacred which surrounded the city and which served it as spiritual wall. To cross the pomerium of a strange city was an impious act, a veritable sacrilege. So long as this religious protection was respected, it was thought unnecessary to build ramparts and towers, the reverence due the pomerium being a sufficient defence. Later it was ascertained that this pious tabu was not always effective and that enemies were prepared to violate it to achieve a victory; thereafter, fortifications were adjoined. The prestige of this forbidden ground remained great enough, however, to make a concession of it for the building of a tomb an inestimable privilege, of which inscriptions would recall the splendid granting; it was still more illustrious if the funeral of this notable citizen were celebrated at the city's expense and with the imposing ceremonial of national obsequies.

Frequently encountered on these Pompeiian tombs are texts like the following that recall this distinction so sought after by the deceased's family, who always derived considerable glory from it: 'Mamia, daughter of Publius, priestess of the people. The ground of her burial has been granted by decree of the decurions'; or 'Marcus Porcius, son of Marcus, by decree of the decurions; the ground to a depth of twenty-five feet and a circumference of twenty-five feet.' (From this it can be seen that the generosity of the decurions was apportioned according to the deceased's civic merits, so that the more important he had been, the larger his plot.) As for Aulus Umbricius Scaurus, son of Aulus, of the Menenius family, the funeral inscription proclaims that, in reward for his zeal in the judiciary office of duumvir, he had received what was probably the maximum in official honours: 'the decurions voted the land for the monument, two hundred sesterces for the funeral, and decided on the erecting of an equestrian statue in the Forum.'

It was not omitted to engrave beside the dead man's names his insignia of rank and his prerogatives, one of the most coveted being the afore-mentioned *bisellium*, the right to a double seat on the tiers of the Amphitheatre. Whether this privilege was intended for the man's greater comfort or to enable him to bring a friend, is not known. Accordingly as officials had or did not have the power of life and death, there was placed after their inscription fasces provided with an axe, or not.

Most of the tombs discovered in the vicinity of the Pompeiian gates belong to the end of the Republic and afterwards, up to 79; but there are also many older ones. Certain of these, the funeral furnishings of which are to be found in the Antiquarium, dated from the Iron Age, from the period when the Oscan and Campanian tribes inhabited the region. Found in the district of Striano or San Marzano, they go back to the seventh and even the ninth century B.C.; their funeral furnishings consist of vases of Etrusco-Campanian manufacture, made of black *bucchero*, Greek ceramics of geometrical design, and bronze jewellery rather primitively fashioned. In the Necropolis of the Porta Ercolano have been found some humble Samnite graves of the third century B.C., in which the corpses were buried unburnt, just in the ground, the rude cover of the grave flush with the surface; they contained simple Italic pottery.

Discovered in 1763, that is to say at nearly the same time as when the excavations began inside the city, the Necropolis situated at the sides of the road leading to Herculaneum, outside the Porta Ercolano, was largely cleared in the course of about a century of investigation. Spread over several hundreds of yards, the most characteristic, splendid evidences of Campanian funeral art were unearthed. Along this route, commonly called the Via dei Sepolcri, were found that bizarre mixture of tombs and stalls peculiar to the Pompeiian cemeteries, as described above. The attention which the Directors of Excavations devote to framing the monuments in a background of pleasing vegetation most suited to them, enables today's visitor to Pompeii to find, instead of melancholy, derelict structures, most beautiful and instructive ruins set among trees and shrubs. Pines grow roundly above the exedrae, cypresses stand beside the statues, living acanthuses are mingled with the sculpted ones of friezes and capitals. In this district of the dead, in a city itself dead, all is life and brightness; and if the sales-talk of pedlars and sellers of cakes or lemonade is no longer heard, nor the wrangling at the open-air stalls of the vendors of funereal articles, nor the music and funeral choirs that escorted the solemn obsequies, at least the singing of birds and the rustling of the wind in the branches of trees is a reminder of the ancient belief that the souls of the dead, light as larks or butterflies, could leave their subterranean asylums to see once again the faces of the loved ones who visited them, or the beauty of a sunset or the brightness of a bunch of flowers.

All styles, all building methods are represented in the Necropolis of the Porta Ercolano, apart from those humble primitive graves in which the urns lay just in the ground, or the lid of which might be jostled by the foot of a passer-by, since the burial had been so superficial. Here we have the cemetery of the most distinguished society of this city where fortunes were made and lost fairly rapidly, which involved a vigorous social fluctuation. Also, the earthquake of 62 had impoverished some of the wealthy, and in the city's reconstruction cunning speculators did profitable business. Freedmen grown rich through trade or banking – even in that period when the interest on money was one per cent, so that the word 'usurer' did not have a base connotation – established themselves in the houses made over to them by nobles who could no longer maintain too expensive a household. These new rich took pride in having built, for themselves or their relations, as beautiful tombs as those of the aristocrats of ancient lineage. As they succeeded to every public office and their fortunes

174

enabled them to shower their bounty on the games, they achieved the highest standing.

Hence, outside the Porta Ercolano the monument to that eminent Umbricius Scaurus, who was so signally honoured with a plot granted by the decurions, national obsequies and an equestrian statue in the Forum. For all his being displayed to view on horseback in the market square, Scaurus was not, as might be expected, a victorious general, but quite simply a *garum* merchant. Garum was a spicy sauce, with a fish base, much used in Roman cooking; and it may be supposed that the neighbourhood of the sea and of the Campanian hills rich in fragrant plants, together with the fact that cargoes of spices were unloaded at Pompeii, had inspired the shrewd Scaurus to establish a prosperous industry of this garum, which was to appear on all festal tables, whether wealthy or humble.[44]

The stucco bas-reliefs decorating this tomb depict circus sports: probably in commemoration of gladiatorial contests for which Scaurus had paid so as to obtain and keep his magistracies, or else simply to recall the fact that this sports enthusiast had democratically shared the passion of the local populace, similar to that of the Romans, for these vile massacres in which men killed one another to divert the idle and gain their applause, or their boos and the turned-down thumb which was the signal for death.

The bisellium figures on the bas-reliefs of the tomb of Caius Munatius Faustus, Augustal and magistrate of his *pagus*: the tomb consecrated by his widow Naevolaeia Tyche to her husband and herself, as well as to all their freedmen, who thus gained the honour of resting beside their masters. The square burial chamber, less than seven feet in length, contained a bench running all around the room, and niches. On the bench and in the niches were placed the urns and amphorae containing the ashes. From the nature of the container can be deduced the social position of the deceased whose ashes these were. In the great glass amphora at the bottom of the tallest niche are doubtless the remains of the magistrate Munatius Faustus himself. Three smaller glass urns had been reserved for his wife and children; as for the ashes of the freedmen, these were humbly contained in terra-cotta urns.

In the glass vases, which were cased in lead, there was discovered, at the time when the tomb was opened, a mixture of wine, water and oil in which the ashes were still bathed, as if in a lustral liquid from ritual libation and in accordance with a magical or religious practice. Beside the amphorae and vases were lamps which were lit during the funeral ceremonies periodically held in the tomb – as is still done today in a number of Italian cemeteries where it is the custom to maintain the light of a lamp set on the tomb, perhaps to symbolize the fragile, tremulous glitter of the immortal soul.

A bas-relief decorating the outside of the funeral monument to Munatius Faustus has, ever since its discovery, excited the curiosity of archaeologists, who still dispute its significance. This bas-relief depicts a ship in which the sailors are busy trimming the sail; some have thought that this imagery alludes to Faustus's profession, which might have been that of a sea-captain or a ship-owner whose earthly occupation was thus reproduced on this sanctuary, his last dwelling-place. A careful study of this sculpture reveals that the unknown artist undoubtedly meant to show a vessel in the grip of a tempest; some of the seamen have clambered up the mainyard, others are clinging with all their strength, and with difficulty it would seem, to the sail, while the pilot, indomitable at the helm, calls out his instructions to them. The anecdotal and picturesque side of this image appear less important than the meaning to be attached to it, especially considering that it is an instance of funereal sculpture. The men of antiquity, more versed than we in allegories and symbols, probably interpreted as a moral lesson this representation which for tourists of today is no more than a miscellaneous piece relating to an episode in the life of the deceased, or a handsome article of sculpture.

What, in fact, is this ship, if not the personification of man himself hurled on the sea of existence to struggle against the unbrindled elements, that is to say against chance and the mishaps and misfortunes inseparable from the destiny of each individual? Storms were not lacking, doubtless, in the life of Faustus, Augustal and pagus magistrate though he was, and of his wife Naevolaeia Tyche. It has also been observed that the actions of the sailors could be those of lowering and rolling up the sails at the moment of the ship's entry into harbour. The harbour is death, which writes finish to this adventurous crossing which is earthly life; similarly, a man breathing his last has done with the hazards of the crossing. He will be at rest in this haven of calm

176

and quiet if not, according to the beliefs of the ancients, of happiness, in the cool darkness of the tomb.

Among the illustrious Pompeiians buried in the Necropolis of the Porta Ercolano we may cite again the priestess Mamia, whose long inscription, all round that semicircular exedra called a *schola*, recalls her religious attainments and her claims on the respectful remembrance of the Campanian people. Beside this exedra stands another devoted to the tomb of the duumvir Aulus Veius, and not far off the monumental mausoleum of the family Istacides surmounted by a circular colonnade, reminiscent of Greek tombs and some of the Roman sepulchres, for example those along the Appian Way. At this juncture, it may be noted that funeral buildings which were circular in shape, tomb, colonnade or exedra, accord not only with a practical function or aesthetic need. Here, as in the bas-relief of Faustus's ship, it is the symbol that determines the object. Everything to do with death was circular, from the prehistoric tumuli to the amphitheatre where were held the sports which, originally at least, had as their object to delight the shades and feed them with the blood spilled; a double meaning remained attached to that geometric form. The circle is the symbol of the infinite, of that which has no end, and it promises to the dead a sure survival, perhaps even immortality, with time closing in a circle upon itself like the serpent gnawing its tail, likewise a symbol of eternity.

The circular tomb and the burial monument built on the plan of the circle, represent the womb in which the infant is prepared for birth. Thus is the dead laid like an embryo in the tomb, from which at the term of required gestation he will be revived to a new life, perhaps even to an eternal one. The ancients' beliefs relative to the after-life have never been exactly defined; they were considerably modified in Italy by the introduction to Rome of the religions of mysteries. As we have seen, the latter, superimposed on the ancestral, traditional religion, spread the doctrine that a man initiated into certain mysteries – of Demeter, Isis, Cybele, Bacchus, Orpheus – could, thanks to that initiation, be assured of an eternal life and escape the danger lying in wait beyond the grave, in the underworld places where the shades wander, for the deceased who has not ensured in advance, during his own lifetime on earth, the certainty of a blessèd survival.

Near the entrance of the so-called Villa of the Mosaic Columns is

177

seen the tomb called that 'of the garlands' in allusion to the friezes of sculpted foliage, exquisite in their accomplishment and light gracefulness, in which a Grecian purity is mingled with an exuberance somewhat Eastern in spirit, which is of course not at all surprising since in this city of commerce and pleasure all or nearly all coastal peoples of the Mediterranean must have had trading establishments.

Beside this tomb is that of the Blue Vase, so named because among the funeral furnishings of the structure, whose occupant is unknown, has been discovered the fine funereal vase, made of a blue-glass paste, which is today one of the treasures of the Naples Museum, where may also be seen an abundant and informative collection of urns, vials and glass funeral vases, of native or Eastern manufacture, in a great variety of shapes, materials and colours.

The celebrated Blue Vase, as famous and beautiful as the Portland Vase in the British Museum, was worked in imitation of a cameo in which the different veins of the stone serve to compose various figures. Here, there are two layers of glass, a dark-blue one constituting the background, and the second of a milky white over the other. It is in this white-glass paste that the artist, working after the fashion of an engraver of precious stones, drew, or rather sculptured with a chisel, a rich decoration of vines in which birds sport and from which are hung masks, while a sumptuous garland of fruits, pineapples, pomegranates and ears of corn runs around the neck. On one of the surfaces is depicted with extraordinary skill a grape-harvest scene in which once again figure those cherubs so often seen, in Pompeiian paintings, as performing the most varied functions – weavers, fullers and bakers. While two of them, perched on small structures that could be funeral monuments, play respectively the double-flute and the Pan-pipes, another is joyously crushing underfoot, in the press, the grapes which a fourth is pouring from a basket.

This vase, which belonged to the owner of the Villa of the Mosaic Columns, where highly remarkable glass objects were found, probably had a symbolic meaning comparable to that of the ship of Faustus. The press, which will recur in early Christian art, is the tomb in which the grape is crushed: as it were, made to die, to be reborn in the shape of wine. The mystic and ritual significance of wine is universal in the religions of antiquity, from which it passed into the Christian religion and even to the mystics of Islam. Dionysos-Bacchus, god of wine, was at the same time god of the dead. We are warranted in supposing that even if the creator of the Blue Vase wished simply to depict a graceful, picturesque scene, the owner of this consummately delicate marvel would have read into the images engraved on it a spiritual message important enough for him to want to take it with him into his tomb.

Beside the tomb of the Blue Vase is a large tomb to which was joined a covered exedra in the form, as already noted above, of an apse, meant perhaps for funeral rites, but also freely at the disposal of anyone who chose to rest there in a cool shade enlivened with pictures. This apse, similar to those which adorn gardens and are called *nymphaea*, was ornamented with shells and sea-creatures, tritons and dolphins, themes which appear frequently in Campanian art, but had perhaps in this tomb, again, an allegorical meaning: existence is a sea not immune from dangerous storms, and the triton and dolphin sport among the waves from amidst which they leap, just as the wise and upright man who knows well how to control his ship, arrives safely at the end of his life. The Greek legend of the poet Amphion was also borne in mind: how, victim of a shipwreck (likened to death), he had been picked up by a dolphin which, taking him on its back, had carried him to the shore (of immortality).

Such are the most important tombs of the Necropolis of the Porta Ercolano; let us now re-cross the city to go out to the south by the Porta di Nuceria, beyond which is another necropolis, recently discovered and unearthed, which has already yielded very fine tombs and which certainly promises today's archaeologists as fine results, when the clearing work is completed, as the Necropolis of the Porta Ercolano vouchsafed the seekers of the eighteenth and nineteenth centuries.

The Necropolis of the Via di Nuceria is situated parallel to the city walls. The tombs retrieved and excavated here present the same architectural characteristics as those already described. The graves are placed at random, according to the inclination or whim of whoever had them built, and are somewhat crowded together, which lessens the effect of imposing monumentality sought by the posthumous vanity of the deceased or his descendants. They are as varying in magnitude and style as those of the Porta Ercolano.

Here are found structures dedicated to the memory of officials: like that of the Tillus clan, in which was laid to rest a certain Caius Tillus, who had been military tribune and duumvir, and his brother, also a military tribune as well as augur. Not far from them, in the mausoleum of the Cellius clan, lies another official, Lucius Cellius, who performed the functions of magistrate and military tribune of the people. Some of the dead made good use of the privilege of free speech accorded them, to extol their own merits, nor did they deny themselves the pleasure of denigrating their political enemies or business rivals. Thus we read on the wall of the last resting-place of the Augustal Vesovius Philer, an inscription in which the unhappy magistrate, who considered himself un-justly charged by a neighbour in some case or other, affirms his inno-cence and calls down the vengeance of the gods on the deceiver; this revenge which he himself had not been able to carry out in his lifetime, either for lack of time or because his slanderer was too powerful to be hit at, the wretched Vesovius entrusted to the deities of Hades and to the Penates, who were to see that truth should be honoured and falsehood punished.

What this case comprised and who Vesovius himself actually was, is unknown. But, due largely to the work and talent of Maiuri, so inde-fatigable in 'reviving' the inhabitants of ancient Pompeii, the banker Lucius Caius Serapion is better known to us: his wife Helvia built him a splendid tomb, in part destroyed, unluckily.[45] Maiuri inferred that this Serapion was, from his name, originally Egyptian. His status was that of freedman, and like many men of that class he practised the profession of *argentarius*; in other words, he lent money at a reasonable interest, but business was so thriving that a fortune could be made without the least infringement of law or morality.

It has already been noted that the houses of bankers were the most beautiful and the most splendidly decorated. The changes effected in manners and in the economic scheme of things, the impoverishment of the nobles, who were obliged to have frequent recourse to money-lenders: all this explains the increasing wealth of a climbing class, who speedily over-reached all the rest, since the latter needed money and came to borrow it of them. Of the wealth of the freedman Serapion, who had probably come from his native Alexandria to seek and find his fortune in Campania, there can be no doubt in the mind of anyone who examines his tomb; in its dimensions, the elegance of its architecture and its beauty of proportioning, it does honour both to the conjugal piety of Helvia and to the fortune which the *argentarius* left to her when for the last time he closed his eyes on the beauty of this world.

The most magnificent of all the monuments hitherto brought to light in the Necropolis of the Via di Nuceria is indisputably the one to that remarkable woman Eumachia. She who lay at rest in this gorgeous structure was the daughter of Lucius, so says the handsome inscription in large and fine letters, and the tomb is dedicated to herself and her people. There is no question of her husband, who is not named. Perhaps the husband of a woman so energetic and forceful in business was a rather modest, self-effacing person. This would explain how Eumachia undertook the direction of family and guild affairs.

When archaeologists entered the burial chamber in which they expected to find the funeral urns of Eumachia and her kin, they found to their great regret that this room was empty. That is, although there were an abundance of niches for statues, and superbly sculpted altars not lacking in effigies of serpents (which in the Greek tradition had been familiar spirits of the house and messengers between the world of the living and that of the dead, from their practice of slipping into all and sundry cracks of the ground), Eumachia's remains were missing. As it is not a tenable supposition that the tomb had been secretly ransacked between 79 and the time when it was opened up, fifty years ago, it must, we imagine, have been emptied before the eruption sealed the door under such heaps of matter. Why so? And where were Eumachia's remains taken? This is one of the numerous riddles still presented by the ruins of Pompeii.

Since before each gate and along the roads leading from Pompeii to the neighbouring towns there were necropoles, it was logical that searches for these should be carried out in the neighbourhoods of the Porta di Nola, the Porta di Stabiae, and the Porta Vesuvio. If these cemeteries have heretofore appeared sparser than those just surveyed, we must however mention the splendid tomb built at the Porta di Nola, and in the most conspicuous place, by the duumvir Herennius Celsius to the Manes and the ashes of his wife Esquillia Pollia, whose marble funeral urn rests like a rare and precious flower at the top of a simple Ionic column which, graceful, slender, feminine almost in its lightness, calls to mind a slim, pliant young girl. Few monuments in the abovementioned necropoles can rival this one in elegance.

Before the Porta di Stabiae stands the mausoleum of a Pompeiian citizen also well-known to us, since it was he, Marcus Tullius, who had built in the Forum, on a plot paid for by himself, the Temple of the Fortuna Augusta.

Near the Porta Vesuvio it is a melancholy shade which awaits us: that of the young aedile Vestorius Priscus whose inscription states that he died aged twenty-two and that his heart-broken mother had a sepulchre worthy of him built for the remains of this magistrate scarcely emerged from adolescence. The Tomb of Priscus is in fact distinguished among all those already cited by painted decoration of great beauty and by stucco reliefs exquisite in their art, which reproduce some episodes from his short life.

We cannot leave the necropoles without saying a word about a man who left no magnificent tomb but whose memory remains associated with the cemetery of the Porta di Nuceria: this is the curious person called Suedius Clementus whose singular history was discovered and related by Maiuri.[46] This Clementus is here represented by a *stele* marking the limits of the *ager publicum*, the public property. To him, after the earthquake of 62, fell the difficult task of determining and fixing property boundaries. Lands had been turned topsy-turvy, archives destroyed, and not a few people, it may be supposed, hastened to claim as their own, plots of ground belonging to their neighbours; some also did not scruple to claim lands belonging to the community.

An officer who had distinguished himself in the Transalpine campaigns, this Clementus was upright, strict, uncompromising. Vespasian, who esteemed him, sent him to Pompeii to set matters straight again, and with the unit of measure to hand, carefully weighing all claims, he established a new demarcation of lands similar to that of before the catastrophe. It is sufficient homage to the memory of a severely honest official to say that the entire population of Pompeii, turbulent and pettifogging as they were, unanimously acknowledged the justice of his decisions.

HERCULANEUM

THE history of Herculaneum is intertwined in many respects with that of Pompeii: the two cities shared the same past, went through the same political vicissitudes, knew the Samnite domination and the Social War, the Roman occupation and the gladiators' revolt. Like so many Campanian cities which have not achieved the renown of these two because excavations have not yet been made in them, Herculaneum was, as much as Pompeii, a victim of the earthquake in 62 and of the eruption of 79. The civilizing process, from the darkness of pre-history, developed similarly in them, and the social evolution was accomplished in nearly the same way. It may be said that the two cities shared and still share the same destiny, but their posthumous fortunes, if such an expression may be used of them, have been altered by different circumstances.

The City of Herculaneum and its Population

Herculaneum was undoubtedly, like Pompeii, an Oscan settlement on which a trade-centre of Greek commerce was grafted, and which progressively became a city where Hellenic civilization by degrees covered up the Oscan foundations. The site at that period was a kind of promontory – the eruption of 79 and that of 1631 considerably altered the terrain – down both sides of which two rushing torrents descended to the sea. As mentioned in an earlier chapter, legend names Hercules as her founder, and the first name under which she appears in history is, in Theophrastus in the fourth century B.C., that of Heracleion. Linking her fate to that of the cities of the Campanian coast on the shore-line of the Gulf of Naples from Cumae to Sorrento, she accepted those masters whom the hazard of politics gave her, from the Greeks of Cumae and Naples to the veterans settled in Sulla's colonies.

The earthquake of 62 produced the same consequences here as at Pompeii, and Herculaneum had as much to suffer from the eruption of 79, but not in the same way. This is explained by the fact that Pompeii was situated on the south-east slope of Vesuvius, while Herculaneum was farther to the south-west. The matter hurled out of the crater of the volcano was distributed differently, according to the direction of the wind and the varying nature of the ground. In this way Pompeii was covered over, as has been related, with a layer of lapilli and ashes spread out to a general height of twenty to twenty-three feet; these enormous mineral masses, weighing on the roofs of houses, broke and crushed them under almost regular strata of an excessively hard substance.

The layer of volcanic matter bursting down on Herculaneum was much higher, reaching up to sixty feet. It is not, however, of the same consistency as at Pompeii, for it is chiefly formed of mud, the torrents of rain that followed the eruption having diluted the lava, slag and ashes – of which the wind hurled the greatest amount on Pompeii – and massed these into a slimy magma which crept in everywhere through the streets and houses, knocking down the flimsier obstructions and stopping and solidifying before those which barred its passage. Herculaneum can be described as having been buried in a deluge of mud which gradually hardened, and under which she disappeared.

In this way the entire city, the surrounding villas and the adjoining countryside were inundated by this vast covering of miry, viscous matter. The mass of mud converted into tufa was so considerable that the inhabitants could not, like those of Pompeii, have had any hope of recovering their lost possessions; although thinner, the cover of ashes and lapilli was harder at Pompeii, but in certain cases Pompeiians got through it, whereas fifty-five or sixty feet of solid mud were sacrcely penetrable. It may also be supposed that under its ashes the general shape of Pompeii remained recognizable; at Herculaneum on the contrary only a great desolate expanse was to be descried, which left no indication of the city's site.

According to the still imperfect knowledge which we have of the actual extent of Herculaneum, its area can however be estimated at a third of that of Pompeii, and the number of its inhabitants at a quarter. Its position on the aforesaid promontory made it less liable than its neighbours to become an important commercial centre; it lacked roads favourable to trade with the interior, a harbour suitable for large merchant vessels, and above all the mouth of the Sarno which formed a natural estuary and enabled shipping to proceed up its navigable stream. From various indications it can be deduced that the population was less dense and traffic less crowded: the paving of the streets nowhere displays the deep ruts which at Pompeii were hollowed out by the chariot wheels, nor are there any of those stepping-stones which served as islands for crossing the road or getting out of the way of galloping horses. It also lacked that element inseparable from real commercial activity: publicity. The Herculaneans had not, like their neighbours, the habit of scrawling publicity notices or electoral propaganda, on walls.

From all this it can be inferred that Herculaneum was a quiet little city, perhaps plunged in a provincial sleepiness, whose inhabitants devoted themselves chiefly to fishing, and whose workshops were made over for the most part, to luxury industries. As everywhere else there were artisans producing the objects in current use, food, wine, oil, but there were no great industrial establishments like those which at Pompeii dealt with wool. The absence of large-scale trade and industry meant also that the class of new-rich and of freedmen achieving wealth was infinitely less here than elsewhere. The distinction was clearly marked between a patrician aristocracy owning fine houses and a humble proletariat. Here the phenomenon of noble houses fallen into the hands of parvenus or debased by the necessity of housing several families in them and of converting rooms into shops or workrooms, is not or at least not often encountered.

This is said with reservations as to what future excavations may reveal, and the possibly different nature of the districts still buried under Resina. The Herculaneum which we describe is that which appears to the visitor of 1960, and it is very possible that in a distant or near future, sensational discoveries may oblige us to modify this judgment.

Visiting the underground parts of the Theatre and encountering prodigious networks of passages circulating between the houses and public buildings of Herculaneum, we get a totally different impression from that which is given to the *surface* visitor by the spectacle of a city whose houses are intact with their ceilings, upper storeys and roofs – which have not in general been preserved at Pompeii, although immense strides were made in this department during the New Excavations, and particularly since 1950. What is unusual in Pompeii is current coin at Herculaneum, where certain insulae allow of our thinking ourselves confronted with modern houses, although these are ancient ones carefully and precisely exhumed from the matrix of mud and restored to the original state, with a complete authenticity and, again, by using elements still in place.

However great the difficulties which they unwittingly prepared for modern archaeologists, those *cavamonti* who opened up this maze of corridors, reminiscent of mine galleries and Roman catacombs, must be unreservedly admired for their courage, tenacity, energy and skill. Under the direction of Karl Weber and of Francesco La Vega, the treasure-hunt was transformed into a true underground exploration, of which old engravings give an accurate idea. Picturesque guides in bell-crowned hats conducted bold curiosity-seekers, by torch-light, through these underground labyrinths, and made them admire paintings which often elicited the exclamation: 'It's more beautiful than Raphael!'

Everyday Life

It would be superfluous to repeat here what the excavations have revealed about everyday life in Pompeii, as regards the features common to both cities. It is of more consequence to point out, in the course of our visit to the houses of Herculaneum, the characteristics special to them, the peculiarities encountered only here, whether these are due to the different state of preservation owing to the fact that the city was deluged by mud and not crushed under a hail of stones, or to the architects' individuality and the different tastes of the population.

Certainly here too it is very interesting, and even moving, to enter shops and find in them mundane objects often intact and awaiting nothing more to come back to life, it would seem, than a hand to grasp them once again. On the counter of the greengrocer Aulus Fufer are beans and corn, with the proprietor's silver ring and a seal in his name; and we see the moulds of the pastry-cook who lived in the same quarter as Fufer, the Insula Orientalis, and whose name, Patuleus Felix, we likewise know, because his pastries were imprinted with his initials. Being superstitious, Patuleus the Happy, so as not to lose his grip on good fortune, had inscribed round the entrance to his bakehouse the magical signs that would ward off demons, since these latter, it was said, amused themselves by spoiling the cooking of tarts or pizza, which were popular then as now in the region of Naples.

Just next to Patuleus's cake-shop was opened a rather smart and inti-mate tavern, where the amphorae of good wine were kept on sets of shelves that were wooden like the landlord's bed. To encourage his clients to drink, he had had painted on his main wall a fresco of Diony-sos carousing at table with Mercury and Hercules. If the gods delighted in getting drunk, you do as much, good people. . . .

In the shop at the sign of the 'drinking Priapus' the clear, sharp wine of Vesuvius was savoured, together with the mountain's fruit. From a country estate, the host received large jars of nuts, which must have been highly popular with his clients; the jars have been discovered nearly full under the counter on which a few portions were set out as samples. Not far from here, at a corner of two streets, there was a large restaurant bar gleaming with polychromatic marbles on which the diners leant their elbows as they ate, unless they preferred to take home the feed that was kept hot on a hearth. The landlord, as well as dealing in drink, sold vegetables and fruit, of which there was a large store in eight pot-bellied jars lined up under the bar.

At each door opening on to the Cardo, which divides Insula V and Insula Orientalis II, we come upon a shop or a tavern: several dyers, grocers, bakeries and retail drink-shops. The most interesting of these shops is that of a cloth-merchant, where among vessels of colouring products fragments of material have been found: precious and fine stuffs, of which hardly more than a whisper is left, but on which still may be recognized, pale and fragile as spider-webs, the traces of a pattern. Extremely moving is the house of the cutter of precious stones, whose wife did graceful embroideries on a frame which is still there, be-side the bed made of rare wood inlaid with Greek keys and arabesques, and on which lies the skeleton of a youth. Corpses are much rarer at Herculaneum than at Pompeii, primarily for the reason that the popula-tion was four or five times less numerous, and perhaps also because the inhabitants had time to flee when the eruption began. Besides the skele-ton of the young jewel-engraver, we shall mention only those of the two thermae door-keepers who were unwilling to leave their post and the bathers' clothes that had been entrusted to them, and who died in their room; and also the unknown cadaver of the House of the Skeleton, dis-covered in 1830, whose owner was in such fear of thieves or of the neigh-bours' prying, that he had had a wire netting erected above the walls of

187

his courtyard. Evidently the poor man was so attached to his earthly goods that he preferred to die beside his nymphaeum with its translucent glass mosaics, rather than survive but leave behind the things he loved.

If these Herculaneans could return, they would find everything in its place. The goldsmith would ascertain that not one precious or semi-precious stone was missing from his collection, and would again take up the rough-carved intaglio, the half-finished cameo, the unpolished carbuncle and the aquamarine in its matrix. The baker would set about turning the mill, since the ass has died on the job and the little stable is empty. The cloth-printing press of the *lanarius* would begin once again to grind, and the weaving trade of the *textor* could easily be re-constituted out of the wreckage of beams and weights. And if he should feel hungry, he would find on a table in the next-door house pastries nineteen centuries old.

There is not a house in Herculaneum where some ordinary detail of the life of the people does not arrest us. In the House of Telephus are the rudiments of a modest lunch: eggs with their shells intact, rolls, cakes. A stout line rolled round its winch formed part of the equipment of a fisherman living in a simple room of the House of the Partition. A collection of writing tablets: some new, enclosed in a box, others written on and carelessly shoved under the bed. In the furnace-room of the women's section of the thermae the large iron shovel, with which the embers were stirred up, is still leant against the door of the boiler, which was extinguished only under the torrential mass of mud, like the fire in the kitchen-grate of the House of the Gem.

We have noted above that, contrary to the custom in Pompeii, the Herculaneans were not in the habit of scribbling on the walls. Here, however, a wag has done it, on the wall of the lavatory adjoining this kitchen, on the occasion of a visit by a famous doctor whose passing through he has immortalized by writing this interesting revelation: '*Apollinaris medicus Titi imperatoris hic cacavit bene*': 'Apollinaris, physician to the Emperor Titus, sh-ed satisfactorily here.'

Private Houses

The most beautiful houses are those which, extensively open to a view of the sea and mountains, crowned the promontory, facing the open

188

sea, and enjoyed at the same time one of the most beautiful panoramas in the world and an air whose healthfulness, famous in antiquity, is extolled by the Roman historians. They were built to the specification of wealthy and distinguished people who chose to reside at Herculaneum by reason of its exceptional position on the Gulf of Naples, and who wanted to enjoy the maximum of what they came here for: sun, fresh air, contemplation of the countryside. Architecture was to defer to this functionality, and to satisfy it did not scruple to abandon the traditional plan, improved on the Greek style, of the Italic house.

The most characteristic of these residences of wealthy folk who wintered here – the House of the Stags, the House of Telephus, the House of the Gem, the House of the Hotel, the House of the Mosaic Atrium, the House of Argus – were designed in such a way as to distribute the daylight, sun and air through the largest number of rooms. The Herculanean house is not, like the Pompeiian town one, a closed cube, but quite the contrary – a happy configuration of terraces, porticoes, peristyles with covered *ambulacra* (for foul-weather days), broad passages, and bays furnished with glass windows. This description does not answer only to the type of the private mansion. At Herculaneum too there were unhappily some patrician houses divided into bourgeois accommodation, and tenements several storeys high, such as are erected in very densely populated cities, like Naples, Ostia and Rome. The large building which has nearly a thousand feet of frontage in Insula Orientalis II was the type of these ancient dwelling-units which changing customs began to introduce into the Campanian cities, and which had reached Naples and Pozzuoli and already invaded Herculaneum when the eruption put an end to such urbanistic advances that threatened to disfigure this charming small city. It is so often the case that a modest, staid aristocratic city like this will allow itself to be won over, in its turn, if tardily, by modern ideas.

The House of the Stags, which attained its current form in the reign of Nero and which was restored but little altered after the earthquake of 62, is the prototype residence both in the lay-out of the rooms and in its collection of works of art. The two groups of stags beset by hounds, which decorate the great triclinium, and also the Satyr of the 'red room', are reckoned among the masterpieces of sculpture in Herculanean collections. It will also be noted how extensively the frescoes of the

189

quadriporticus represent cherubs busy at various tasks – that theme already encountered at Pompeii – employing a treatment of space that is complex and subtle.

The small atrium into which we first enter, and the small triclinium which follows on it are virtually banished to a corner of the house with the kitchen and accessory quarters. The most important part, by far, where the inhabitants mostly live, is comprised by the great triclinium extensively opening on one side to the garden framed by the quadriporticus, on another to the *pergula* and *viridaria*, which is extended along that façade's entire length in the sunny promenade called the *solarium*. The splendour of the pavings of polychromatic marble, the luminous brilliance of the glass mosaics, the warm colours of the frescoes flawlessly set off the beauty of the marble or bronze statues happily left *in situ*.

The House of Telephus was so disposed as entirely to provide a view of the Gulf, while making best use of the unevenness of the terrain on that crest of promontory upon which it was built. The largest and most luxurious rooms are not so much the atrium, although it is attractively and subtly decorated, but those opening on to the south of the peristyle; here can be discerned an idiosyncrasy of the master of the house: his predilection for marbles, which he prefers to frescoes. The *oscilla* – those medallions swinging, with their figures of maenads and satyrs, in the wind – hung between the columns of the atrium, the great bas-relief of Telephus, the bas-reliefs depicting chariot races, are the best indication of this; but the most flawless and original room was that which, between the loggia and the peristyle, displayed the most dazzling marble decorations, of colours never before seen in Campania or even at Rome; the paving and walls were covered over with a kind of marquetry, of antique green, of pavonazzo, porphyry, serpentine and that African yellow which seems full of sun and fire. Other rooms, less grand and splendid than this one, which is nearly thirty-five feet long, had marble facings of which the effect was sometimes majestic, sometimes charming, but always in exquisite taste.

Just beside the House of Telephus is situated the House of the Gem, so named because of an intaglio engraved with the portrait of a woman, perhaps the mistress of the house, that was found there. As was the case next-door, the out-offices and subsidiary quarters were established on the lower storeys, while the terraced part, with the sea providing the backdrop, was reserved for the living-quarters and rooms of state.

Here there is not that extravagance of marble which characterizes the House of Telephus; the decoration is more restrained and makes skilful play of the black and white mosaics of the pavings and the red and black paintings on the walls. The keynote here is a concern for elegance, harmony and proportion quite different from the ostentation of wealth that appears in the house next-door.

Again in this southern part of the city, which was pre-eminently the residential quarter because it was extensively open to the sea, sun and fresh air, the House of the Mosaic Atrium exhibits the characteristic plan of these Herculanean mansions built for the enjoyment of people wintering here. Clearly the main part is the solarium, the uncovered terrace for walking, where the owners chatted with their visitors while looking at the Gulf and where they also enjoyed the beauty of the nights. For respite from the sun, when it was too hot and strong, small, cool, quiet bedrooms, bathed in a soft chiaroscuro and designed for peaceful siestas, were laid out at the two ends of the solarium; these were called *diaetae* or *cubicula dierna*, that is, day-bedrooms. Here too the triclinium, of enormous size, is located, between the solarium and the wide portico in the middle of which are the garden, the fountains and the piscina. Around the portico, agreeably decorated rooms give an impression of charming intimacy of *dolce far niente*. The mosaic paving of the atrium and of the entrance passage is partly comprised of geometric designs and partly of that illusory carpet, a veritable *trompe l'oeil*, which is also found in the House of the Gem.

The House of the Hotel, situated on the other side of the Cardo, is informative firstly by virtue of its dimensions, so huge that this was initially believed to be some public building, such as a basilica. An enormous terrace covering the top of this house provides a view which was probably the most beautiful in Herculaneum; below were laid out the living-rooms, and there was an extremely ingenious installation of baths. Unhappily the House of the Hotel had fallen victim to that democratization which had ended by reaching Herculaneum; before being pierced through and through by the exacavation tunnels of Alcubierre, Weber and La Vega, the house had been much spoilt by this clumsy division of a private mansion into modest lodgings. The new

191

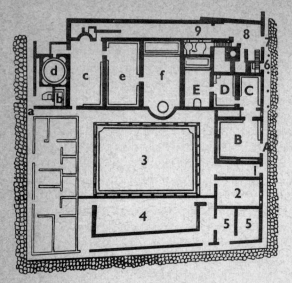

a   men's entrance
b   latrine
c   *apodyterium*
d   *frigidarium*
e   *tepidarium*
f   *caldarium*
A   entrance to the women's baths
B   vestibule
C   *apodyterium*
D   *tepidarium*
E   *caldarium*
1   entrance to the *palaestra*
2   dressing rooms for the gymnasium
3   *palaestra* (gymnasium)
4   *sphaeristerium* (games room)
5   rooms belonging to the *sphaeristerium*
6   keeper's lodge
7   entrance to the furnace-room
8   well and *castellum*
9   furnace

PLAN OF THE THERMAE

tenants, unable properly to keep up the luxurious decorations made for the previous owner, who was dispossessed or impoverished and forced to sell, let the pictures and stuccos little by little become damaged – the mosaics were more resistant – and the Bourbons' treasure-hunters completed this unfortunate work.

Looking at the houses discovered in the eighteenth century and at the beginning of the nineteenth, we cannot help but notice their dearth of works of art and the mediocre state of preservation of the apartments thrown into confusion by *cuniculi* bored more or less at random through the walls. Frescoes were ripped out, statues carried off, and little trouble was taken about restoring partitions, bracing ceilings or replacing beams that were charred in those cases where they still were in place. After having visited the House of the Genius, the House of Argus and the House of Aristides, ransacked of old in this way, we admire all the

192

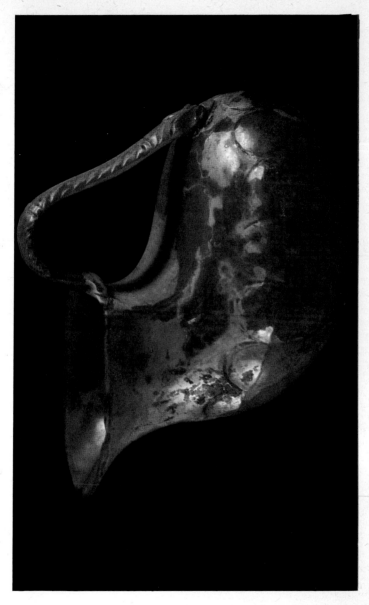

9 Glass jug. Naples Museum.

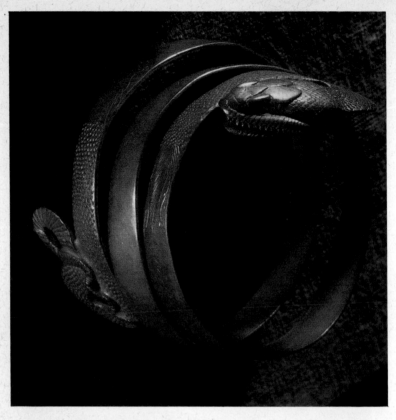

10 Gold bracelet. Naples Museum.

11 Villa of the Mysteries, Pompeii. Fresco depicting the preparations for the initiation ceremony.

12   Mosaics of animals. A wild-cat devouring a partridge, above; and below, wild duck, fish and shellfish. Naples Museum.

13 Detail from the Battle of Alexander mosaic. Naples Museum - found at Pompeii.

14   Fresco depicting Jason and Pelias. Naples Museum.

15   Decoration of one of the triclinium walls in the House of the Vettii, Pompeii.

16 Fresco from the Villa of Boscoreale, depicting a landscape. Naples Museum.

more the patience and skill of modern archaeologists, whose House of the Partition and House of the Wooden Partition are their masterworks.

Of greater interest to historians and archaeologists than to lovers of painting, sculpture or mosaics, these two houses boast the exceptional advantage of preserving evidences of the techniques employed by the Campanian artisans. Certain sections of wood providentially intact have enabled the restitution of special features of construction which are wonderfully revealing for us. The visitor attracted by the aesthetic beauty of the rich houses just seen, might tend to cast an indifferent glance over these plebeian houses, were the considerable value of these discoveries not pointed out to him.

Let us take for example the House of the Wooden Partition of Insula III. If the interior has rather beautiful decorations, it is for its façade primarily that we admire this flawless, precise restoration of a building of noble character, with its projecting beams, its roof considerably overhanging the street, its finely sculpted cornice and its low benches on both sides of the door. In the interior the phenomenon is observed, unique in the revived Campanian cities, of an entire partition of wood – from which the house derives its name – which completely enclosed the tablinum. The panels of two of these three double doors were quite well preserved in the blocks of mud, which did not remain hot for long enough to char them; and it has proved possible, not without difficulty as may well be imagined, to dig them out of this hard, solid matrix, repair them and put them back in place. For the first time in the history of Campanian archaeology, we find ourselves in the presence of wooden doors whose leaves still turn on their hinges, and near which bronze bracket-fittings, on which lamps were hung, are still to be seen.

For the unique example which it provides us of the *opus graticium*, the House of the Partition, next-door to the preceding, deserves the attention of all those interested in details, apparently modest but in reality significant, of the construction of buildings at Herculaneum. The *opus graticium* appears in the shape of walls formed inside by a framework of wood or reeds covered over with earth and plaster. Houses thus built at Pompeii disappeared, by the very fact of their fragile construction which was not resistant to pressure, as a result of the eruption.

193

In general the *opus graticium* was used for the partitions of upper floors, so as not to impose too heavy a weight on the ceilings, but was also utilized in houses of the people because it was a material vastly more economical than the Sarno stone, tufa or brick which were the ordinary materials. Extreme lightness was achieved by the use of these lattices of reeds and wood, and this also enabled the superimposing of numerous storeys: a highly useful combination, since the growth of the population and the influx of foreigners into the Campanian cities had considerably increased the cost of land and that of labour.

The House of the Partition, marvellously preserved in a matrix of mud and now expertly cleared, provides the first complete example of a technique cited by Vitruvius and of which no model as perfect and as well-preserved had heretofore been found. The parts facing the street afford the exact prototype of those economical houses rapidly constructed of materials that were not very durable, certainly, but extremely cheap. A loggia with roofing and balustrade, supporting a room lit through a window on to the street, and propped up by brick pillars, overhangs the whole breadth of the pavement. Since this arrangement is rather frequently encountered, undoubtedly the Campanian cities of antiquity offer the prototype of the arcaded streets which began to be built in Italy in the Middle Ages and which have remained in favour to this day with a people who like being able to go out even on rainy or sultry days and walk about without getting wet or being troubled by too strong a sun.

Inside, the walls are composed of thin uprights, the spaces between which are filled with a brickwork plastered and stuccoed in vivid colours; brick pillars gave solidity to the corners of main walls. It is no paradox that this house, surely one of the most fragile in Herculaneum, withstood the deluge of fiery mud from the ground-floor paving to the ceiling of the first floor, and that in an apartment of just this house which was more vulnerable than most others, a room preserving its furnishings entire was found on the first floor: with its wooden bed, its lararium with the images of the familiar divinities, and the crockery cupboard. Just as the House of the Bicentenary, previously mentioned, was probably one of the first Christian sanctuaries ever to exist, so the House of the Partition is that in which the simple realities of everyday life can be felt in their most touching immediacy.

194

The House of a Humanist Collector

Leaving these modest dwellings which, however, have the virtue of representing with an utter exactness the details of the average Herculanean's way of life, let us turn to a grand house of which unfortunately only a part is known even today, for the clearing has not been finished: the famous Villa of the Papyri so-called, celebrated for numerous reasons in the annals of Herculanean archaeology: for the library of philosophic works, written on papyrus, which give it its name; for the remarkable collection of sculptures, one of the first to embellish the Villa of Portici; and for the fact that it probably belonged to a Roman of illustrious family, whom we believe to be that Lucius Calpurnius Piso who was the father-in-law of Julius Caesar.

The considerable dimensions of the villa, the façade of which exceeded eight hundred feet, much larger than the Pompeiian villas of which we have spoken, and the fact that from 1750 innumerable cuniculi were bored here in the search for valuables, make it very difficult to achieve a complete clearing, which alone will enable us to understand the arrangement of the various sections, or to comprehend it better, at all events, than we now can do by relying on the plan, excellent though it is, drawn up by Karl Weber when he directed the work.

The remarkable wealth of works of art extracted, in a few years, from this mine of treasures ought to have encouraged the searchers to push on with their explorations; but the emanations of carbonic gas were extremely noxious, even deadly, and the workmen abandoned the site. In consequence of this desertion, everything that had been achieved was annulled; as the galleries were no longer propped up nor the air-shafts carefully cleared, the ground fell in and the villa disappeared once again. Heavy expenditure and strenuous exertions will be necessary to give back life to this remarkable dwelling which, from what is already known of it, is indisputably the vastest and most beautiful in all antiquity. Indeed, judging the grandness and splendour of the apartments by what was taken from the rooms excavated by Weber and noted on his plan, we may imagine what riches await the searcher in rooms yet unknown, which constitute the intimate, family section where the masterpieces would doubtless have been collected. It is in this living quarter, in a quite small room laid out as a library with its shelves on the walls, that the papyrus rolls which comprised the favourite works of

Calpurnius Piso were discovered, carefully ranged one beside another.

The humanist collector was rewarded for his love of books, in that it is to them that he owes having his name known to us and being immortalized by the discovery of the Villa of the Papryi. Are we, moreover, to accept the theory of Comparetti, who sees a portrait of Piso in the so-called bust of the pseudo-Seneca which was in the peristyle and is today, with the entire Piso collection, in the Naples Museum? I do not think so: the expressionist and dramatic realism of this bust is too excessive for it to be really a portrait; with its theatrical anguish, carried to a level of distress and despair, the pseudo-Seneca is a character from tragedy, not a wealthy Roman patrician, cultivated and hedonistic, as we imagine Piso to have been.

A sequence of deductions comparable to those of a detective story enabled Piso's name to be put forward, though it remains hypothetical, for all this rests only on conjecture. Among the literary and philosophic works in the library were found books by Philodemos, the philosopher of Gadara. Their number, in proportion to the other treatises, would indicate that the owner had been a friend or disciple of Philodemos. Besides, Cicero informs us that Lucius Calpurnius Piso constituted himself the protector and patron of Philodemos, who certainly enjoyed a great reputation but not to such a level that a Roman not particularly connected with him would have owned his complete – or nearly so– works in a library whose books are very well chosen but hardly numerous. To connect the name of Philodemos with that of Piso, and make the latter the humanist collector of the Villa of the Papyri, appeared a quite natural solution.

The reading of the papyrus rolls comprised an extremely difficult task: especially in that second half of the eighteenth century which was unversed in the subtle techniques today employed in archaeology, enabling the reading of what is written on a completely charred piece of paper. These charred rolls have been compared to briquettes of coal, and the image is entirely apt. The fiery mud which engulfed the library also consumed the manuscripts but did not completely destroy them. Distracting problems were, however, raised: how to unroll these *volumina* without reducing them to dust, how to decipher the faded words on this fragile material scorched by the lava.[47]

The painter Paderni, artistic adviser to King Charles III, was consulted,

196

and he applied himself to the task of unfolding; he succeeded in deciphering several words, but at the cost of irreparable losses, on account of which the experiment was interrupted. Charles III then replaced Paderni by an authentic specialist in antique manuscripts, Piaggi of the Vatican Library, who began by constructing an ingenious apparatus, which, he held, would unroll the papyri without damaging them. In fact, after four years of trial and at the cost of numerous rolls destroyed, it was contrived to unroll three and to read a fragment of the Treatise on Music of Philodemos.

This was little enough; but the Academy of Herculaneum, founded by the King, succeeded in gaining an adequate knowledge of about two thousand rolls, in which most of the great writers of antiquity were represented. It is a curious story, at once comic and saddening, that of the investigation of Piso's library, from 1753 to the present. George IV of England became interested in it and engaged scholars like Hayter and dangerous amateurs like Sicklet in the deciphering, up to the time when a truly scientific policy in the treatment of the papryus was instituted, profiting by advances made in other countries in this subject.

As regards the works of art, their exhumation comprised fewer risks, and more than sixty bronze statues were taken out of cuniculi traversing the peristyle of the Villa. To picture that part of the house, we may imagine a rectangle well over a hundred yards by thirty-five, at the centre of which there were trees, flowers, fountains and a long piscina of more than sixty-five yards, all encircled with harmonizing colonnades, under which strollers preferring coolness could walk in the shade. Between the columns, on plinths of precious marble, stood those masterworks of ancient sculpture today seen at the Naples Museum. Infinitely varied, this collection includes admirable pieces of animal sculpture, the Deer, for example, in which each muscle vibrates and quivers; portraits of a remarkable animation, like those of Scipio and Seleucus Nicator; enchanting female figures that have been named Berenice and Sappho; the moving Dionysoplato, at once divine and human, the woeful pseudo-Seneca, and those figures destined for world-wide renown, the Mercury at Rest, the Sleeping Satyr, the drunken Faun, the Wrestlers and, exceeding all the rest in majesty and beauty, the five monumental female Dancers, hieratically grave, which have an intimidating, well-nigh terrible look in their inlaid eyes.

On one end of the peristyle, in which the fountains were supplied by a wonderfully ingenious system of hydraulic pipes which even today astounds us, the living-apartments and rooms of state opened. At the other end, a long terrace of dimensions almost equal to those of the peristyle served as an open-air promenade and terminated in a round tower, a belvedere the top of which must have commanded a view on every side of the whole of the country surrounding the villa; it is there that we can imagine Calpurnius Piso, glad to be far from Rome, politics and public affairs, reading his beloved Philodemos, facing the setting sun.

Public Buildings

Numerous public buildings, as yet unearthed, will enlighten us on the complete plan of Herculaneum. At present the only important public buildings known to us are the Thermae, the Palaestra and the Theatre. Only this last gives us an idea of the luxury prevailing in the city and placed at the general disposal of the people who thronged to attend the spectacles, all classes being assembled, each on its suitable tier, in this vast cavea today stripped of its decorations, which at the beginning of the eighteenth century went to adorn the villa of the Prince of Elbeuf.

There is no question here as at Pompeii of a theatre restored to its original state and in which it would not today be difficult to give performances comparable to those of the past, but of a structure which appears subterranean to us when we visit it by the light of lamps, because the edifice built – and not hollowed out, like that of Pompeii – on several storeys of arcades is completely merged with the hardened mud; only the shafts and tunnels bored in the eighteenth century still traverse this mass, this fairly homogeneous matrix in which marbles, painted columns and stucco bas-reliefs are contained.

Everything that could be removed has been taken, the statues from the niches, and the slabs of porphyry, antique green, pavonazzo and alabaster from the walls they covered. The equestrian statues have been broken, the Corinthian capitals hurled to the foot of the columns that they crowned. Vaguely recognizable during this walk through passages reminiscent, again, of mine galleries or catacombs are the entranceways to the tiers and the masonry of the stage's majestic façade. The plans and lists of Weber and La Vega are a help in finding one's bearings in this subterranean, puzzling, rather painful world, where half the population of Herculaneum could be seated, and which today is reached by the descent of a staircase going down over ninety feet below the surface.

While we visit the monuments of Pompeii all on a level, we descend into those of Herculaneum. If we recall that the city was covered by the hardened mud up to a height exceeding sixty feet, we will understand that the exploration here is still done vertically. When the thermae were identified in 1942 and the effective clearing begun on them after 1955, it was necessary to dig deep shafts, all the deeper since the building was already lower than the general level of the city: it had been lit by round windows opening in the vaults. The glass of these windows had been shattered under the burning mire, and the torrent of mud had poured into all the rooms, hermetically sealing them before it solidified and took on the hardness and consistency of stone.

It was by following the same route as the lava – that is, by going through one of those dormer windows – that the clearing of the laconicum and the sudatorium was begun. It is most fortunate that the architectural structure of the whole building has thus been preserved in its unity, for it attests the originality and boldness which the unknown architect showed in superimposing several series of arches on the four columns of the vestibule, to raise the vault higher and give more light.

The traditional arrangement of the rooms follows the same succession as we have seen at Pompeii, corresponding to the various stages of the bath. There was a bath for women, separate from the men's and smaller and more simply decorated. Built at the beginning of the reign of Augustus (that is, slightly less than a century before the eruption), these thermae are of inferior dimensions to those of Pompeii, which is explained by the much smaller number of the population; but the decoration, which was completed in the reign of Nero, is as luxurious as that of the Pompeiian thermae and in as good taste. The frescoes and stucco bas-reliefs, the pavings of marble mosaics, the fine capitals of the columns are of an exquisite perfection. Particularly to be admired is the ingenious and enchanting 'illusion' of the frigidarium, where in the piscina the bather had the impression of diving into the midst of shoals of live fish. These were in reality painted on the vault with a striking verisimilitude and animation which would indicate that, anticipating the under-sea explorations practised today, the painter went to study his octopi, eels and lampreys in their natural habitat, in the waters of the Gulf. The bottom of the piscina was painted blue, the frescoes of the vault were reflected in it, and the agitation of the water stirred up by the bathers moved the painted fish in a strange and wonderful fashion.

If the 'pool of live fish' is the curiosity and masterpiece of the thermae, the fountain of the serpent-dragon, discovered in 1952, is the Palaestra's finest ornament. This place, which had been previously reconnoitred by La Vega, was named by him, overimaginatively, the Temple of the Mother of the Gods. It is in fact a municipal sports-ground which complemented the palaestrae existing in the thermae, the latter being reserved for patrons of the establishment, while the public Palaestra was open to all. As at Pompeii, handsome colonnades give this stadium an air of grandeur and majesty which caused it to be taken for a religious building.

In the middle of the great pool of considerably over a hundred feet, which served as swimming-bath, was discovered an immense serpent-dragon that functioned as a fountain; quite different from the motifs of known fountains, it represents the following remarkable composition: around a bronze tree seven feet in height, wind the enormous coils of a giant reptile whose multiple heads sprout among the branches. More wonderful than the ingenuity of the hydraulic installation, causing the water to gush from the heads, is the savage, menacing eccentricity of this unprecedented work of art, which perhaps was inspired by the famous bronze serpent of the Bible. This figure, given a patina by nineteen centuries in the earth, is altogether imbued with a kind of infernal horror, and the viewer cannot but wonder about the identity of the unknown sculptor capable of so audaciously strange a concept and of giving to this sinuous body, and to the slender throats terminating in small, ferocious and evil heads, the very throb of life.

ART AT POMPEII AND HERCULANEUM

DURING the visits that we have paid to the houses, shops and public buildings of Pompeii and Herculaneum, we have encountered a profusion of works of art, and we know besides that a great number of museums and private collections in Europe and America have been enriched with paintings and sculptures found in the Campanian ruins. There is no question of sketching here even briefly an over-all view of Roman art at the period of the end of the Republic and the beginning of the Empire, for such a study would overrun the limits of this book; but it is necessary to trace the general lines of this art, so as to emphasize the considerable privilege that we have today of being able to know it extensively and thoroughly, thanks to the Campanian cities.

Judging by results, it can be said that the barbarian invasions, wars and revolutions have done much more harm to the countries on which they have been unloosed than the eruption of Vesuvius brought to the cities which it buried. Sacked by the Vandals, the Ostrogoths and many other peoples who saw in the artistic wonders of the Imperial City rich plunder, Rome herself has preserved far fewer works of art than Pompeii and Herculaneum, because for centuries hers were at the mercy of whoever wanted to take them and was strong enough to do so.

It is not then paradoxical to say that a visit to Pompeii and Herculaneum, as well as to the Naples Museum, is more necessary to an understanding of Roman art than a visit to Rome itself, although the latter undeniably possesses a larger number of famous works of art.

The catastrophe which caused such great damage to the houses of Pompeii and Herculaneum had, however, the great advantage of preserving in a fashion that could almost be called miraculous the paintings with which they were invested; to such an extent that, given the great rarity of Greek and Roman works, it can be said that the most important part of what we know about that art, such as it was practised in anti-

201

quity, was transmitted to us by the Campanian cities. Let us imagine that the great compositions painted by Polygnotus in the Leskhe of Delphi, and which today are no longer known except from the descriptions of Pausanias, had been as carefully sheltered from ravages of the weather and of men as the frescoes of the Villa of the Mysteries, for example: the considerable lacuna which is responsible for our knowing nothing, or almost nothing, of great Hellenic painting, would then happily be filled. As to this Hellenic painting itself, it is thanks to reproductions and copies made at Pompeii, where the artistic hegemony of Greece lasted for a long time and even after the triumph of the Roman aesthetic, that we know what techniques were used in it, what its plastic sense was, what subjects it chose for preference, and in what manner these were treated.

It can be affirmed, without exaggeration, that the very large majority of Pompeiian and Herculanean houses, from the villas of the aristocracy and the wealthy bourgeoisie to the shops of dealers and artisans, from the temples to the brothels, were covered in paintings. Not only because the inhabitants of the Campanian cities had a most unerring and discerning taste, an artistic sense as common among the ordinary people as among the upper classes, but above all because painted decoration was virtually a necessity. Most rooms, in fact, even in wealthy homes, were of modest dimensions. At Rome, even in that Palatine mansion which is called the House of Livia because it is thought that the Empress lived there, the rooms are surprisingly constricted.

This constrictedness was related to the character of intimacy which the Latins were pleased to give to their homes. Living much outside, passing the greater part of their day in public buildings, in the Forum, at the Amphitheatre and in the thermae, when evening fell they were glad to return to those narrow rooms where they felt agreeably at home. But these rooms might well have been claustrophobic, if the space here had not been enhanced, artistically enlarged. The expanse which was lacking materially was compensated for by imaginary spaces created by the paintings.

The latter opened up, beyond the walls, vast perspectives of streets and palaces, porticoes and gardens; fields, woods, the sea itself and the sky *entered* in profusion into these apartments. The natural surroundings of which the town dwellers were deprived, for they were too much monopolized by work or the pleasures of the city to have time to go out into the country, came to them and were established in their rooms. With an art skilled in perspective – a perspective quite different, moreover, from that which we understand by the term and which has prevailed in Western painting since the Renaissance – the Pompeiian frescoists made the walls 'disappear' and covered them over with landscapes which cleverly imitated nature and gave the actual illusion, without it being necessary to go out of the house, of walking in vineyards or under shady trees, or of looking on at the bustle of ports with their ships, fishermen and dockers.

The taste which the Campanians of the coastal cities had for all aspects of life, elegant or picturesque, was largely satisfied by the representations of every kind with which their walls were adorned. It was not a question solely of satisfying an aesthetic requirement, but of responding to what could be called a physiological and psychical necessity, which demanded the creation of illusory and illusionist spaces. An analogous occurrence took place, which explains the evolution of Pompeiian art, in Holland of the seventeenth century: the feeling for nature had become very strong and accorded ill with the small, narrow, low-ceilinged houses darkened by greenish and almost opaque windows. It was for this reason that the painters composed so many seascapes and landscapes of plain and wood, of meadow and canal spread out under an immense sky which often occupies four-fifths of the canvas, giving the bourgeois of Delft, Haarlem or Amsterdam the impression that other windows, looking directly on to the sea or fields, had been opened up in their walls.

The Campanians, however, wished their illusory landscapes to be illusionist to boot – that is, giving the impression of reality. It is a highly curious and amusing singularity of ancient painting, in Greece and Rome, this esteem in which the *trompe l'oeil* was held. The anecdotes related by Greek and Latin authors on ancient artists gave these a particular credit when the painted object so effectively resembled the original as to create a confusion in the mind of the viewer. A proof of the artist's excellence of talent was seen in the fact that a visitor, having made as if to drive away a fly from a picture, perceived to his great confusion that the fly was painted on the canvas. It is also related in praise of an artist that birds having entered his studio rushed down to peck at a painting depicting grapes. We shall see presently to what extent the Pompeiian still-lifes remained faithful to that tradition of illusionism inherited by Rome from Greece.

We would be mistaken, however, in imagining that Italic painting of the great Pompeiian epoch was only the prolongation and repetition of the Hellenic painting which had served as its model. It must not be forgotten that if Greece had the ascendancy in southern Italy as in Sicily, there were also local aesthetic traditions which were never completely annulled. If little remains of Oscan or Samnite works of art, if we have scant evidence of an infiltration of the Etruscan aesthetic into Campania, this is because the cities which had contained these works of art were completely modernized at the time when Pompeii and Herculaneum entered on their prodigious development, in the Imperial era.

In spite of the disappearance of the genuinely native art in favour of an imported one, traces of the first are found in the divergence of currents that motivated Campanian painting according to the public for which it was intended. Of these two currents, one was cultivated; it is this one which is seen in the decoration of public buildings, temples, thermae, theatres and in those of the houses inhabited by the upper classes: bankers, big businessmen, high officials, magistrates, priests or the idle rich. These people required an art refined in its forms of expression and drawing its subjects from the mythology known by every cultivated person, or from the poems that appeared in the libraries of the erudite.

These distinguished folk were not afraid to lower themselves on occasion by accepting vulgar, comic, licentious, sometimes even blasphemous and sacrilegious subjects in which the gods were ridiculed. This leads us to conclude that a considerable part of the wealthy classes were of rather low extraction: slaves who having made money, had bought their liberty from their masters and become influential and rich, owners of grand residences. Although these new-rich had had it in mind to imitate the nobles in everything, and though the mansions of these latter were scarcely distinguishable from their own, the new-rich retained nonetheless a certain vulgarity: of manners, if not of feelings. It thus came about that sacred things were mocked with a cynicism highly reminiscent of the *Satyricon* of Petronius, who described in his famous hero Trimalchio one of the grotesque, impudent and ostentatious parvenus of which there were certainly many at Pompeii. A fresco in the House of Menander represents the gods as absurd puppets, sparing neither Jupiter, Juno, Apollo nor Minerva, all caricatured in a farcical spirit which shows what scant deference the master of the house felt for the guardian divinities of the city, since Venus herself, the Pompeiian Venus, watching over the security and prosperity of the city, is depicted under the lineaments of an old woman, hirsute and ugly.

It was natural that the personages of the Bible should be little respected, since the raillery did not spare Olympus: one Pompeiian fresco portrays in grotesque fashion the Judgment of Solomon. Here, as in the House of Menander, the characters have enormous and distorted heads on tiny, deformed bodies, a process of distortion which was to be taken up again by the caricaturists of the nineteenth century. It is possible that these irreverent scenes reproduce episodes from theatrical performances. It is in fact known that to relax the audience after tragedies had been played to them, farces parodying these tragedies themselves would then be presented to them. The spectators laughed heartily at these, and only a few peevish souls would censure such disrespectful take-offs. We have seen, in surveying the religious life of the Pompeiians, that the official cults of the Empire enjoyed no more than a formal, conformist and conventional devotion and that true piety was to be found in the religions of the mysteries which prepared the way for Christianity.

Beside the refined, cultivated art of the aristocratic and bourgeois houses, an art in the Hellenic tradition and copying Greek models more or less faithfully, there also existed a popular painting, much freer in its modes of expression, probably close to the Samnite or Oscan, perhaps even Etruscan, prototypes, and choosing its subjects from current events and no longer from mythology. This popular work describes with a swift and entertaining verve, as if merely dashed off, the endlessly diverting spectacle of every-day life. It is in this style of painting, expressionist, far-removed from formal academism and very modern in spirit and accent, that the parodies just spoken of are treated. In this style, too, are painted the works of artisans, rather than artists properly speaking, which adorn the shops.

Sometimes the two styles are associated, without however being mingled. Studying a work characteristic of this eclecticism, like the sign of the Pompeiian Venus which decorated the shop of Verecundus, we can distinguish in it two clearly distinct parts. In the upper register we see Venus mounted on a chariot drawn by four elephants and leaning on a rudder, emblem of the ships over which her protection extends; beside her an Eros in a yellow robe is playing with a crystal ball; cherubs flutter about in the sky. Apart from the naturalistic, almost expressionist treatment of the elephants' bodies, this painting is in conception and realization perfectly classical. In the lower register, on the other hand, are depicted workers in the weaving and dyeing shops that belonged to Caecilius Verecundus, and portrayed in the wholly natural attitudes of artisans, shop-assistants and purchasers seated in front of the counters while waiting their turn.

Despite the exquisite delicacy and most charming beauty of some of the Campanian paintings, which are true works of art, while many others are evidently 'jobbings' done by pupils or imitators of the masters, the creators of these noble pictures remain unknown. The artists of this epoch were not in the habit of signing their works; one only inscribed his name on the fresco in the House of Loreius Tiburtinus representing the death of Pyramus and Thisbe, though he contented himself with modestly setting down his praenomen: Lucius. For Tiburtinus in whose garden there was even a small temple with rather curious fountains, Lucius painted not only the sad history of Pyramus but also that of Narcissus and some episodes from the *Iliad*.

The decorative function was, we have seen, the chief purport of these paintings which enlivened the public and private buildings of the Campanian cities. It is necessary, however, to specify the nature of this decoration and the various forms it borrowed. To define the different processes of decoration, four styles have been distinguished which it is necessary to describe briefly, for the terms 'First Style, Second Style' etc., always come up when the various Pompeiian paintings are mentioned. These four styles, which remained in use concurrently, constituted however a very clear evolution of aesthetics and taste, a development of the spatial sense of the Campanian artists. This feeling for space utilizes basically the *trompe l'oeil*, but illusionism progresses from the most simple forms – simulated materials – to the most subtle and complicated, the latter of a baroque extravagance which found its last echo in the polychromatic stuccos of rococo decoration in the eighteenth century. These styles are not to be considered, in an artificial search for unity, as mutually exclusive: some apply to particular kinds of apartments: a household temple, a lararium, would not be decorated in the same way as a dining-room, a bathroom or a verandah.

The First Style, also called the Samnite or 'incrustation' style, had been the longest in use, and has remained associated, even in the terminology employed by art-historians, with the Samnites. This explains why naturally it is dominant in the 'Samnite House' of Herculaneum (where is likewise found a magnificent 'Rape of Europa'). It is this element too which gives its monumental character to the decoration of the Great Nave in the Basilica of Pompeii, and to that of the House of the Faun.

The main characteristic of the First Style is the imitation, in paint, of exotic and rare marble panels which were too difficult or costly to be obtained. In the Samnite House of Herculaneum, perfect imitations of alabaster, porphyry, antique green and Numidian black marble are thus encountered. The skill in imitation does not comprise the only merit of this style: even more to be admired is the expert feeling for proportion, for harmonies or contrasts of colour used by the painter in the arrangement of the simulated marbles. These slabs being sham inlay, a play of subtle reliefs is contrived which, competing with the polychrome, delights the eye and the understanding in a purely abstract fashion and without its being necessary to have recourse to figures or anecdotes; the First Style was long to remain admired and practised for this motif.

The progression from the First Style to the Second marks a considerable change in taste and particularly in the plastic sense. The pseudo-marbles of the previous period simply used colour contrasts and tactile illusionism which suggested the finish and grain of basalt, breccia and serpentine, but this scarcely went further, aesthetically, than the simulated woods of today's decorators. On the contrary, the spatial illusionism of the Second Style rests on a more subtle invention: the wall does not merely change its substance, it disappears, giving way to architectonic vistas so effectively disposed that the occupant of the house can believe himself in a street or public square. The glass wall so frequently used in our contemporary architecture and which does away with the hindrance of opacity between the interior and the outside, has been realized only in our time and was unattainable in that of the Pompeiians, who replaced it by a fiction: the painter represents on the

207

wall those things which are located on the other side of it – or, more accurately, which could be found there, since these painted architectures are imaginary and do not reproduce real buildings – exactly in the same way as if the wall were transparent.

'The Roman or Pompeiian painter,' writes Amedeo Maiuri, 'here accomplished a great victory in the art of wall decoration. Without having a precise knowledge of the laws of perspective, he nonetheless conquered space; for the blind wall he substitutes a spacious and luminous arrangement. Such an effort to enhance space is especially impressive in certain dark, small rooms. Without the decorations of vistas, these might well give an impression of prison cells; deprived of all other source of light, they receive it only through the door.' Maiuri justly points out as one of the best examples of Second Style painting the double-alcoved cubiculum in the Villa of the Mysteries.

On the partition of the cubiculum, we find a wall of sham marble, according to the principles of the First Style, with the glow of pavonazzo, antique green and porphyry; but between this wall and ourselves the spectators, the painter had designed a sort of colonnade of high Corinthian pillars with long fluted shafts and, resting on the capitals of these, a light architrave and graceful arch. A similar colonnade seems to stand out from the rear wall, while that wall itself is pierced, in its upper part, by a circular opening, a large dormer-window through which can be descried the top of a round temple similar to the Temple of Vesta at Rome, or that of the Sibyl of Tivoli. Thus there are four planes insinuated between the background and ourselves.

The paintings of the Third Style are composed in a still more complicated fashion, since, to the architectonic vistas of the Second, they add landscapes painted on the panels of these rooms, and illusionist landscapes presented as if seen through a window or between the columns of a portico. We notice that objects are delineated on the plinths or cornices in such a way as to emphasize the impression of a real third dimension, and that the elements of the architecture are less plausible and less realistic. The artist portrays unusual columns, vaguely resembling Egyptian lotiform or campaniform ones, which indicates that this style could have come from Alexandria.

The visitor to Pompeii will be able to study this style at leisure in the tablinum of the House of Lucretius Fronto and the atrium and cubiculum of the House of the Ceii, which contain excellent examples of it. At the back of Lucretius Fronto's garden will also be seen a grand 'exotic' picture such as the Pompeiians loved, showing an Africa of fantasy, this too perhaps of Egyptian inspiration. 'Real' landscapes and others painted in the Hellenic tradition neighbour one another, in Fronto's atrium and tablinum, and the artist has denoted with great skill the difference in atmosphere between the two modes, and contrasted the open air of the garden (made to seem real) with the *pictorial* air of the mythological paintings affixed to candelabra.

In the House of the Ceii, the painter was still more clever and skilful, for he rejected these easy and almost infantile artifices of the *trompe l'oeil:* the projecting lintels on which wine-cups are balanced, the birds posed on garlands. His composition in the cubiculum is almost entirely abstract; simply by a most adroit play of vistas, without pilasters or jutting-out columns, he makes us see the architecture as displayed in the manner of a screen from which certain panels have been removed.

The lustrous black backgrounds, shining with that remarkable brilliance dear to the Campanian painters, give these architectural views a sort of fantastical backdrop, from which the architectonic elements stand out with a powerful impression of relief. Not to be missed in the New Excavations, is the house (Region I, Insula 9, No. 5) where one of these Third Style pictures with a black background is located. Here the scene is very lightly represented, barely suggested, giving to the implied space all its breadth and striking effectiveness. This recalls to us the boldest and most powerful creations of modern scene-painting: today the decorator of that house would surely have been an *avant-garde* stage-designer.

The influence of the theatre on the paintings of the Third Style appears indubitable when we study, for example, that Pompeiian fresco which depicts a public square, with a palace façade or city gate, very cunningly *hollowed-out* in space. Tall, delicate columns and thin, light walls stand out against a great expanse of sky of a supple, warm blue-green which makes the ochre, faded rose or red-brick tones of the structures vibrate.

This still-restrained theatricalness of the Third Style, which is content merely to suggest, becomes insistent, cluttered with ornament, weighted by its own opulence, in the decorations of the Fourth Style. Deliberately it turns its back on reality and draws its components from imagination

209

and fantasy. These paintings are distinctly *baroque*, compared with those of the preceding style, which preserved a simplicity and restraint comparable to what might be called the Renaissance spirit. Campanian baroque such as it is manifested in the paintings of the Fourth Style displays characteristics analogous to those of Roman or Neapolitan Baroque of the seventeenth century: a rhetorical, bombastic emphasis, overburdened with unfunctional, superfluous detail. Through excess of skill, misusing a virtuosity grown more and more considerable, the artist means to show that for him there are no impediments and no difficulties. If the frescoes just spoken of in a Pompeiian house of the New Excavations may be compared with present-day *avant-garde* stage settings, when we look at a celebrated decoration from Herculaneum which is now in the Naples Museum we are surprised to find that this work, which is so very characteristic of the Fourth Style, resembles opera scenery of the 1900s, with its ostentatious, turbid splendour, its heavy curtains and its colonnades suspended against a void.

Such painting is evidence of a plastic art that has arrived at extreme mastery of its devices, knowing no limit in the suggestion of planes laid out to an ever-increasing distance, and observed as if under arcades between columns. The profusion of sculpted or stuccoed details, bas-reliefs, statues, acroteria, friezes and mascarons is astonishing, and there would even be some danger of the viewer being wearied by it, if the painter's virtuosity did not ceaselessly discover new spatial resolutions which evidenced the wealth of his imagination and which delight ours, drawing us endlessly into the boundless distance, to infinity.

The remarkable state of preservation of these Pompeiian and Herculanean frescoes which, after having remained for nearly two thousand years under layers of matter, emerged so fresh and intact that they might seem to have been painted yesterday, inspires the visitor to wonder what process the artists of the first century A.D. used, to give their works this lasting brilliance and durability. At Pompeii, as also in the Etruscan tombs, it is found that the paintings become damaged or discoloured on contact with the air, on being exposed to thermic and hydrometric changes, which they were spared as long as they stayed buried in the ground. Flawlessly preserved up to their discovery, they pose difficult and even agonizing problems of conservation, for the question always arises whether it is better to leave them in the place for which they were made, or to transfer them to a museum where they would have the benefit of every protective measure.

As regards the Etruscan frescoes, it seems that archaeologists are more and more in agreement to detach them, thus shielding them from temperature and humidity changes where these are harmful to them. For the Campanian paintings, however, the question does not arise in the same fashion, since those which are still *in situ* are in nearly the same state as two thousand years ago. The excellence of the materials and of the colour preparations used by the artists, makes these frescoes almost as immutable, theoretically at least, as the mosaics.

Is it correct to say *frescoes*, as one commonly does, when speaking of the Pompeiian and Herculanean paintings? These are not frescoes in the literal sense of the word, and in that which the painters of the Middle Ages and Renaissance understood by it. The Italian term *al fresco* indicates that water-colour is incorporated into the still-damp mortar, which serves it as fixative. This precludes going over the work and re-touching when it is dry, and calls for a sureness of eye and of touch in the artist, as his work must be irrevocable. Retouching after drying, or even in oils, as was done in the second half of the Renaissance, constitutes a kind of heresy in the art of the fresco. But the water-colours mixed with the fresh mortar sustain a matt, simple, almost austere effect, in which resides the nobility and even the beauty of the fresco.

So as to obtain all the effects of glitter, shine and brilliance that they sought, the Campanian painters would not limit themselves to the fresco proper. It was wax painting, such as it had been practised by the Greeks, which gave a picture the indestructible firmness and brilliance of enamel. On the other hand, the demands of this art imposed corrections, retouching and effects of thickness of actual substance impossible in the pure fresco. These artists were thus impelled to combine the various pictorial techniques of fresco, distemper (done on dry mortar and not on damp as with the fresco) and encaustic for the application of certain colours, especially vermilion.

The preparation of the wall on which the colours were applied was itself the object of expert workmanship. If, looking at the Pompeiian-Herculanean paintings, we wonder how they were executed, the various stages of the operation must be considered. Workmen first spread separate coats of rough-cast on the wall, mixing dust of alabaster and marble into the last layer, which was thus given both brilliance and firmness. This completed, the painter set to work, in fresco or distemper according to whether he was working on damp or dry mortar, strictly determining the proportions of hydrated and saponified lime.

Ancient authors, especially Pliny and Vitruvius, have left useful advice on the choice of colours, their nature and the method of using them. The palette of the Campanian artists was much richer than that of the Greeks who, according to Pliny, utilized only four colours: Melosian white, yellow from Attic ochre, Pontic sinople for reds, and ink black.

The last operation was polishing, which consisted in levelling the painted surface and making it smooth as glass and shiny as enamel. To get an idea of the difficulty which the artist had in obtaining the materials from which colours were derived, and in preparing them, we must hear the counsels of Pliny, who recommended taking the glue from the ears and genitals of bulls – bewaring always of counterfeits, for certain unscrupulous manufacturers would make this out of old skins or even boiled shoes. To re-whiten the walls, Chian earth mixed with milk was used; and to obtain vermilion, *purpurissimum* and egg were mixed on a base of sandyx. To give minium its final protection against discolouration by effects of the sun or moon, declares Vitruvius, the following delicate and difficult operation must be performed: once the wall has thoroughly dried out, a coat of very white Punic wax blended with oil must be applied with a silken brush and heated again to the sweating point by burning coals of nutgalls close to it; then it should be smoothed by rubbing with tallow and lastly with scrupulously clean cloths, as is done to a marble when it is desired to make it brilliant.

All these preparations, briefly indicated, make the visitor to the Campanian ruins understand that the paintings whose beauty, lustre and state of preservation he admires owe all these merits to the fact that the artists were at the same time chemists who perfectly comprehended the nature of the substances they used, and that the studio formulas comprising the traditional techniques rested on a precise, genuinely scientific body of knowledge, which explains the excellent state in which they still are today, whereas so many modern works spoil and fade rapidly. Easel-paintings, that is the non-mural ones, were more affected by the catastrophe of 79, as they fell from the walls on which, like pictures today, they were hung, and were lost in the ashes and molten lava; the wood which formed their support was destroyed. Paintings on marble, on the contrary, have survived. Those discovered at Herculaneum are, if not Attic originals, at least faithful copies of Greek paintings. Just as we know only one author of frescoes, Lucius, so Alexander the Athenian, the artist who executed the 'Knuckle-bones Players' of Herculaneum, signed this sensitive, enchanting masterpiece.

Of small dimensions, inserted as rare and precious objects in walls, these paintings on marble were executed in the same fashion as the Greek *lithostrota* of the fifth century B.C., that is to say in outline, on a base of pure marble, with a rare few monochromatic lightings; their impression is one of supreme, subtle delicacy and gentleness. The 'Knuckle-bones Players' is a very characteristic and fascinating example of these little pictures called by the Greek term of *pinakes*, their accomplishment being generally superior to that of the decorative paintings which sometimes give the impression of jobbery. The value attaching to the pinakes is emphasized by the fact that they were not framed like modern paintings but enclosed in a kind of small cupboard, the shutters of which were opened when it was desired to contemplate the masterpiece which they contained. On a wall of the triclinium in the suburban Villa of Porta Marina, destroyed by the earthquake of 62 and undergoing repairs in 79, there is the representation, in *trompe l'oeil*, of one of these pinakes complete with its wooden case and its doors open.

What were the preferred subjects of the Campanian painters? We can understand that these were extremely varied, according to the character of the room which they adorned and its dimensions. From the advent of the Second Style, the sham windows and pseudo-colonnades multiplied, replacing actual apertures and, as we have seen, substituting an imaginary landscape for a real one viewed through a genuine window. Here is found again that love of nature which impelled Virgil to write his Georgics and Bucolics, and which made Latins prefer their rural villas to an overcrowded Rome.

The Roman and Campanian painters are to be credited with having invented landscape painting, which was to be raised to such great heights in the centuries to come: it corresponds to a phenomenon at once psychological and social. These prototype landscapes are painted very lightly, creating an atmosphere that might be called poetic or musical quite as much as pictorial, or even more so. Delicate trees,

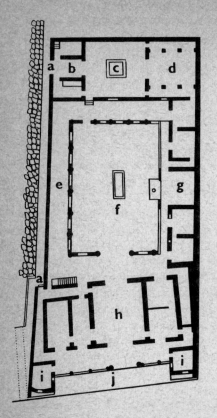

a-a   entrances
b   *fauces*
c   *atrium*
d   *tablinum*
e   *portico*
f   garden
g   *exedra*
h   *triclinium*
i-i   *diaetum*
j   *solarium*

rocks scarcely outlined, the sea indicated by barely perceptible waves, are its customary elements: fine examples are to be found in the fresco from the House of the 'Cupid Punished' and in that other Pompeiian one representing Pan amidst nymphs.

These are *classical*, decorative landscapes, somewhat conventional, requiring no effort of imagination from the artist, no search for realism: from time to time only, a fresh breath of sensitivity reminds us of the Impressionists. But there are other landscapes, which could be called Expressionist, painted with greater boldness and freedom. The scene called 'House at Midday' shows the painter's desire to create original and vigorous effects of lighting. In this work, the Campanian dominant, what could be called the native genius, is affirmed, while the classic landscape remains a survival of Greek art.

Also found at Pompeii, and especially in the House of the Orchard, are paintings on dark backgrounds, wholly comparable to those Flemish and French tapestries of the Middle Ages and the Renaissance called 'verdures'. Cleared in 1954, the House of the Orchard (Region I, Insula 9, No. 5) belonged most probably to a horticulturist, of modest status, for his house is small. It is touching to see how this person who probably spent the whole day in his garden chose to encounter his favourite trees all over again inside the house. On the walls of his cubiculum he had painted the various species which he cultivated: sorb-trees, cherries, figs, and plums, drawn to the life with, as well as their verisimilitude, a delightful, touching gracefulness. Sometimes too these 'verdures' were dotted with animals: thus we see a snake climbing along the trunk of a pear-tree in the House of the Orchard; and in another house with 'verdures', also situated among the New Excavations (Region II, Insula 6, No. 3), marvellously lifelike herons stalk among pomegranate-trees in flower and orange-trees laden with golden fruit.

These examples, and many others besides, bear out that the Campanian painters were, as much as landscapists, good animal painters. Their predilection is naturally for familiar creatures such as dogs or birds, but they frequently portray the exotic beasts to be seen rending one another apart in the circus sports, including those brought over for the celebrations at great trouble and expense: hippopotami, rhinoceroses, giraffes, tigers and lions. The anonymous creator of the sacred Bull from the Temple of Isis at Pompeii rivals the Dutch Paul Potter and the most celebrated English animal painters of the eighteenth century, James Ward and Thomas Weaver, whose bulls were famous. Likewise crocodiles from Egypt enlivened those Egyptian scenes of which the Roman world was fond; and possibly the artist had observed in nature that extraordinary combat between a cobra, hood swollen, and a heron with its feathers bristling, the figures standing out with dramatic vividness against the brilliant black of the background.

All subjects are represented in these Pompeiian and Herculanean frescoes, from the holiest to the most ordinary. Some relate to religious ceremonies, like the 'Sacrifice to Dionysos' from Herculaneum, the

'Pompeiian Venus' of the House of Marcus Lucretius Fronto (in place), the 'Adonis' of the House of Adonis (in place). From the Temple of Isis come ritual episodes, the portrait of the priest and the holy retinue. The figures, from Pompeii, of young priestesses, are charming and accurate images.

With religious subjects can be ranged mythological scenes, of which there are so many *in situ* and in the museums that it is impossible here to enumerate them, for these are chiefly documents of initiation and of the traditions of sacred import forming the basis of the myths. A considerable place is given to Homer, whose epics were known by all educated men, and perhaps even by the people, and to the celebrated Greek legends: that of Theseus, from Herculaneum; of Icarus, in the House of Amandus; of Dirce, in the House of the Mosaic Atrium; and very many others. Sometimes these are dramatic scenes suggestive of theatrical episodes which might have served the painter as models, like the 'Centaurs in the Palace of Pirithous' from Pompeii; the 'Andromeda and Perseus', also Pompeiian; the 'Achilles at Skyros' from the House of the Dioscuri; or the 'Loves of Venus and Mars' of the House of Lucretius Fronto.

Among episodes from the *Iliad* and the *Odyssey*, the strangest and most striking is the 'Trojan Horse', so modern in its idiom and so bold in execution; *in situ* at Pompeii are still to be found representations of the most celebrated passages from these poems: in the House of Siricus, the House of Menander, the House of the Tragic Poet, the House of the Cryptoporticus, the House of the Lararium, the House of Loreius Tiburtinus.

In passing we must mention the delightful figures of young girls, goddesses, priestesses and personifications of the Seasons, which were discovered at Stabiae, and which are in their charming simplicity among the most accomplished works of Campanian art. The huntress Diana on a background of turquoise blue, the Spring gathering flowers in a meadow of fresh green would be worthy of the brush of Botticelli or Titian.

In the House of Julia Felix were exhumed those everyday scenes, treated in brown or tawny *camaieu* with some rare highlights of colour, which in an ironic, terse spirit depict men on horseback, the matron going round the market followed by her little slave carrying the baskets

216

of provisions, the carrier saddling and loading his mules, the pedlars thronging the Forum with their displays of vegetables, bundles of shoes and bronze or clay vessels.

Elsewhere is seen the baker, installed in his shop, distributing large round loaves to his customers. Still elsewhere are dice-throwers bent over a flimsy table. The signs crying up the wine of a tavern or the cuisine of a restaurant have all the spontaneous liveliness, the jollity, the comic verve of a slice of life taken from the tumult of square and street and transported, just as it was, on to the plank of wood or on to the wall with its six rough coats underneath. The verisimilitude of the attitudes, the intensity of expressions, the naturalness of gesture are the same whether it is a question of circus sports, of hawkers' wrangling, of musical performances (suburban Villa of Porta Marina), of idle chit-chat in the gynaeceum (Imperial Villa, triclinium), of the childish games of cherubs imitating artisans (House of the Stags, House of the Vettii) or of the interview between a courtesan and a comic valet wearing a theatrical mask, as in that house of the New Excavations (Region I, Insula 6, No. 2).

If there is occasionally something theatrical about these popular scenes, despite the genuineness which inspires them, that is not surprising, for the Italian people were always inclined slightly to exaggerate the comic or tragic in their modes of expression, and of course in Campania as at Rome spectacles occupied a very great place in the life and preoccupations of the inhabitants. Even when the paintings do not directly reproduce a theatre scene, they are often inspired by the theatrical spirit, in the same way as Fourth Style decorations derive inspiration from the scenography in use at that period.

It would be surprising if a people so attached to the reproduction of the real, to the suggestion of what is most original and most personal in an individual, did not accord an important place to the portrait; and indeed in Campanian painting from the second century B.C., to the first A.D. there existed very numerous and fine portraits. The most celebrated, and rightly, is that of a baker and his wife, discovered painted on the wall of their shop in Pompeii. The character of these two is delineated with much sincerity and vigour; the faces, that of the man especially, have a sort of proletarian robustness, and it is understood that the painter was not trying to flatter his model. The wife,

217

of a more refined type, holds wax tablets and a style in her hand; this could indicate literary tastes; as in the portrait of the young Pompeiian girl who is depicted in the same attitude and has been named Sappho. In both cases, the baker's wife and the poetess, the young women are holding the style close to their lips, in the attitude of reflective hesitation, of someone pondering on what he is going to write. The Pompeiian 'Woman with Curls' has a more dramatic and romantic aspect than the two just cited. The painting is freer, with bolder and more expressive modelling, and Maiuri has noted here 'a provocative expression, a troubled, sensual aspect'. It is evident that the 'Woman with Curls', of which the expression is so strange that the picture has been sometimes interpreted as an image of the shepherd Paris, is quite different from the photographic portraits of the baker couple; in her is something more than exactitude of features, the perfect resemblance demanded by these artisans proud of displaying their likeness in their shop or their apartment adjoining that shop, and this something is perhaps soul, so often absent from Campanian painting, as from Roman painting generally.

This Roman painting is as a whole anecdotal and decorative; it aims to please rich and cultivated people, decorate their homes attractively and recall to them the lovely landscapes that they might have seen or imagined. True, authentic dramatic feeling without theatrical emphasis rarely appears in Pompeiian art; it is scarcely encountered save in the portrait just mentioned, in the 'Philosopher' from the Villa of Boscoreale, and in that portrait of an actor or dramatic author, sometimes named Menander, still in place at Pompeii, in the so-called House of Menander.

These two figures are too original to be seen as conventional heads. The philosopher of Boscoreale is a real living being: his Socratic head, his unquiet eyes searching the riddles of the universe, his heavy person ponderously leant on the twisted staff are, it might be said, portrayed to the life. The Menander of Pompeii is less striking, but his physiognomy is quite strongly individualized, and it is very possible that this is a portrait of the celebrated Menander, the likeness having been handed down by tradition or repeated from a known portrait of which copies were frequently made.

Mosaics

With the exception of some famous pieces, like the 'Battle of Alexander' in the House of the Faun at Pompeii, the mosaic is used for rather humble decorations, pavings, fountains or grottos, and could not be compared with painting, either in its artistic significance or for excellence and refinement of technique. Only one mosaicist is known to us by name: Felix, who signed himself on the threshold of the House of Siricus at Pompeii.

At Pompeii are found all possible kinds of mosaic, from the simplest and most primitive, which aspire nonetheless to an agreeable effect of shapes and colours, to the grandiose compositions, executed with admirable virtuosity in the use of small cubes of stone or glass, of which the most magnificent example is that 'Battle of Alexander'. For the fineness with which it reproduces the texture of a tapestry, for the vividness of colours and strength of the attitudes, this work enjoys a deserved fame; but it is probably only a copy or replica of a Greek original: the archaeologists judge it to have been executed not at Pompeii but on an Aegean island, or at Alexandria. Possibly damaged during its transport from the place of origin to the Campanian port, it was restored rather clumsily by a local mosaicist, who did not have at his disposal the stone used by the original artist. Since its discovery, in 1831, it has been variously attributed to Nicomachus, to his pupil Philoxenus of Eretria, to Aristides of Thebes, and even to a woman artist, Helena of Alexandria, who enjoyed a great renown, without it being possible to establish any certain identification. In its technique, the 'Battle of Alexander' recalls the mosaics of the suburban villa called Cicero's at Pompeii: these latter are enchanting copies of Greek originals attributed to a certain Dioscorides of Samos, which also aim obviously at giving the effect of tapestry, both by the colouring and by suggesting the very substance of the fabric.

The mosaics of pavings, grottos or fountains were more often artisan than art work properly speaking; this comparison, intended primarily as a definition, has nothing pejorative in it. At Pompeii as at Naples, Palestrina, Rome or Piazza Armerina in Sicily, the artisan-mosaicists possessed skill, ingenuity, verve and talent. They could succeed in creating the illusion of a relief by means of an adroit play of shade, especially in those colourful decorations of dining-room pavings which

219

appear covered with all sorts of fragments thrown on the floor by care-less guests: oyster-shells, fowl-bones, fish-bones, bread crusts, pieces of meat, nut-shells, fruit peel. The real artistic quality of these comic com-positions lies in the proficiency of the *trompe l'oeil* which we have already noted in the paintings of the three last styles. The tactile illusion is so great that some naïve visitor unprepared for this decoration might quite seriously have bent down to pick up what a diner had let fall.

There is, moreover, something picturesque and fanciful in the figures of dogs which adorn the thresholds, warning visitors to 'beware of the dog'. The inscription *cave canem* which, as we have seen, accompanied the image of the watch-dog, was superfluous, his aspect was intimidating enough in itself. The *cave canem* of Pompeii with his lead of tawny leather, and the *canis catenarius* (dog on a chain) of the vestibule in the House of Proculus at Pompeii, are images full of vividness and colour. The mosaicist of the House of Proculus portrayed the animal crouched in front of a door, shown in perspective, with one leaf open, thus im-posing a still greater vigilance upon the dog.

A well-known habit of the Romans was that of passing from hand to hand, at the end of a banquet, either silver vessels decorated with skele-tons, like that of the Boscoreale, or skeletons of wood, ivory or metal, sometimes jointed so as to make their aspect more impressive. These figures embody the poet's counsel to enjoy life here below, for we do not know what awaits us in eternity, nor even if there is an eternity. Thus we must hasten to take advantage of all the pleasures which life can give, and these pleasures were varied for the Latins, as evidenced by frescoes representing guests at table, eating and drinking and at the same time caressing women lying beside them on the triclinium couches, while musicians are playing and dancers doing their turns.

Instead of inspiring melancholy, these skeletons at the end of the feast only further aroused the revellers' impatience to exhaust all pleasures. There exists in the Museum of the Thermae at Rome a triclinium-paving mosaic in which the image of the skeleton, raised on its elbow and facing the spectator and sneering, bears in Greek the inscription 'Know thy-self'. The mosaic skeleton of Pompeii is a fearsome thing: on the white background framed with black it stands out in its terrible simplicity; in each hand it holds a pitcher of wine. It is Death which supplies drink to man, to make him forget all cares.

Portraits too in mosaic existed in Pompeiian houses: for example, that likeness of a woman found in the alcove of a cubiculum; undoubtedly this is the mistress of the house and the occupant of the room, and it is an image of remarkable verisimilitude, full of life and expression. Utilizing an extremely clever technique, placing his highlights, with stones of brighter colour, on the bridge of the nose and in the corners of the eyes, the artist made this mosaic truly eloquent. It has sometimes been compared to the funeral portraits of the same period found in the Egyptian tombs at Fayoum. Without it being necessary to posit an interchange between two centres of culture as far removed from each other as Campania and Egypt, it can be noted once again that the principal characteristics of Roman art such as it was practised in Italy and in all dependent countries, politically or aesthetically, of Rome, is realism, that is to say an accentuation, together with a photographic accuracy, of the special detailed features of the subject.

The theatrical scenes often repeated in painting appear also in mosaics. We find an example of this in that fragment of paving which represents Silenus sitting astride an ass which is collapsing under the weight of the old drunkard, and which two men are trying to lift up: memorial to a farce which probably had had considerable success in the Theatre and which the artist enjoyed perpetuating in the tablinum of the House of Proculus. Another theatrical scene portrays strolling musicians, one of whom shakes a kind of tambourine, another castanets, while a woman plays the double-flute. The presence of a thin, wan, sickly child with an ugly and prematurely wrinkled face emphasizes the wretchedness of these poor people struggling to entertain the passers-by so as to earn a bit of money. An inscription attributes this work to the Greek artist Dioscorides of Samos, as previously mentioned, but it is difficult to know if this Dioscorides is the author of the mosaic itself, discovered in the Villa of Cicero at Pompeii, or the creator of a celebrated original of which this would be a copy. Whichever it is, copy or original, the work is very beautiful, most cunningly executed, rich in colour and highly diverting by the drollery of the buffoons' gestures. The famous and splendid frieze of the House of the Faun, depicting tragic masks hung from garlands of flowers and fruit, can also be related to the theatre. To the circus games pertains the mosaic of wrestlers, found in the Forum Thermae, showing the pugilists in attitudes that are characteristically natural and colourful. But the most beautiful of the 'theatrical mosaics' is that Pompeiian one introducing us into the wings before the performance; a musician is rehearsing on his flute, two dancers disguised as satyrs try out new steps, and a manservant is dressing an actor in the vast robe which will lend him authority and majesty, while a bearded old man, perhaps the author of the piece, gives the actors his last admonitions, choosing from among the masks piled at his feet those which they will be wearing just now on the stage. This episode in the daily life of theatre folk is stamped with the utmost conviction and a most charming liveliness; from the aspect of technical execution, as well, it is a masterpiece among Campanian mosaics.

The customary themes of the mosaic, it is seen, are – with the exception of the *cave canem*, the skeleton and the unswept paving – the same as those of painting. Historic scenes, views, genre pictures, portraits; to this list must be added still-lifes, numerous and remarkably fine as they are. We here mention, from among the best and most representative of works decorating triclinia with subjects suitable to a dining-room: the birds of the House of the Faun, three tame white turtle-doves perched at large on the walls of their cage, a cat devouring a partridge, ducks biting water-lily stems amidst a crowd of multicoloured fish, a cock-fight.

Sculpture

The observations just now made on the realism which dominated the painting of portraits in Campanian art apply equally to sculpture. Although the Naples Museum and the Antiquarium of Pompeii are very rich in bronze and marble sculptures, discovered at Pompeii and Herculaneum, and although in these two cities there are also extant a great number of them which were left, or put back, in place, their abundance does not equal that of the paintings. For a very simple reason: on the day of the eruption of Vesuvius, certain inhabitants fled with all that they could take in the way of statues and statuettes, providing these were not too heavy or unwieldy. After the catastrophe, some fugitives returned to retrieve such objects as were recoverable from the ruins of their houses: these naturally included statues.

Moreover, when the first excavations began to break open the ground of Herculaneum and Pompeii, it was again portable objects, rare and valuable ones worthy to grace collections, which the clandestine diggers sought. They troubled little about paintings which could not be detached from walls and which often could not be distinguished in the rooms filled with every kind of rubble. The sculptures, moreover, easily found buyers and emigrated most often to foreign museums. Until the time when Italy took very strict measures to prevent or control this dispersal of works of art, the treasures of Pompeii and Herculaneum continued to be sent off to adorn the showcases of public and private collections.

It can also be noted that with the exception of some very beautiful pieces which will be spoken of presently, Campanian sculpture like that of Rome was often content with copying famous Greek originals. All public buildings, thermae, temples, forums, theatres being decorated with an incredible profusion of statues, in their hundreds and thousands, it is easy to understand that not all were of an equal artistic value. The new-rich of Pompeii, who frequently possessed but little culture and taste, were satisfied with mediocre works manufactured for them by clever artisans rather than by artists properly speaking. The best sculptures were those brought from Greece or Egypt, since Alexandria had become one of the most active centres of Hellenistic art and culture. The local product could not compete with the creation of foreign masters, and we are not acquainted with a single Roman sculptor of true genius; but the especial talent of the Campanians was practised, as with painting, in the portrait.

Portraits in marble or bronze, through the artist's will to discover the individuality of the sitter and to express his especial nature distinguishing him from all others whether physically or spiritually, constitute the best of Campanian sculpture. This need of material and psychological individuation is a phenomenon of very general character, since it is encountered equally in Egypt and in the Eastern countries marked by Graeco-Roman culture, at Antioch, Pergamum and Alexandria. What distinguishes the Campanian artists is this popular animation, this verisimilitude carried almost to the level of caricature – so loath was the artist to idealize his subject – and the liveliness of facial expression, the whole personality of the model concentrated in the bust.

The bust of the banker Caecilius Jucundus, that of the actor Norbanus Sorex, that of the gentleman Cornelius Rufus, are numbered among the masterworks of this Pompeiian sculpture. Most often these busts which were portraits of the master of the house or of a famous person, were placed on a plinth or a pedestal at the rear of the atrium. Often freedmen had a bust done of their master, in gratitude for the act which had given them their liberty, and presented to him.

This was the case with Jucundus's bust, which discloses to us in a few minutes all we want to know about his character. The artist has defined it admirably, with that authoritarian and wily look, and the wrinkles of cupidity and avarice betraying the false good-nature of the sensual, thick-lipped mouth. The low forehead, the loose ears and an air of vulgarity 'place' Jucundus.

The gentleman Cornelius Rufus whose bust is still in place in the atrium of his Pompeiian residence was a quite different character. The balding forehead, hollowed by deep wrinkles but broad and high, and the gravity of the regard, meditative and thoughtful, would be those of an intellectual; the lower part of the face, with receding chin, pinched and almost lipless mouth, and cheeks ploughed deeply by emotions and cares, reveals an unquiet, tormented nature, almost woeful or anguished by dint of its complexity.

Again different is the actor Norbanus Sorex. In the bronze bust the eyes, formerly inlaid in the sockets, are missing. For these, mother-of-pearl, ivory, onyx or ebony would faithfully render the colour of the iris and the brilliance of the gaze. Despite the empty sockets, the bust of the actor is extraordinarily animated; in it may be recognized a man accustomed to embody very diverse characters and to move the auditors by his voice and gestures. Even if we did not know the profession once practised by Sorex, this portrait would tell us it, so expressive and revealing is the work. This is not only a Pompeiian actor of the first century A.D. whom we have before us, but much more, the actor himself, the actor in his consummate essence, in the specialness of his profession and his art.

Realistic also, but at the same time idealized, as is only fitting when it is a question of personages of the Imperial family, are the portraits of Livia and of Marcellus, nephew and adoptive son of the Emperor, which are in the Pompeii Antiquarium. Marcellus, sung of by Virgil, showed great promise but died at Baia aged scarcely twenty years; here he is depicted in pontifical garb, his head covered with a veiling that falls

17. House of the Bicentenary at Herculaneum. The upstairs room, with the Cross and the little wooden cupboard-altar, supposedly Christian.

18. Detail from the bronze statue of the Citharist Apollo. Naples Museum.

19.   Bronze statue of a young wild boar. Naples Museum.

20. House of the Stags. Herculaneum. Marble statuette, representing a drunken Hercules.

21. House of the Stags, Herculaneum. One of the marble groups, representing a stag beset by hounds, from which the name of the house is derived.

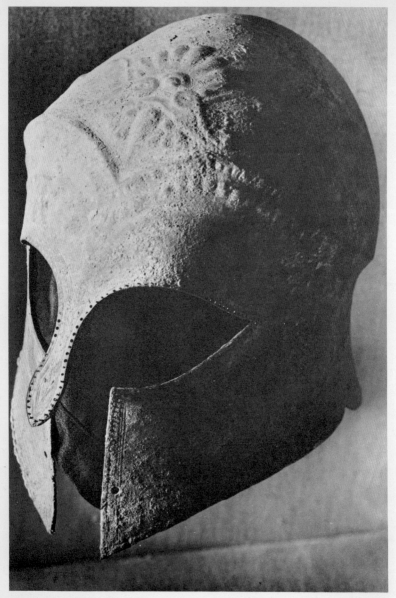

22.   Bronze helmet, of the type worn by Greek hoplites. Naples Museum.

23. Head of a woman, in marble. Naples Museum.

24. Bronze statue of a flamen. Naples Museum. — found at Herculaneum.

to his shoulders. The title and functions of *pontifex* explain this solemn, almost hieratical gravity which darkens his young and pleasant face; for similar reasons, a like expression is found in the portrait of Livia. The Pompeiians, as we have observed, had dedicated a cult to the Emperor's wife, the personification of all Roman feminine virtues. She was considered as the model of piety because, extremely attached to the old religious customs, she supervised their scrupulous observance. Thus she is represented here in the garb of a priestess, almost of a divinity, in this statue which was discovered among the remains of the Villa of the Mysteries, whose lararium it had adorned.

Also on view at the Antiquarium is the portrait of one of the Istacides who were, it is thought, the owners of the Villa of the Mysteries. Their 'family vault', from which this statue comes, was a splendid mausoleum, erected in the Necropolis of the Porta Ercolano, and in its centre stood a little circular temple, restored not long since, where the statues of the deceased were assembled.

Pompeii was not alone in possessing numerous statues; a great number, of considerable beauty, have been found at Herculaneum. The most remarkable is surely the equestrian statue of Marcus Balbus,[48] in which the horseman has the severe, austere and chilly majesty of exalted personages of Roman society. The pictorial realism is linked here to a kind of official formalism which stiffens the individual in a conventional attitude which is that of *function*. The horse, on the other hand, like the horses of the famous bronze quadriga, is admirable in its truth and naturalness; details of the mane, veins, the play of muscles beneath the skin, bear witness to the fact that the anonymous sculptor, or sculptors, of these works were great animal artists.

Also at Herculaneum, an archaic statue of Athena Promachos was discovered in the suburban Villa of the Papyri, where the ambulacrum of the peristyle was a veritable museum of sculptures, proving at once the taste, wealth and eclecticism of the villa's owner. Among the masterworks of this collection must be numbered the fine bronze bust of the poet Eschinus or Pseudo-Seneca, remarkable for the dramatic vividness of the very expressive face of a hirsute and fleshless old man; also the graceful Mercury in Repose; the Wrestlers, copy of a celebrated Greek statue; the delightful female dancers; and the likenesses, bronze or marble, of animals, among which the group of Deer is the best.

There are a great number of fauns as well, in all postures, dancing, sleeping, drunken. From the Villa of the Papyri also come the bronze bust of a woman, believed to represent Sappho; a charming statue of a young Roman woman, her draperies done with exquisite taste and her hair in the fashion of the reign of Tiberius; and a precious Greek original, probably the most remarkable of all those yielded up by the ruins of the Campanian cities: the bronze bust of an athlete, dating from the fifth century B.C.

Coming back to Pompeii, it must be remembered that before the Roman domination, at the time when the Samnites were masters of Campania, there already existed a refined art here. The best examples of this Oscan-Samnite art, strongly influenced and instructed as it was by the Greeks, are in the Antiquarium: the remains of the Temple of Dionysos, the altar and pediment; the capitals, coloured or not, with figures, very different from the usual Roman art and much more so from Greek art; and the terra cotta temple decorations which comprise the most ancient evidences of Pompeiian plastic art, since certain of these decorative objects go back to the fifth or even sixth century B.C. It is known that there existed in the Forum, as early as the sixth century, a temple dedicated to Apollo by the Greeks of Cumae who, as has been related in a previous chapter, took Pompeii; this temple was enlarged and restored after the victory of 425 B.C. over the Etruscans.

The capitals with sculpted figures, which sometimes are painted as well, are commonly placed in Samnite art. Those on view in the Antiquarium are from various houses: the House of the Bull, the House of the Figured Capitals, the House of the Coloured Capitals and House 17 of the Via Consolare. The figures sculpted on these capitals sometimes display affinities with Etruscan art: especially that portraying a couple in the attitude which the Etruscans used for portraits of the deceased on tombs. Others, like that of the Maenad, are frankly Campanian, Samnite in their robust and straightforward realism.

The altar and pediment of the Dionysiac sanctuary, found in 1947 on the Hill of Sant'Abbondio a little apart from the city, are of a more complex character. The rites of the cult of Dionysos had been prohibited, it will be recalled, by the *senatus-consultus* forbidding the Bacchanals, a chief element of this cult. The figures of the pediment, pre-dating this epoch – the Dionysos-Liber, the Ariadne, the Eros holding a *flabellum* –

226

are interesting in that they show the very clear imprint with which the Oscan or Samnite character, an Italic one at all events, marked the Hellenic art introduced into Campania by the Greeks. The altar had been dedicated, as the inscription in the Oscan tongue shows, by Maras Atiniis, a municipal official of the Samnite period. By his order, probably, the pediment too was scuplted in the vigorous, original and touching style of those early inhabitants of southern Italy.

The technique of decorative reliefs in stucco, an old Italian tradition which has remained in favour to this day, was extensively employed at Pompeii and Herculaneum for the decoration of public and private buildings. The finest remains elsewhere of this clever, subtle, exquisite art, of which the Roman masterpiece is the Basilica of the Porta Maggiore, cannot rival this marvellous underground sanctuary at Pompeii. The most beautiful decorative and figured stuccos are those of the apodyterium of the Stabian Thermae and of the tepidarium in the Forum Thermae.

As for art objects belonging to what are called the 'minor arts' or the 'decorative arts', they are innumerable and to be found in all the museums – having escaped the various disastrous fates of spoils in the barbarian invasions or to clandestine diggers, or of plunder to the conquerors who melted down unnumbered quantities of gold, silver and bronze vessels simply to utilize their metal.

If large sets like the silver plate of the House of Menander or the treasure of Boscoreale are rare, nonetheless at the time when the prospecting of the ruins at Herculaneum and Pompeii began, there were precious vessels, candelabra, tables, beds and bronze seats in all the houses, and everything of a splendid, exquisite workmanship. We proceed with amazement and, ultimately, a slight, sated weariness through the halls of the Naples Museum where these objects are displayed; and there also exist storerooms where pieces, also very numerous, of interest only to specialists are kept. I do not refer to that so-called 'secret' part of the Museum, where particularly indecent objects are shown only to the few.

The character of luxury cities which Herculaneum and Pompeii possessed, inhabited as they were by wealthy merchants and art-lovers of refined taste, brought it about that most ordinary objects became things of beauty in their materials and workmanship. The gladiators, for example, must have been vain indeed to wear – for the procession, if not in combat – bronze helmets adorned with fine relief figures, as are seen at Naples, with the greaves delicately worked and the cuirasses splendid. A similar ostentation characterized the new-rich in the banquets they gave, of which the famous banquet of Trimalchio is scarcely a caricature. With this reservation, we can only praise the desire of these Campanians and the people who came to spend the winter here or for the cures, to have the merest utility object made into a pleasure for the eye and to the touch.

The sculpted and chased silver cups, the precious and fragile glass flagons, of which a number have survived, the carved cameos and the intaglios are works of art of high quality. What still further manifests the refinement of the Campanians are those table stoves, similar to braziers, of which several examples exist in the Naples Museum; these burned a special wood, called by a Greek name, *akapnon*, which did not smoke and so incommode the guests. On these braziers certain dishes were re-heated or even cooked, the Pompeiians having got from Rome a love of complicated cuisine, of rare and expensive foods the preparation of which involved great pains, and over which the master of the house himself would sometimes preside.

Lamps too were monumental, and it could even happen that a bronze statue, a Greek original, like the Ephebus, might serve as central support. In other candelabra, these supports are in the shape of trees realistically depicted with their roots and knotted branches, or of columns with delicately sculpted capitals, or of sphinxes, Silenuses or infants.

If the civilization of a people is measured in the beauty of material and form of ordinary objects, the Pompeiians and Herculaneans had reached that level which sometimes seems even to be the beginning of decadence. Decadence occurs when the functionality, the utility value of an object is sacrificed for the benefit of ornament, which then becomes superfluous and detrimental. Seeing the dishes and cups whose backgrounds are decorated with figures in high relief, very beautiful too, which are called *emblemata*, we wonder if such cups and dishes were really used, or if they were simply displayed on a table or sideboard to rouse the admiration and envy of visitors.

Jewellery

In antique jewellery the artist's workmanship was prized more highly than the largeness or beauty of the precious stones which went into the making of the jewels. This was probably because Roman civilization did not enjoy that profusion of diamonds, emeralds, sapphires and rubies such as were extracted from South African and American mines; and India did not readily export her most beautiful gems. The Hellenic taste that formed Campanian society rejected as vulgar all ostentation of material wealth: it was well enough for Orientals, for Barbarians.

In Greece, therefore, as with the Etruscans and at Rome, what was esteemed above all was the goldsmith's talent at working in gold, at modelling and chasing minute figurations in which all the detail nonetheless remained recognizable. Filigree, which is a very ancient technique, enables the creation of tiny masterpieces, representing cupids, heads of bulls or lions, or bunches of fruit, to form necklaces and ear-rings.

Pearls were much sought after, and through the Latin authors we know what zeal the Empresses and Roman great ladies displayed in getting them from the Orient; but it must not be forgotten that Rome had long been a State in which simplicity, even austerity, counted as supreme values. Sumptuary laws periodically chastised excesses of gastronomic greed or of elegance; rusticity, even, was for a long time the rule, in keeping with the precepts of the elder Cato, who exalted the 'Republican virtues'. The pleasure of wearing magnificent jewels was long considered reprehensible, and inimical to the people, who frequently criticized the luxury of the nobles and the rich and counted it as a grievance against them.

When the Empire replaced the Republic, and progressively as the influence of the Orient, Egypt, Syria and Asia Minor became preponderant, this severity lessened and relaxed. Exotic cults brought, with their strange idols, colleges of priests and priestesses covered with splendid jewels. As happens today, power and prosperity softened the descendants of the old Romans, who had had an exaggerated simplicity of manners and tastes; and those absurd, repugnant excesses at table, as described by the ancient authors, and that excessive wearing of magnificent clothing and jewels, came into force, already presaging the Later Empire and Byzantium.

229

In Campania, where the population was very mixed and Easterners were numerous, it was natural that luxury should not be proscribed as rigorously as at Rome. The Pompeii known to us is that of the Empire, and customs had changed considerably since the fall of the Republic. We will not then be surprised to find the art of the goldsmith himself presenting little originality now; lazily he works in the shadow of Etruscan and Ionian jewellers, those, in other words, inspired by an aesthetic more Eastern even than Greek, so that it is most frequently Syrian, Egyptian, even Aegean motifs that recur in the necklaces, rings, ear-rings and pendants issuing from Pompeiian workshops and it is not easy to distinguish imported jewels from those made by local artists.

Scantily supplied with precious stones, antiquity highly esteemed the semi-precious ones, like the agate, cornelian, jasper and lapis lazuli. At Pompeii as in all the great ancient cities these semi-precious stones were worked with a very considerable skill. The art of the intaglio, with its meticulous, minute precision, was confined to an upper artisan group, like that of the cameo, which requires still more virtuosity. The cameos found in the workshops of gem-cutters, or among 'treasures' abandoned at the moment of the eruption, are of great interest: here in fact may be observed the skill with which the artist utilizes the veins of an onyx or sardonyx, the different strata of the stone and its varied colours, to create compositions with numerous figures, highly animated. Most often, however, these are ring settings comprising images of gods, allegorical characters or magical signs protecting the person wearing this ring against the evil eye, and conferring on him all the advantages of a favourable talisman.

Surveying as a totality the art of Pompeii and Herculaneum, we note that its chief manifestation, the one most to be admired for the originality of its forms and for its diversity of expressions, was painting. In the province of sculpture, the Campanians did nothing which the Greeks had not already done better, and often they were content with copying Hellenic statues. In the fresco, on the contrary, they invented a new conception of space and new modes of expressing it; and in the world history of painting, the Campanian masterpieces deserve a place of honour.

CONCLUSION

The Pompeiian Decoration Conquers Europe

IT was not only archaeologists and historians who came hastening to survey and study the remains of Pompeii and Herculaneum as soon as the news of their discovery spread throughout cultivated society in the European countries. This phenomenon, extraordinary enough in itself, of a civilization miraculously preserved under the ashes of a volcano, had the power to capture men's imaginations. They readily – and somewhat immoderately – pictured intact houses with all objects remaining exactly where they were at the moment of the eruption; they imagined they were going to enter into intimate contact with a people vanished all those long centuries ago and to learn the secrets of their daily life. There was not a traveller to southern Italy who did not set aside several days of his stay at Naples for a visit to these strange and moving wonders. To visit the Theatre of Herculaneum by torchlight, under sixty-odd feet of earth, to go through those cuniculi similar to the underground passages that they had already explored in the Roman catacombs, was a fascinating adventure for the English, German or French tourist.

Artists also experienced this, but, not content with the superficial emotional reaction, they analysed the essential characteristics of Pompeiian art and wondered what could be salvaged out of it to nourish a new art inspired by antiquity. At the same period when architects were enthusing over the temples of Paestum, to the point of filling the European capitals with Doric colonnades out of their element under the skies of London, Paris or Berlin, as did the Adams, Chalgrin and Schinkler, painters marvelled at those delicate, graceful decorative motifs, full of imagination and fantasy. Pompeii set the tone for everything relating to decorative art, and the stuccoer now often replaced the cabinet-maker.

Robert and James Adam were familiar with Piranesi's collection, and they prided themselves on having 'with some success captured the spirit of beautiful antiquity and made it prevail in a new fashion in all their works'. They also plumed themselves upon having 'tried to introduce a mode of decoration different from all that had been done up to now in Europe: style and ornaments borrowed from vases and urns of the Etruscans'. The confusion prevailing in the eighteenth century over the Etruscans, some of whose tombs had been discovered and excavated, caused almost everything relating to ancient Italy to be called 'Etruscan'. For a long time the Greek vases found in tombs in Tuscany and Umbria continued to be so called. This passion for the Tuscans' ancestors, these highly mysterious Tusci, likewise inspired Wedgwood to give the name 'Etruria' to his porcelain works, where he imitated antique models.

The Neo-classical style dominant at the end of the eighteenth century does not owe a great deal to the Neo-classicism, derived from Nero's House of Gold, which inspired Giovanni da Udine and Raphael's *loggie* at the Vatican. The antiquity with which Renaissance artists and humanists were smitten did not really suit the taste of the rococo period; but the *Pompeiian style*, as the decorators who adapted it in the great capitals called it, was exactly what perhaps unconsciously was wanted – because it embodied the rococo period of Roman art – by a society tired of the plumes and fountains and fantastical boughs of dying baroque.

Pompeiian decoration became the background on which all decorators anxious to do something 'modern' were to draw. Medallions in the antique style were affixed everywhere, stucco motifs were placed on ceilings and walls. There was no longer any other concept of beauty comparable with the antique; its excellence and superiority in all spheres were laid down as laws. Painters and sculptors from every country made their pilgrimage to Pompeii, whereas fifty years earlier they would scarcely have gone farther south than Rome; and, with the seal of approval of Mengs and Winckelmann, the Portici Museum was renowned for presenting the aesthetic of supreme perfection.

It is Goethe who best reflects this new-born sensibility in describing his visit to Pompeii and Herculaneum, in his *Italian Journey*. He also admires the accord between nature and works of art in these cities, and he yields alternately to pleasure in contemplating the frescoes and sculptures, and to an inclination to philosophize on the fragility and precariousness of beauty, of gladness, of sensual and aesthetic joy.

We find the same admiration, the same delight, a hundred years later in a traveller who is not a poet but a painter: Auguste Renoir. 'Leaving Rome, I took the Naples road,' he wrote to Ambroise Vollard. 'You have no idea of the respite it was for me when I arrived at that city absolutely filled with Pompeiian and Egyptian art. I was beginning to be a little tired of Italian painting, always the same draperies and the same virgins. What I so admire in Corot is that he gives you everything in a treetop. And, you know, it was Corot himself whom I found again intact in the Naples Museum, with that Pompeiian and Egyptian simplicity of workmanship. Those priestesses in their silver-grey tunics could be taken absolutely for Corot nymphs.' It is spirit rather than form, the vibrancy of Pompeiian painting, which causes Renoir's delight, proving that that art, delicate, restrained and tremulous as it is, retains an extraordinary vitality, since modern painters can discover a beauty always contemporary in it.

This immediacy of effect rather than a retrospective one is the prime feature of the 'Pompeiian experience' felt by today's visitor. It would be a mistake to compare Pompeii and Herculaneum with museums: the latter are necropoles, however ingeniously laid out they may be; in them the past appears irremediably dead. In the Campanian cities, however, it is otherwise; and this effect enhances their art, with its altogether dazzling grace of perpetual youth.

NOTES

1. See, in Marcel Brion, *La Révolte des Gladiateurs* (Paris, 1952), the history of Spartacus and his associates. Also, everything relating to the general situation of the gladiators, their armaments and fighting method, and the way in which the games were organized.

2. On the situation of slaves, see Paoli, *La vie quotidienne dans la Rome antique* (*Vita Romana*), (Paris, 1955) and the ancient historians. According to Athenaeus, certain rich Romans could sometimes own up to 20,000 slaves. Horace, although of simple habits, had three to wait at table; but Tigellius had 200. Men of modest status would be accompanied by three when they went to the *thermae*. The cruellest punishments were inflicted on those slaves who committed serious offences, and it was not until the reign of Hadrian that the master's power of life and death over his servants was annulled, and not until that of Constantine was the murder of a slave punishable like an ordinary homicide.

3. The best known Vesuvian growths were the Pompeianum and the Lympa Vesuvina. The vine does not seem to have been natively Italian. It is traditionally believed to have been introduced there by an Etruscan who brought it from Marseille. The Italian wines that were most famous in antiquity were the Caecuban, Falernian, Massic, and those of Mammerto, Sorrento and Spoleto; also the wines of Latium were highly esteemed in Tuscany. Heavy, rather indigestible wines were imported from Spain, Africa and Greece. Very thick, resinated or mixed with honey, these could not be drunk undiluted: they were normally mixed with four parts of water. To drink neat wine appeared the height of alcoholism.

4. The pine to which Pliny compares this smoke cloud is the genus called parasol pine, very common in southern Italy.

5. Jérôme Carcopino's *Études d'histoire Chrétienne* (Paris, 1953) contains a most interesting theory on the origin of the graffito 'Sodom, Gomorrah' which was found – for it has disappeared since its discovery – in house 26 of Region IX, Insula 1. This author believes these words to have been written after the eruption, probably by one of the diggers who had risked a return to the ruins now that the catastrophe had abated. 'Unless we endow Pompeii with Jews or Christians possessing second sight, this consigning of the pagan Pompeii to that punishment visited by God on

Sodom and Gomorrah is the unmistakable type of *post eventum* preaching, and would have been directed only after the event at the buried city.'

6. With the exception, of course, of the animal skeletons found in the Foro Boario, the Bovine Forum.

7. The funeral feast was part of the obsequies (Festus, 295) on the actual day of the ceremony, and was repeated on certain anniversaries: notably, on the ninth day after burial, when it was called the *cena novemdialis*, and a year later, as the Festival of the Parentalia. Those present ate and drank to the health of the deceased. While tombs were still of a simple kind, these meals took place either in front of the monument itself or in the family home. Later when monumental tombs were the thing, the feasts were celebrated inside.

8. That quite a number of inhabitants returned to dig in the ruins after the catastrophe, and that throughout antiquity looters drawn here by the rumour of treasures took the risk of sinking shafts, is indubitable. Della Corte published a most authoritative essay on this subject in the Mélanges Parvan (Bucharest, 1934): *Esplorazioni di Pompei immediatamente successive alla catastrofe dell'anno 79*. Certain graffiti in the House of the Golden Cupids were most probably scribbled by one of these clandestine diggers; in particular, this phrase, analogous to the 'Sodom, Gomorrah' previously mentioned: 'The place where the harlot drank is no more than a heap of stone and ashes'. The words *'domus pertusa'* ('house broken through') deciphered here were perhaps a direction given by one of these diggers to another. On this question, see the statements of Carcopino, op. cit., pp. 62 et seq.

9. An extremely handsome work was produced by the French engraver Charles Nicolas Cochin, *Observations sur les antiquités d'Herculanum*, and published in Paris in 1755.

10. See, in the Letters of Pliny the Younger (II, 17), the description of the ideal villa, which in fact resembles the plan of Pliny's own villa at Lavinium – as re-established by Winnefeld – rather than his Tuscan villa also spoken of in his letters (V, 6) and likewise reconstituted by Winnefeld. In Letter IX, 36, comes the account of the life led by the cultivated gentleman in his country residence.

11. Some streets were designated in antiquity by the kind of shops most numerous in them. Particular trades or industries would group themselves preferably in certain quarters. The denominations indicate this: Vicus Sandaliarius (Street of Cobblers), Vicus Turarius (Perfumers' Street), Vicus Bubularius (Cattle-dealers' Street), Vicus Materarius (Timber Merchants' Street), Vicus Frumentarius (Street of Corn Chandlers), Vicus Alliarius (Street of Garlic Merchants), for example.

12. Altars to the Lares situated in the streets were available for the devotions of those who, whether poor folk or slaves or travellers, had no Lararium at home. Their

Lares were hence the Lares Compitales, those 'of the cross-roads'; in their chapels the Compitalia, the festival of the lowly, was celebrated in January.

13. On the question of Oriental religions, see Franz Cumont, *Les religions orientales dans le paganisme romain* (Paris, 1929). Also: N. Turchi, *La Religione di Roma Antica* (Rome, 1939); M. Rostovtzev, *Mystic Italy* (New York, 1927); G. Wissowa, *Religion und Kultur der Römer* (Munich, 1921).

14. Were there Christians at Pompeii? On this strongly controversial and much disputed question, the most valid conclusions would seem to be those of J. Carcopino, in the *Études d'historie Chrétienne* already cited. Was the cross in the House of the Bicentenary at Herculaneum actually a Cross? This symbol was adopted slowly in Christian society; according to some authors it did not appear before the fifth century. As to the sign marked on the amphora found in the House of Venus, which sign Maiuri sees as the monogram of Christ, the two Greek letters *chi* and *rho* linked together, Carcopino is of the opinion that these are figures indicating the weight of liquid content of this receptacle.

'To begin with, it is more than doubtful that Pompeii and Herculaneum harboured Christians before disappearing. Certainly in the last chapters of the Acts of the Apostles St. Paul is seen to land at Pozzuoli, final port of call on his voyage to Rome, and there be immediately welcomed by co-religionists who begged him to "pass seven days with them." But despite the nearness of Pozzuoli, on the north of the Bay of Naples, both to Herculaneum and to Pompeii, there is no comparison between the great port which drew the convoys from the East to Rome, a port whose mixed population comprised all the races of the Empire, and on the other hand cities of bourgeois retirement and holiday-making. At all events, it is a fact that Tertullian denied at the end of the second century that a hundred years earlier Christians had been on the scene when Pompeii was asphyxiated.' Carcopino, op. cit., pp. 49–50.

If St. Paul had thought he would find Christians at Pompeii, it is perhaps there that he would have disembarked — or at Herculaneum. In any case, the question is not fully resolved.

15. For definitive enlightenment on the origins and significance of the 'magic square,' see the work cited above by J. Carcopino, which contains a penetrating, exhaustive discussion of this problem.

16. On the *periplus* of Ptolemy, see Marcel Brion, *La Résurrection des Villes Mortes* (new edition, Paris, 1959), Vol. 1, pp. 161 et seq.: especially in regard to the curious Roman trading-posts in India, Cranganore, Muziris, and Arikamedu.

17. On this conception of Venus as mother and fecundating power of the whole universe, see the splendid invocation of Lucretius at the opening of his *De Rerum Natura*.

18. 'The Lararium was originally a simple hollow, a niche or an unpretentious cupboard above the ancestral hearth (*focus patrius*) where the sacred fire burnt

perpetually; it contained the waxen statuette of the Lar Familiaris – often depicted as a young man in a short tunic and high boots, poised on one foot, crowned with laurel and holding a horn of plenty or a *rhyton* (drinking-cup) – which guarded the house and the whole family, together with the statues of the two Penates, represented as two seated youths, who were the protectors of wealth and abundance, if their name is in fact derived from *penus* (provision). Subsequently the Lararium was magnified often to the point of faithfully reproducing in miniature the image of a temple.' Paoli, op. cit., pp. 232–3.

It is in this form that the Lararium appears in the Pompeiian houses where it is still to be found *in situ*. A serpent is often portrayed on it, this creature representing the domestic genius, the *genius familiaris*, in keeping with a very ancient tradition common to all the peoples of the Mediterranean basin, notably the Greeks. The reptile here functions as a Chthonian symbol.

19. On the cult of Isis in Campania, and its representations, the reader is referred to Olga Elia, *Le Pitture del Tempio di Iside* (Rome, 1941).

20. The best analysis of the ancient mysteries and in particular of the Mysteries of Dionysos, such as they were celebrated in southern Italy in the first century A.D., is to be found in Leopold Feiler, *Mysterion* (Vienna, 1946).

21. The street leading from the sea; in antiquity it undoubtedly bore the same name as today.

22. The various working techniques of the fullers are known from the signs representing them, which are very realistic and completely accurate. And also by the workshops which have been found installed in certain houses, as will be seen farther on.

23. The Latin word *venatio* designates the hunt in general: from it, of course, the word 'venison' is derived. It was applied to those circus games imitating a hunt, in which the horsemen pursued and slaughtered savage beasts; the term was extended, subsequently, to include those contests in which animals were set on one another, and in which men no longer participated. For people unable to afford the luxury of real hunting, this great battle provided the spectacle and excitement which actual sportsmen so adored, but with the added advantage of there being no danger. 'Bulls and maddened rhinoceroses stampeded through the arena, enraged by the display of large, red-cloth scarecrows called *pilae*, and pursued by the animal-fighters and their dogs. Nero came down to brave and kill a lion. A remarkable piece of boldness, unless this was a "prepared lion" (*praeparatus leo*): that is, a wretched creature made harmless in advance and fit only to be slaughtered; but the public went wild.' Paoli, op. cit., p. 370.

24. The simplest and oldest machines were those that imitated thunder and lightning, marking the appearance of supernatural personages on the stage. There

was also the elementary winch, which the Greeks had employed, and which was called *mechane*, from whence the expression *deus ex machina;* thus would Medea be seen appearing in her chariot drawn by dragons at the *dénouement* of the Euripidean tragedy, which has been faulted for excessive use of the machine. A trap-door called 'Charon's stairway' communicated with the stage-pit. The settings were painted on three-sided flats, which could thus show three different places according to which way they were turned. The use of machines at Rome does not antedate 99 B.C., at which date they were introduced there by Claudius Pulcher. It is possible that with movable adjuncts the ancient stage ended by slightly resembling the Elizabethan one.

25. The building of stone theatres also came rather latterly in the history of Rome; the first was built by Pompey on the Campus Martius in 55 B.C., an imitation of the Mitylene one, the plan of which he had reconstructed. That of Marcellus dates only from 2 B.C.

26. The base tradition of gladiatorial combats was often severely judged by ancient writers. In a well-known letter (Letters to Lucilius, VII) Seneca describes one of these spectacles: 'Chance had led me to the Ampitheatre at midday; I was expecting games, jokes, those interludes in which the spectator's eye is rested from seeing human blood flow. But the opposite happened: the morning's contests had by comparison been humane. Now, no more trifling: these were sheer slaughters. The gladiator had nothing with which to cover himself; all parts of his body were exposed to blows, and no encounter failed to leave its wounds. Did the majority of spectators prefer this kind of combat to that which the usual or extra pairs of gladiators undertook? How could they but prefer it? No helmet, no shield against the sword. What need of protective armament or of a struggle according to rules? These are only ways of delaying the kill. In the morning, men had been delivered to lions and bears; at midday it was to the spectators that they were thrown. After having killed, the combatant must fight again to be killed in his turn; even the victor was earmarked for death. For the contestants there was one outcome only, death, carried out by fire and sword. And all this occurred during the interval.'

The execution of criminals also provided spectacles of extraordinary savagery. 'Among the most popular effects attending executions were spectacles culminating in the murder or slaughter of the protagonist. But while in ordinary performances the hero's death was simulated, with a dummy being substituted at the last moment for the supposed victim, at the Circus the actor portraying a character doomed to die did so in earnest. For example, genuine wild beasts, just as in the myth, followed a flesh-and-blood Orpheus playing the lyre, until an equally real bear tore him to pieces. The story of Daedalus and Icarus was also re-enacted. The latter, his wings torn, was hurled from the sky and fell crashing in the middle of the circus: a flight, a fall, a shapeless heap of palpitating flesh in a pool of blood. If Icarus finished in this way, Daedalus himself was not rewarded for his caution: a wild beast sprang

239

out at the appropriate moment to tear him to pieces. The effect was magnificent and the people were in transports of enthusiasm.' Paoli, op. cit., p. 371.

27. The *thermae* generally opened at midday, and the opening was announced by ringing of bells or sounding of gongs, and the cries of slaves assigned to this duty. At Rome, the Emperor Hadrian ordered that the opening should be put back to two o'clock, but invalids had access to the bathing rooms before the appointed hour. In theory, closing time was at twilight. For the *thermae* to be open during the night was considered a big advance at Pompeii.

28. Among especially colourful sobriquets are those referring to physical defects: Paulus, the small; Balbus, the stutterer; Luscus, the one-eyed; Strabo, the squinter; Silo, the flat-nosed; Scaurus, the club-foot; Pedo, big-feet; Labeo, the thick-lipped; Bibulus, the tippler; Varus, the knock-kneed; Claudius, the cripple; Chlorus, the pale, etc. In the long run, these nicknames would become family names, some even distinguished ones.

29. The invention of glass was accomplished in Egypt, from which glass-ware and panes were imported in great quantities. Before the use of window-panes, transparent sheets of selenite were utilized, or lapis specularis. Window-glass was in current use from the first years of the Empire but the substance was as yet rather coarse, and the sheets were normally one-fifth of an inch thick; they were inserted in the wall or placed in movable sashes, bronze or wooden ones, turning vertically around a pivot. Glass being very costly, windows were usually protected by a sort of curtain or blind or by wooden shutters.

30. The ancient Italian cuisine was rather different from our own. The cookery book of Apicius, a celebrated gourmet, speaks for instance of pigeons cooked in a stew of melons, dates, honey, wine, vinegar, oil and mustard; with fowl and game, a sauce of oil, raisins, wines, mint, melon and aromatic herbs was served. Mushrooms were flavoured with honey, and peaches pickled. Ancient authors speak of roast wild boar stuffed with live thrushes, and peahens' eggs stuffed with beccaficos. All meals began compulsorily with an egg dish, the phrase 'from eggs to apples' meaning from the start to the finish of the feast. Such a feast would often last for several hours, and be interspersed with 'attractions.' Seneca remarked that the Romans 'ate to vomit and vomited to eat.' The philosopher also deprecated such culinary extravagances, over and above rare, costly foods, as *pâtés* of song-birds' tongues, stews of nightingales' livers and dishes of parrots' heads, camels' heels or elephants' trunks.

31. The Pompeiians were highly superstitious, as indeed were all the Romans. They feared the evil eye, believed in witchcraft that could turn men into animals, and in lucky and unlucky days. Sign and presage were all-important. If one stumbled going out of one's house, it was best to go in again and stay there until the next day.

240

Fire must not be spoken of at table; if it were, the guests must be sprinkled to exorcize the bad luck. To upset a bottle of oil presaged a misfortune, as did also a sneeze at the moment when a dish was offered to one. The sale of charms, amulets and talismans was highly profitable; there were some for every use or circumstance in life.

32. On this subject, see F. Oelmann, *Haus und Hof in Alterthum* (Berlin, 1927) and M. Rostovtzev, *Social and Economic History of the Roman Empire* (Oxford, 1926).

33. Latin authors, including Cato himself, greatly prized the presses manufactured in Pompeii.

34. Bread varied greatly in form and quality, as has been ascertained from that discovered in bakeries and baker's ovens. Before the second century B.C., cereal porridge was eaten instead of bread, which was not in general use. The names of various kinds of bread are known: *acerosus, plebeius, rusticus, castrensisi, sordidus, secondarius, clibanicus, mundus, candidus, siligeneus*. There was even dog-biscuit: *furfureus*.

35. The practice of drinking mulled wine is attested by actual installations of *thermopolia* where the drinks were heated up or kept hot on stoves.

36. The main significance of the graffiti lies, often, in their revealing to us how the ancients pronounced Latin; for certain words were written down phonetically just as they were spoken.

37. The *domus* was the private home, the house inhabited by a private person and his family – the family also including slaves employed at various trades, since many things were made at home. The *insula*, as we have seen, was a building divided into apartments, or a block comprising several private mansions.

38. The bed occupied a special, virtually ritual place in the *cubiculum*: sometimes an alcove or even just a niche. The situation of the bed can be divined in Pompeiian and Herculanean houses, though rarely found in place here, from that part of the ceiling which was above it being lower than the rest and vaulted, the walls being painted in different colours from the others, and the paving mosaic being uniformly white.

39. Jucundus's tablets have lent themselves to analysis of the way in which these writing-pads were made, the wax being pressed into the wooden frame and smoothed thoroughly. Writing was done with a pointed reed called *stilus* or *graphium*, or a style of metal, bone or ivory with, at the other end, a flat, spatulate surface for rubbing out what had been written and restoring the wax to its unblemished state. When a piece of writing comprised several of these plaques, they were bound together by a string.

40. See the description of the country house and the life led there in the Letters of Pliny the Younger, particularly II, 17 and IX, 31.

41. A plan of the Villa Boscoreale will be found in Blümner, *Römische Privatalterthümer*, p. 74.

42. The best description of the frescoes of the Villa of the Mysteries and the most reliable commentary are in Feiler, op. cit.

43. 'The place where the dead received the last honours had to be situated outside the *pomerium*. The Law of the Twelve Tables stipulated in fact: "*Hominem mortuum in urbe ne sepelito neve urito*." Paoli, op. cit., p. 223.

44. Pompeiian *garum* was renowned throughout the Empire and exported everywhere. Here is the recipe for it, from a manual of Greek agriculture, the Geoponica: First, the liquamen was prepared by mixing entrails and small fish or small bits of fish in a vessel, and beating this to a homogeneous pap. Exposed to the sun, this pap was stirred and beaten frequently, so as to set it to fermenting. When evaporation had considerably reduced the liquid content, a small basket was plunged into the vessel of liquamen. The liquid which filtered slowly into the basket was the essential part, the garum; what remained, the lees as it were, was the *allec*. 'Variations of flavour depended partly on the quality of fish used and partly on the method of preparation.' See also Paoli, op. cit., pp. 180–1.

45. The description of it will be found in Maiuri, *Fra Case ed Abitanti*.

46. See Maiuri, *Fra Case ed Abitanti*.

47. Originally from Egypt, the papyrus was rough and uneven. To make it smooth, it was beaten with wooden hammers, and the leaves, formed from fragments of stems placed and squeezed together, were condensed in presses. From this, a rather coarse wrapping paper, called *charta emporeutica*, and various qualities of increasing fineness up to the really splendid *hieratica*, were made. The Roman papyrus manufactories were called *officinae chartariae*; the best known was that of a certain Fannius who had achieved considerable advances in the making of paper. Before being written on, it was made smoother by rubbing with a shell or a bit of ivory. The ink was of varying qualities. That of the Herculanean papyri was excellent and has withstood the centuries.

48. Marcus Balbus held high political offices: Proconsul of Cyrenaica and Crete, he played an important rôle in the administration of the Roman Mediterranean colonies. Thus, that votive statue erected to him in the Basilica of Herculaneum, and another, of which no more than the base is left, in the Theatre.

GLOSSARY

All words given in the first column in italics are in Latin unless otherwise stated

acroteria	pedestals or ornaments at the top or side angle of a pediment
aedile	magistrate (for municipal affairs)
alae	recesses for conversation (*lit.* wings)
albus	tablet on which official announcements were posted
ambulacrum	walk planted with trees
andron	corridor
apodyterium	cloak-room
apotheca	storehouse (esp. for drugs)
argentarius	banker, money-lender
atellanae	farces of a type which was the forerunner of the *commedia dell'arte*
atrium	central hall of the house
atrium testudinatum ..	central hall with closed ceiling (lacking an impluvium)
ballista	military sling
basalt	greenish- or brownish-black igneous rock
biscae	gambling houses
bisellium	double-width seat at the theatre
breccia	composite rock consisting of angular fragments of stone
bucchero (Ital.)	a kind of terra-cotta used for the early Etrusco-Campanian vases
caldarium	hot room (at the baths)
camieu (Fr.)	a painting in monochrome or in simple colours not imitating nature
campaniform	bell-shaped
cardo	road crossing Pompeii, now called Via di Stabiae
cartibulum	a kind of sideboard
castellum	reservoir
cavamonti	the underground excavation diggers of Herculaneum
cavea	auditorium of a theatre
cella	store-room
chalcidicum	portico with double row of columns, as with Eumachia's Building in Pompeii

243

Chian	of or from Chios
comitium	electoral assembly of the people
compitalis	cross-roads
compluvium	opening in the atrium roof to let in the light, and through which also the rainwater was diverted into the impluvium
Cryptoporticus	covered gallery
cubiculum	bedroom
culina	kitchen
cuniculi	excavation tunnels
curia	usually Court of Justice
decumanus major	the longest street (today called Via dell'Abbondanza) of Pompeii
decurion	member of the Senate (orig. Roman army officer)
diaetum (properly *diaeta*).	dining-room (possibly summer-house)
dolium	large earthenware vessel or jar (often used for flour)
duumvir.............	one of two co-equal magistrates
emblemata	figures in high relief (often on dishes or cups),
ephebus	a youth
eurypus	an ornamental water
exedra	hall or waiting-room, with seats
fauces	passages
flabellum	a fan
fondaco (Ital.)	a kind of guildhall-cum-inn, usually pertaining to some particular nationality
frigidarium	cooling-room (in thermae)
fronton	pediment
groma	surveyor's measuring apparatus
gynaeceum	women's apartments
impluvium	basin in the atrium to receive rain from the compluvium
lanarius	a worker in wool, a fuller
lanista	a trainer of gladiators
lapillus	pebble
lararium	shrine for the Lares
lithostroton (Gr.)	5th-century Greek painting on marble
lotiform	shaped like the lotus-leaf
lupanar	brothel
Macellum	provision market
Melosian	of or from Melos
minium	vermilion, red lead
mofeta	an exhalation of poisonous gas
mythraeum	temple devoted to Mithra
naumachia	mimic sea-fight

nymphaeum	a kind of grotto (dedicated to the nymphs)
oecus	reception room
oscilla	medallions (with portraits of deities, etc.) which were generally hung under the portico of a house and so 'oscillated' in the breeze
pagus	village; province under an official
palaestra	gymnasium
parmula	small round shield
parmularius	gladiator who used a small round shield (the *parmula*)
patera	bowl
pavonazzo (Ital.)	a kind of marble
pergula	balcony or pergola
pinake (Gr.)	a painting on marble: of great value, these were enclosed, not by a frame, but in a little individual wooden cupboard
piscina	bathing pool at the thermae
pistrinum	bake-house
pomerium	'green belt' on both sides of a city wall
Pontic	of or from Pontus
pontifex	member of the College of Priests
posticum	the great doorway of a house
praefurnium	the furnace-room in the thermae
purpurissimum	a dark purple colour
putti (Ital.)	paintings or sculptures of children
retiarius	gladiator who carried a net to entangle his opponent
Samnites	the warlike people who dominated Campania until their defeat by the Romans
sandyx	red pigment
senatus-consultus	a decree of the Senate
sinople	an iron oxide used for colouring
sistrum	a kind of rattle used in the worship of Isis
situla	urn
solarium	uncovered terrace along the side of a house
sparsiones	perfumed showers to cool the spectators at the theatre
sphaeristerium	games room
stele	column
strigil	scraper (used in the hot-air bath)
sudatorium	sweating-room (in the baths)
suggestum	public cryer's platform in the Forum
taberna	shop
tablinum	room containing the nuptial bed and the dining-table
tepidarium	'warm' room (in the thermae)
thermae	public bathing establishment
thermopolium	tavern serving warm drinks

tholus	a small round covered market
thrax	a gladiator (originally Thracian), heavily armed, with short, visored helmet of bronze, and shield
thyase (or *thyad*)	a Bacchant
thyrsus	a bacchanal's staff
travertine	white limestone
triclinium	dining-room
trompe l'oeil (Fr.) ..	a painting creating an illusion of tangible reality
tufa	volcanic rock
venationes	sham hunts in the Amphitheatre
vestibulum	entrance hall
vicomagistri	the 'street officials'
viridarium	pleasure garden
volumina	books, in the form of rolls

BIBLIOGRAPHY

BECATTI, G.: *Pitture murali campane* (Florence, 1955).

BECCARINI, P.: *Pompei pagana e Pompei cristiana* (Rome, 1923).

BOISSIER, G.: *Promenades archéologiques* (Paris, 1904).

BRETON, E.: *Pompeia, décrite et dessinée* (Paris, 1870).

BRIGGS, R. A.: *Pompeiian Decoration* (London, 1912).

BRION, M.: *La révolte des gladiateurs* (Paris, 1952).

BUREN, A. W. VAN: *Companion to the Study of Pompeii and Herculaneum* (New York, 1938).

CARCOPINO, J.: *Études d'histoire chrétienne* (Paris, 1953).

CARINI, P. B.: *Pompei* (Milan, 1921).

CAROTENUTO, S.: *Herculaneum* (Rome, 1932).

CHEVALIER C.: *Herculanum et Pompéi; scènes de la civilisation romaine* (Tours, 1880).

CHEVALIER, E. J.: *La cité romaine* (Paris, 1948).

COCHIN, C. N.: *Observations sur les antiquités d'Herculanum* (Paris, 1755; translated into English by C. N. Cochin & J. C. Bellicard, London, 1753).

(DELLA) CORTE: *Pompéi. Les nouvelles fouilles* (Rome, 1927).

(DELLA) CORTE, M.: *Case ed abitanti di Pompei* (Rome, 1954).

CORTI, E. C.: *Vie mort et résurrection d'Herculanum et Pompeii* (Paris, 1953; translated into English, *The Destruction and Resurrection of Pompeii and Herculaneum*, by K. & R. Gregor Smith, London, Routledge & Kegan Paul, 1951).

CUMONT, F.: *Les religions orientales dans le paganisme romain* (Paris, 1929).

ELIA, O.: *Pitture murali e mosaici nel Museo Nazionale di Napoli* (Rome, 1939).

ELIA, O.: *Le Pitture del Tempio di Iside* (Rome, 1941).

ELLABY, C. G.: *Pompeii and Herculaneum* (London, Methuen, 1930).

ENGELMANN, W.: *New Guide to Pompeii* (London, 1926).

FEILER, L.: *Mysterion* (Vienna, 1946).

FIORELLI, G.: *Descrizione di Pompei* (Naples, 1875).

FIORELLI, G.: *Pompeianorum Antiquitatum Historia* (Naples, 1860-4).

FISCHETTI, L.: *Pompeii Past and Present* (Milan, Beccarini, 1907).

FRANCISCIS, A. DE: *Il ritratto romano a Pompei* (Naples, 1951).

GABRIEL, M. M.: *Masters of Campanian Painting* (New York, 1952).

GUSMAN, P.: *Pompéi, la ville, les mœurs, les arts* (Paris, 1906; translated into English, *Pompeii. The city, its life and art*, by F. Simmonds & M. Jourdain, London, Heinemann, 1900).

GUSMAN, P.: *La décoration murale de Pompei* (Paris, 1924; translated into English, *Mural Decoration of Pompeii*, London, Batsford, 1925).

HELBIG, W.: *Wandgemälde der Städte Campaniens* (Leipzig, 1868).
HITTORFF, J. I.: *Mémoire sur Pompéi et Petra* (Paris, 1879).
LUGLI, G.: *Forma Italiae. Campania.* (Rome, 1926–8).
MACCHIORO, V.: *La Villa dei Misteri in Pompei* (Milan, 1926).
MAGALDI, E.: *Pompei e il suo dolore* (Rome, 1930).
MAGALDI, E.: *Le iscrizioni parietali pompeiane* (Rome, 1931).
MAIURI, A.: *Pompei* (Rome, 1956; also Novara, 1957; translated into English by
    V. Priestley, Rome, 1953).
MAIURI, A.: *Pompei ed Ercolano. Fra case ed abitanti* (Milan, 1959).
MAIURI, A.: *Ercolano* (Novara, 1932; translated into English by V. Priestley, Rome,
    1945).
MAIURI, A.: *Ercolano* (Rome, 1955).
MAIURI, A.: *Studie ricerche sulle fortificazioni di Pompei* (Rome, 1930).
MAIURI, A.: *La Villa dei Misteri* (Rome, 1931).
MAIURI, A.: *Passeggiate campane* (Florence, 1950).
MAIURI, A.: *I nuovi Scavi* (Rome, 1948).
MAIURI, A.: *La Peinture Romaine* (Paris, 1953; translated into English by Stuart
    Gilbert, Geneva, Skira, 1953).
MAIURI, B.: *Museo Nazionale di Napoli* (Novara, 1957).
MAU, A.: *Pompeii in Leben und Kunst* (Leipzig, 1908).
MAU, A.: *Pompeianische Beiträge* (Berlin, 1879).
MAU, A.: *Geschichte der dekorativen Wandmalerei in Pompei* (Berlin, 1882).
MAYER, E. VON: *Pompei in seiner Kunst* (Berlin; translated into English, *Pompeii as
    an Art City*, Langham Series, 1903).
MAZOIS, F.: *Les ruines de Pompéi* (Paris, 1824-38).
NICCOLINI, F. A.: *Le case ed i monumenti di Pompei* (Naples, 1854–91).
NISSEN, H.: *Pompejanische Studien zur Städtekunde des Altherthums* (Leipzig, 1877)
NOACK, F.: *Baugeschichtliche Untersuchungen am Stadtrand von Pompei* (Berlin,
    1936).
OELMANN, F.: *Haus und Hof im Altherthum* (Berlin, 1927).
OVERBECK, J. A.: *Pompeji in seinen gebäuden* (Leipzig, 1856).
PAOLI: *La Vie quotidienne dans la Rome antique* (Paris, 1955).
PARPAGLIOLO, L.: *Campania* (Milan, 1930).
PERCICE, E.: *Pavimente und figurliche Mosaïken* (Berlin, 1938).
PESCE, G.: *Il Museo Nazionale di Napoli* (with English translation, Naples, 1932).
PETERSON, R. M.: *The cults of Campania* (Rome, 1919).
PIGANIOL, A.: *Recherches sur les jeux romains* (Strasburg, 1923).
RIZZO, G. E.: *La Pittura ellenistica-romana* (Rome, 1929).
ROSTOVTZEV, M.: *Social and Economic History of the Roman Empire* (Oxford, 1926).
RUSCONI, A. J.: *Pompei* (Bergamo, 1929).
SCHEFOLD, K.: *Die Wände Pompejis* (Berlin, 1957).
SOGLIANO, J.: *Pompei e la regione sotterrata* (Naples, 1879).
SOGLIANO, J.: *Gli scavi di Pompei dal 1873 al 1900* (Rome, 1904).

SPINAZZOLA, V.: *Le arti decorative in Pompei e nel Museo Nazionale di Napoli* (Naples, 1939).

SPINAZZOLA, V.: *Pompei alla luce degli scavi nuovi di Via dell'Abbondanza* (Rome, 1953).

THEDENAT, H.: *Pompéi. Histoire. Vie Privée. Vie Publique* (Paris, 1910).

TUCKER, T. G.: *Life in the Roman World* (London, Macmillan, 1910).

VIEILLARD, R : *Recherches sur les origines de la Rome chretienne* (Paris, 1926).

WEICHARDT, C.: *Pompei vor der Zerstörung*.

WIRTH, F : *Der Stil der kampanischen Wandgemälde* (Berlin, 1928).

WRENCH, F.: *Recollections of Naples* (London, 1839).

INDEX

Accius 113
Adonis 97, 99, 165
aediles 22, 102, 107–8, 139
Agathemerus 96
Agrippa 121
Alcubierre 50–1, 52, 53–4, 191
Alexander the Athenian 213
Ambivius 113
Amphion 179
amphitheatre 9, 46, 79–80, 112, 114–19, 120, 122, 150–1, 173
Andromeda 101
Antiquarium 102, 173, 222–6
apodyterium 120, 122, 227
Apollinaris 188
Apollo 97, 122, 205, 226
Arceus Arellianus 110
Ariadne 102, 159, 167–8, 226
Arikamedu 89
Aristides of Thebes 219
Art 201–30.
Asellina 134
Atella 113
atellanae 112–13, 155
atrium 11, 147, 158, 190
Augustales 109, 175–6
Augustus 20, 95–6, 102–4, 137
Aulus Umbricius Scaurus 173
Aulus Veius 177

Bacchanals 97, 102, 165, 167–70, 226
Bacchus 39, 101–2, 159, 165, 167–9, 177, 179
Balbus 225, Note 49

Basilica 108–9, 207
Bianchini 47
bisellium 117, 173
Bonaparte 57
Boscoreale *see* Villa Boscoreale

Caecilius Jucundus 23–4, 92, 223–4, Note 44
Caesar 98
Caesius Bassus 29
Caius Munatius Faustus 175–6
Caius Tullius 180
caldarium 123
Caligula 20, 98
canis catenarius 220
Capitolium 94
Capri 21
Capua 18
Carcopino 88, Note 5, Note 14
cardo 65, 82, 187
Casca Longus *see* House of C. Longus
Catulus 109
Celadus 119
Championnet 56
Christians 86–8, Note 14
Cicero 53, 138, 196
Claudius Pulcher Note 24
Clodius Flaccus 110
comitium 107–8
compluvium 11, 147
Concordia Augusta 84, 96, 106
Cornelius Rufus 223, 224
Corti 162
Crassus 19

255